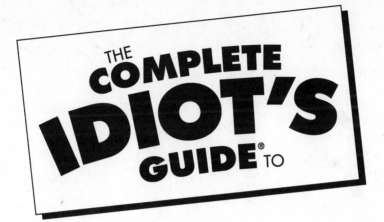

Intermediate Spanish

Second Edition

D1297101

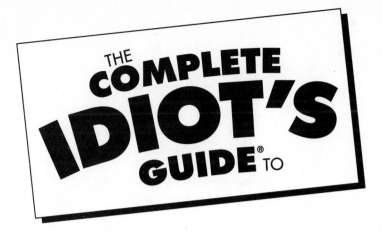

Intermediate Spanish

Second Edition

by Steven Hawson

ALPHA

A member of Penguin Group (USA) Inc.

ALPHA BOOKS

Published by the Penguin Group

Penguin Group (USA) Inc., 375 Hudson Street, New York, New York 10014, USA

Penguin Group (Canada), 90 Eglinton Avenue East, Suite 700, Toronto, Ontario M4P 2Y3, Canada (a division of Pearson Penguin Canada Inc.)

Penguin Books Ltd., 80 Strand, London WC2R 0RL, England

Penguin Ireland, 25 St. Stephen's Green, Dublin 2, Ireland (a division of Penguin Books Ltd.)

Penguin Group (Australia), 250 Camberwell Road, Camberwell, Victoria 3124, Australia (a division of Pearson Australia Group Pty. Ltd.)

Penguin Books India Pvt. Ltd., 11 Community Centre, Panchsheel Park, New Delhi—110 017, India

Penguin Group (NZ), 67 Apollo Drive, Rosedale, North Shore, Auckland 1311, New Zealand (a division of Pearson New Zealand Ltd.)

Penguin Books (South Africa) (Pty.) Ltd., 24 Sturdee Avenue, Rosebank, Johannesburg 2196, South Africa

Penguin Books Ltd., Registered Offices: 80 Strand, London WC2R 0RL, England

International Standard Book Number: 978-1-59257-583-1
Library of Congress Catalog Card Number: 2006940217

09 08 07   8 7 6 5 4 3 2 1

Interpretation of the printing code: The rightmost number of the first series of numbers is the year of the book's printing; the rightmost number of the second series of numbers is the number of the book's printing. For example, a printing code of 07-1 shows that the first printing occurred in 2007.

Printed in the United States of America

Note: This publication contains the opinions and ideas of its author. It is intended to provide helpful and informative material on the subject matter covered. It is sold with the understanding that the author and publisher are not engaged in rendering professional services in the book. If the reader requires personal assistance or advice, a competent professional should be consulted.

The author and publisher specifically disclaim any responsibility for any liability, loss, or risk, personal or otherwise, which is incurred as a consequence, directly or indirectly, of the use and application of any of the contents of this book.

Most Alpha books are available at special quantity discounts for bulk purchases for sales promotions, premiums, fund-raising, or educational use. Special books, or book excerpts, can also be created to fit specific needs.

For details, write: Special Markets, Alpha Books, 375 Hudson Street, New York, NY 10014.

Publisher: *Marie Butler-Knight*
Editorial Director: *Mike Sanders*
Managing Editor: *Billy Fields*
Acquisitions Editor: *Michele Wells*
Development Editor: *Ginny Bess Munroe*
Production Editor: *Kayla Dugger*
Copy Editor: *Emily Bell*

Cartoonist: *Shannon Wheeler*
Cover Designer: *Bill Thomas*
Book Designer: *Trina Wurst*
Indexer: *Julie Bess*
Layout: *Brian Massey, Matt Dufek*
Proofreader: *John Etchison*

Contents at a Glance

Contents

Foreword

There is no question that a strong working knowledge of Spanish is becoming increasingly important in the United States and Canada for cultural, commercial, and political reasons alike. Many English-speakers who have a basic knowledge of Spanish need a text that can serve as a bridge between that knowledge and any advanced material they may need to focus on, such as in the fields of medicine, law, business, or literature.

Steven R. Hawson's *The Complete Idiot's Guide to Intermediate Spanish, Second Edition*, is just such a text, explaining grammar and syntax in an innovative way and continuing to provide benefits through repeated readings.

The Complete Idiot's Guide to Intermediate Spanish, Second Edition, is an ideal text for students who have already studied the fundamentals and are eager to enhance their knowledge and skills.

—Prof. Carl Fehlandt
Graduate School of Translation and Interpretation, Monterey Institute of International Studies, Monterey, California.

Introduction

Welcome to *The Complete Idiot's Guide to Intermediate Spanish, Second Edition*. But wait … isn't there already *The Complete Idiot's Guide to Spanish?* Well, yes, there is. *The Complete Idiot's Guide to Learning Spanish on Your Own*, by Gail Stein, has become a popular textbook for beginning students of Spanish. Similar teach-yourself guides have also enjoyed great success in recent years. With so many "advanced beginners" out there, we realized that it was time to offer an intermediate resource to those students who are ready to progress to the next level. That's where *The Complete Idiot's Guide to Intermediate Spanish, Second Edition*, comes in. This book has been specifically designed to take you beyond the basics and introduce you to many of the finer points of the Spanish language.

You don't have to have read *The Complete Idiot's Guide to Learning Spanish on Your Own* to use this book. This is not a "volume two." In fact, the only requirement is that somewhere along the line you have acquired a basic knowledge of Spanish (no matter how rudimentary or rusty your skills might be) and that you feel ready to learn more. If this sounds like you, you've come to the right place. Hang on to your *sombrero* and get ready for *The Complete Idiot's Guide to Intermediate Spanish, Second Edition*.

About the Second Edition

No, there was nothing really wrong with the first edition. However, in the years since *The Complete Idiot's Guide to Intermediate Spanish* was first published in 2000, a few things have changed. First, over 50 percent of the Internet sites that appeared in the first edition have gone belly up. So, we went through the book and replaced the dead Internet sites with active ones. There have also been several political changes in the various Spanish-speaking countries, rendering some of the statistics from the first edition out-of-date. A handful of minor typos that got past us in the first have now been corrected, and a number of the examples have been improved throughout the text. The second edition also contains a workbook section, rather than quizzes at the end of each chapter, thus making it easier for you to keep your work together. Other improvements have also been made here and there as needed.

How This Book Is Organized

Studying a new language is always a challenge, even under the best of circumstances. To make the experience as pleasant as possible, I have tried to make this book fun and easy to read—without compromising its content. Yes, you'll find grammar, vocabulary lists, quizzes, and activities. But there will also be jokes, timesaving hints, and new perspectives about the language that you probably weren't exposed to when you were a beginner. I promise that it won't be all dry linguistic stuff.

The Complete Idiot's Guide to Intermediate Spanish, Second Edition, is divided into five parts:

Part 1, "So You Want to Learn Intermediate Spanish: ¡Qué Bueno!" prepares you for the rigors of the book by reviewing in detail some of the nuts and bolts of the language, such as pronunciation, spelling, stress, and accent marks. You'll also find suggestions for getting the most out of your learning experience.

Part 2, "Getting to Know the Spanish-Speaking World," introduces you to your first Spanish texts. Each reading deals with some aspect of a country or region where Spanish is spoken. You'll also learn some basic facts about the various countries that make up *el mundo hispanohablante.* The grammar sections review nouns, verbs, adjectives, and other basics, but with a new perspective that I hope you will find refreshing.

Part 3, "La Vida Cotidiana (Everyday Life)." The readings in these chapters relate to family, friends, religious customs, food, and *fiestas.* The grammar sections move away from verbs and nouns and discuss issues such as *por* versus *para,* the use of prepositions, *tú* versus *usted,* and so forth.

Part 4, "Arts and Leisure," includes texts relating to literature (*Don Quixote*), sports, the Prado Museum, and other such topics. Grammar sections introduce (or review, depending on your experience) the past subjunctive and show you how prefixes and suffixes can be used to build new Spanish words.

Part 5, "Money, Science, and Politics," presents some of the most challenging readings in the book. We'll look at computers, business correspondence, a political document, and other complex texts. As for grammar, we'll check out homonyms, cognates, and polite expressions, and I'll give you my own perspective on reflexive verbs.

What You'll Find in Each Chapter

As previously mentioned, the chapters in Part 1 are devoted to fundamental issues about pronunciation, spelling, accentuation, and facts about the language. Thus, they seem to dance to the beat of their own *conga.* But the chapters in Parts 2 through 5 all follow the same basic format. After a few paragraphs of introduction about the subject at hand, you'll find the following subsections:

◆ *Lectura* **(The Reading)**

Most chapters include a Spanish text, known from now on as the *lectura*. Each *lectura* will be related in some way to the chapter's main theme. The *lecturas* vary in length, difficulty, and style, becoming generally more difficult as the book progresses. These *lecturas* are "real live" Spanish texts; they were written for native Spanish-speakers.

◆ *Vocabulario Útil* **(Useful Vocabulary)**

From the *lectura*, a list of vocabulary words will be generated. Not all of these words will be directly related to the general topic, but they will be selected based upon my hunch that you might not know what they mean. If the English definition starts with "here, ...," this means that the word or phrase might have another meaning in a different context.

◆ *Análisis del Texto* **(Text Analysis)**

In this section, I focus on some of the more interesting parts of the *lectura* and discuss what they have to teach us. Translations may be provided for the more difficult passages.

◆ *Gramática* **(The Grammar)**

No book such as this could be complete without some discussion of grammar. But the good news is that many of the topics I'll be covering probably won't be entirely new to you. Intermediate Spanish grammar is really just beginning grammar explained in greater detail. I'll expand on your current knowledge, explain things in a new and more detailed way, and provide examples of how the rules of grammar can be applied. I'll do my best to make it as painless as possible.

◆ *Diálogo* **(The Dialogue)**

Some chapters contain one or more dialogues. These have been included to give you additional exposure to how the language is actually spoken. Most of the dialogues are followed by a translation.

◆ **The Idiot's Guide to Idioms**

The chapters in Part 5 include an "Idiot's Guide to Idioms." Soon you'll be able to amaze your friends with the Spanish equivalents of phrases like "There's more than one way to skin a cat" and "A bird in the hand is worth two in the bush."

◆ *Risa del Día* **(Laugh of the Day)**

I'll be doing my best to ensure that the material in each chapter is interesting and upbeat. But just in case I get a little long-winded (as my wife will tell you that I often do), you'll have a chance to laugh off your frustrations with a section devoted to Spanish humor. It's amazing how much Spanish you can learn from reading jokes. That's why a short Vocabulario Útil section will also follow the jokes. Of course, I can't promise that these jokes will be "good," but I'll do my best.

Approaching the Material

The most important thing to keep in mind as you read this book is that you should not expect to understand everything the first time through. If you come across something that doesn't make sense, move on and come back to it later. Most of us go through a "two steps forward, one step back" process when learning a new language, so unless you have superhuman powers of memory retention, you'll find it impossible to master the contents of this book after only one sitting.

After you read the entire book, I strongly suggest that you go back and read all the *lecturas*, grammar sections, and jokes again. You'll be amazed how much easier everything is the second time around.

Extras

You'll find many interesting facts about grammar, word usage, Latin culture, and linguistic pitfalls set aside throughout the book in our famous sidebars. Look for the following:

Acuérdate

Here you'll find helpful hints and definitions of words and concepts. These sidebars will help you to better understand grammar and word usage. They may also gently remind you of things you learned during your days as a beginner.

Ten Cuidado

These boxes mention words to avoid and common grammar pitfalls. Read these to avoid making unnecessary mistakes or wasting time when you could be having fun.

Cultura Latina

Look here for information about Latin culture, geography, regionalisms, and local customs.

Algo Nuevo

This is a longer sidebar. Read these for lots of fascinating commentary about things that "I bet you didn't know."

Acknowledgments

I would like to thank the following individuals for their support and contributions during the writing of this book: Marga Vaquer (Spain), Lorena Martin (Panama), Norayda de Leon Jones (Cuba), Nataly Romero (Ecuador), Hermann Grunbaum (Colombia), Oscar Gioino (Argentina), Pedro Misner (Cuba), Tony Iglesias (Spain), and Jaime Lembach (Chile). I would also like to thank my agent, Andree Abecassis, whose hard work and guidance made the original book, as well as the second edition, possible. But most of all, my deepest gratitude goes to my wife, Kristin, for her input, ideas, help with the manuscript, and nearly unwavering patience during the writing process. *Muchísimas gracias* to everyone.

Special Thanks to the Technical Reviewer

To help us ensure that this book gives you everything you need to know about intermediate Spanish, *The Complete Idiot's Guide to Intermediate Spanish, Second Edition*, was reviewed by an expert who double-checked the accuracy of what you'll learn. I would like to thank Carl Fehlandt for his work on this book. The great part about this for me is that if something goes really wrong, I've got someone else to blame!

Trademarks

All terms mentioned in this book that are known to be or are suspected of being trademarks or service marks have been appropriately capitalized. Alpha Books and Penguin Group (USA) Inc. cannot attest to the accuracy of this information. Use of a term in this book should not be regarded as affecting the validity of any trademark or service mark.

Part 1

So You Want to Learn Intermediate Spanish: ¡Qué Bueno!

¡Vámonos! Let's begin the book with a review of the fundamentals. First we'll take a look at some statistics about the Spanish language, and then we'll move on to pronunciation, spelling, and accent marks. Now that you're at the intermediate level, I'll let you in on a few secrets about Spanish pronunciation and spelling that they probably didn't tell you when you were just starting out. I'll also suggest some creative ways for you to practice your *español* in addition to reading this *libro*.

A Closer Look

In This Chapter

◆ Similarities and differences between *español* and *inglés*

◆ Spanish from Spain—and elsewhere

◆ Regionalisms

◆ Making yourself understood on both sides of the Atlantic

◆ Culture: is it important?

Okay, here we go. Let's start by looking at the Spanish language itself. This chapter begins by comparing and contrasting English and Spanish. You know that Spanish and English are very different—if they weren't, there would be no need for me to write this book. But you may be surprised to learn that both languages also share some common ground.

After we examine the two languages, you'll see why all Spanish is not created equal. You'll also learn what you can do to make sure that everyone will understand you when you're *hablando español*.

Spanish vs. English

Sometimes it may seem as though Spanish and English are worlds apart. But believe it or not, the two languages actually have a few things in common:

Ten Cuidado

Take care when saying that something or someone is *Spanish*. Technically, *Spanish* refers to Spain. If you say, "I am talking to a Spanish person," that means that this person is from Spain. Just because you *speak* English doesn't mean that you *are* English. If you're not sure which country someone is from, say "Spanish-speaking" instead.

♦ **Spanish and English are both Indo-European languages.** This means that many thousands of years ago, they both had a common linguistic ancestor. Although much has obviously changed since then, you can at least take some comfort in knowing that Spanish and English are distant cousins.

♦ **Both Spanish and English use the same Roman alphabet.** Yes, I know that you already knew this. But hey, you could have chosen to study Arabic, Chinese, Thai, or some other language that uses a vastly different writing system from the one you already know. So count your blessings.

♦ **Spanish, being a Romance language, is made up mostly of words that started as Latin.** English also contains a huge number of Latin words (blame it on William, Duke of Normandy … 1066 and all that). In fact, in almost every English sentence, you will find common words that were born in ancient Rome.

Of course, I must admit that the differences between Spanish and English outweigh their similarities. The following section discusses how Spanish and English are not so similar:

♦ **Spanish pronunciation differs from English pronunciation.** Naturally, you will find yourself producing sounds in Spanish that you never make in English. But the good news is that Spanish is actually easier to pronounce than English, even though you might not think so at first. There are 11 distinct vowel sounds in Standard English, whereas in Spanish there are only 6. Spelling rules in Spanish are logical and fixed, with virtually no exceptions. Once you know how to read and spell, you will always know how to pronounce a word. Wouldn't it be lovely if this were true in English as well?

♦ **Spanish nouns all have gender, while most English nouns do not.** In Spanish, all nouns are classified by gender. In English, unless we're talking about living things, nouns don't have a gender classification. But don't panic; although the concept of a gender for inanimate nouns may seem rather odd to you at first, it eventually will make perfect sense.

Acuérdate _____

Gender is not just a bizarre way of trying to see the universe in terms of masculine or feminine. This gender thing actually helps to hold Spanish sentences together. When dealing with inanimate nouns, don't think of them as "boys and girls," but rather as words with similar endings that belong to two different classes. You'll see later how gender will actually be very helpful to you.

♦ **Spanish verbs change more than English verbs do.** Spanish expresses time and aspect ("do," "will do," "was going to do," "might do," "could do," "would do," "will have done," "did do, but my dog ate it") differently from English. While English tends to use other helping words before verbs such as *will*, *would*, *might*, and *could*, Spanish usually indicates these differences at the end of the verb by adding endings such as *–ó*, *–ía*, *–aba*, and *–ría*.

♦ **Verbs in Spanish don't have a "to" part at the beginning.** English verbs in the infinitive form need the word "to" at the beginning, as in "I want *to go* home." In Spanish, the "to" part of the verb is at the end of the word in the form of *–ar*, *–er*, and *–ir*.

♦ **In Spanish, you don't always have to use the words** *I, he, she, we, they,* **and so on, with the verb.** Unless you're sending a telegram, English sounds odd if you don't indicate who is doing what. We must say "*I* want to go" and "*They* like to play" and "*He'll* put out the cat tonight." If you leave out the *I*, *They*, and *He'll* parts ("want to go," "like to play," "will put out cat") you'll start sounding like Tarzan. But in Spanish, the verb by itself can indicate the person or thing that is doing the wanting or liking or putting by its ending, so the pronouns (*yo, tú, usted,* and so on) may often be omitted without sounding as though you were raised by wolves.

♦ **Spanish words must "agree" with each other more often than English words.** Although Spanish-speakers themselves may vehemently disagree about many things, agreement within their language is mandatory. In English, we also have situations in which words must "agree." For example, according to the rules of Standard English usage, it is grammatically incorrect to say "I wants" or "He know" or "We done" or "I is." In Spanish, though, the need for words to agree is much greater. Not only do the pronouns and verbs have to correspond, but the adjectives must also agree in gender and number with the nouns they modify. The word used for *it* must have the same gender as the thing it refers to. This isn't true in English because we don't classify our nouns by gender (except for living things, when we use *he* and *she*).

◆ **Word order in a Spanish sentence is usually different from that of an English sentence.** For example, in English we say, "I gave it to him," while in Spanish we say, "I to him it gave." Also, when something in Spanish is being described, we usually put the adjective after the noun, rather than before it. Instead of "I see the blue car," we must say, "I see the car blue."

Spanish: An International Language

Spanish, like English, is spoken by millions of people who live in many different places around the world. And, just as folks in Mississippi speak differently from those in Manhattan—who, in turn, speak nothing like the good citizens of Manchester or Melbourne—it only stands to reason that the way Spanish is spoken varies greatly from place to place. Mexicans speak differently than Chileans. Spaniards don't sound at all like Guatemalans.

In fact, differences in pronunciation can exist even within the same country. People who live in the mountains speak differently from those living in the valleys or along the coast. The accents in some regions are so strong that people can immediately identify someone as being from a particular area from the very first word he or she utters.

Two principal varieties of Spanish exist: the Spanish of Spain (known as "Peninsular Spanish," or "Castilian Spanish") and the Spanish spoken in that country's former colonies. Some people say that Castilian is the "real" or "pure" form of Spanish: "I don't speak Spanish," they say, "I speak Castilian," as if this should somehow impress us. Nonsense! There are only two ways to speak Spanish: you can speak it well, or you can speak it badly. Remember that not everyone in Spain speaks Castilian—some Spaniards speak Basque, Galician, or Catalán.

With respect to Spanish pronunciation, we can make the following generalizations:

◆ **Castilian**—The chief distinguishing feature of Peninsular Spanish is the way that the letters *c* and *z* are pronounced. Most people in Spain pronounce the letter *c* (when written before the letters *e* and *i*) and the letter *z* much like the *th* in our words *fifth* and *think*. Thus, *zapato* sounds like "*th*ah pah toh," and *ciudad* sounds like "*th*ee oo dahd." Another feature of the Spanish from Spain is the way in which most Spaniards pronounce the letter *s*. The *s* in Spain has a distinctive whistle or buzz to it, a bit like the *sh* sound in *trash*. This sound is not found natively in Latin American Spanish.

◆ **Latin American Spanish**—The Spanish spoken in Latin America is so varied that one can't possibly say there is a single "Latin American" Spanish that includes all speakers. What we might call "New World Spanish" can really be identified only by contrasting it with Peninsular Spanish: the *c* and *z* are not pronounced as "th," and the *s* is not buzzy as it can be in Spain. I include more information about variations in pronunciation in the following chapter.

Acuérdate

The second person plural *vosotros* (y'all) form of address is used only in Spain. Except for religious ceremonies and old literature, you won't hear Latin Americans saying *vosotros* (or *vosotras*). Depending on the materials you used when you were studying Spanish as a beginner, you might have skipped this form. If you want to sound like a Spaniard, then you need to master the *vosotros* forms. If not, you can continue to skip it.

Regionalisms

Pronunciation is not the only thing that varies from place to place. Quite often, certain words and phrases that are used in one country may be entirely unknown elsewhere (although television and film have changed this somewhat). Some words that are perfectly acceptable in one country may have an entirely different meaning (or no meaning at all) in another. So, while a particular word may have worked just fine in Spain, it could provoke blank stares in Puerto Rico, unbridled laughter in Argentina, and righteous indignation in Mexico. Just think of all the different words and phrases used in Britain that are practically unknown in the United States.

Such issues are known as regionalisms. As a beginning student, you didn't have to be too concerned about this. However, now that you've progressed to the intermediate level, you should become more aware of regionalisms.

One example of a regionalism is the verb *coger*. Generally, it means "to get" and is quite common in Spain, the Caribbean, Colombia, and a few other areas: *Sonó el teléfono y María lo cogió* ("The telephone rang and Maria picked it up"). However, in much of Latin America, especially the Southern Cone, this seemingly innocuous little verb refers to the sex act and is quite vulgar. Avoid *coger* and use *agarrar* instead in most of Latin America. I will be pointing out some of the more important regional variations throughout the book.

What This Means to You

So should you try to speak like a Spaniard or a Mexican? A Colombian or a Chilean? Well, that's entirely up to you. The way I see it, you basically have two choices. If you know that you'll be staying in a particular country for an extended period of time, then you might wish to fully adopt the Spanish pronunciation and usage of that country. When you return home, you will most likely feel a certain kinship with the people of that nation, and you probably will want to reflect that in the way you speak your Spanish. If you're in Spain, please learn Castilian. If you're in Mexico, learn Spanish the Mexican way. In Argentina? Learn to speak it like the natives do. Later, other Spanish-speakers will detect your regional accent, and you'll have a great way to break the ice at parties.

On the other hand, if you're one of those free-spirited individuals who hates being associated with one country in particular, then you probably would do best by adopting a Spanish that travels well and is place-neutral. I would *not* recommend that you adopt a Castilian accent if you plan to spend most of your time in Latin America. A "standard" Latin American Spanish will be far more useful to you in the long run, and people in Spain will have no trouble understanding you.

Being Understood Everywhere

The key to communicating effectively in Spanish is simple. No matter where you are—Mexico, Spain, South America, or even Equatorial Guinea—the rules are the same. Make sure that you always speak at a reasonable pace and enunciate your words clearly. Don't worry if you have a strong accent. People *will* understand you and will appreciate your efforts to speak their language.

Cultura Latina

Not all Spaniards pronounce c and z like our *th*. Many people in southern Spain pronounce these letters the same way that Latin Americans do. Also, some Spaniards don't make the whistle-like s, either; it's a regional thing. In fact, the Spanish of southern Spain sounds a lot like the Spanish spoken in the Caribbean.

What About Culture?

Edward Sapir, a noted linguist, wrote in 1928, "People who speak different languages live in different worlds, not the same world with different labels." He believed that language and culture were inseparable. More recently, other scholars have maintained that a language can be studied and understood without the need to take any cultural considerations into account. The truth, I am sure, lies somewhere between these two theories.

Unfortunately, speaking universally about "Spanish culture" is practically impossible. Spanish is spoken by many people who come from extremely diverse social, ethnic, and economic backgrounds. A *campesino* in Mexico may have very little in common with the president of Uruguay or a businessman from Spain—and yet they all speak essentially the same language.

When I started studying Spanish in junior high school, our exposure to the language and culture of Spain and Latin America was limited to an ancient textbook, black-and-white filmstrips, and a few tattered Mexican *sombreros* dangling on the wall. Boring! Today, things are much different. Students of Spanish have access to so many resources that learning the language doesn't have to be as painfully dull as it used to be. Welcome to the twenty-first century!

While it is true that understanding the people who speak a language will be much easier if you are familiar with their culture, the nuts and bolts of the language tend to remain consistent. Spanish-speakers might not always share a unified culture, but their language is basically the same, in spite of the occasional, though not unimportant, differences in the way it is spoken from country to country.

The Least You Need to Know

- Linguistically speaking, Spanish and English actually share some common ground.
- Certain key structures in the two languages are, however, very different.
- Not everyone speaks the same Spanish; pronunciation and word choice can vary considerably.
- Culture is always a factor, but it can be considered as a separate issue from the basics of the language.

Chapter 2

ABCs, etc.

In This Chapter

◆ An in-depth look at the sounds of Spanish

◆ What they never told you about Spanish pronunciation

◆ Capitalization

◆ Punctuation

Most introductory books and courses tend to simplify the sounds of Spanish in order to get you speaking as fast as possible. This is as it should be, because there is no need to overburden you with too many details at the beginning. But now that you've moved beyond the basics, it's time to talk about the sounds of Spanish in greater detail.

If you're at all uneasy about pronouncing your Spanish, you've come to the right place.

The Sounds of Spanish

Although it may sometimes feel as though your tongue has to dance the *salsa* when you speak, Spanish pronunciation is relatively straightforward in most cases. What's more, Spanish spelling is also very logical; the way a word is written always indicates its pronunciation. Once you're comfortable with the sounds of the letters, you'll know how any word is pronounced. This certainly can't be said of English, where *daughter* rhymes with *water*, and *laughter* sounds like *after*.

Knowing the names of the letters in Spanish can be very useful, especially if you have to spell something over the telephone such as your name or street address. If you need to review the names of the letters, consult Appendix A.

Los Vocales (Vowels)

Let's begin by clarifying the sounds of the Spanish vowels.

Ten Cuidado

Don't stress too much about pronouncing Spanish diphthongs (two vowels pronounced together as one syllable in English words such as "boil"). Actually, diphthongs (and even triphthongs, three vowels together) are pretty easy. Just try to pronounce each vowel quickly but with its full value. The diphthongs will practically pronounce themselves. Don't make this harder than it needs to be. I'll discuss more about diphthongs in Chapter 3.

a

The letter *a* is always pronounced like its name, "ah," and never like the *a* in words such as "wait," "Amy," "able," "ant," "at," and "apple." The sound is actually closer to the *o* in "hot," as pronounced in Standard American English. Thus, the Spanish word *amar* (to love) sounds like "ah mahr," and "blah blah blah" is written as *bla bla bla* in Spanish and sounds exactly the same.

e

The letter *e* is generally pronounced like its name, "ay" (sounds like "day" and "way"): *le* ("lay"), *me* ("may"), *se* ("say"). However, *e* is pronounced like the *e* in "Edward" when it begins a word. Thus, *esto* is not "ay stoh," but "eh stoh"; *entonces* is not "ayn tohn sayss," but "ehn tohn sayss." It will also take this sound in the middle of a word if the word has more than two syllables: *excelente* is "ehk seh lehn tay." Only the last *e* sounds like "ay." You may find that the actual sound in such cases is somewhere between "ay" and "eh." When Spanish wants to make absolutely sure that the "ay" sound is made, the diphthong *ei* is written.

i

The Spanish *i* always sounds like the "ee" sound in "sleep" and "cheap," never as in "pin" or "pine."

o

The *o* always is long, as in "stone," never like "pop" or "too."

u

The *u* sounds like the "oo" sound in "to," "too," and "two." It's never short, as in "cut" or "put."

When the letter *g* is followed by the letter *e* or *i*, it makes the "h" sound, as in *gente* ("hen tay"). When the letter *g* makes its hard *gato* ("gah toh") sound before *e* or *i*, Spanish places a silent *u* between the two letters: *gue* is "gay," *gui* is "ghee." You will pronounce the *u*, however, in the combinations *gua* and *guo* ("gwah," "gwoh"). If the *u* has dots on it, it will also be pronounced, as in *güero* ("gweh roh").

You probably already know whether you are able to make the trilled "rrrr" sound. Try as they might, some people just can't make this sound. If this sounds like you, don't worry. Just pronounce the *r* and *rr* the same as you normally do in English, but with as much emphasis as you can. People *will* understand you.

Las Consonantes (Consonants)

The following group of letters makes the same sounds in Spanish as they do in English. No need to worry about these—just follow your instincts:

f, k, l, m, n, p, t, "ch"

Now take a look at the following letters. While similar to English in many ways, a few words of explanation are needed for accuracy.

b and v

At the beginning of a word, the English and Spanish *b* sounds are nearly identical. Elsewhere, the sound of the Spanish *b* and *v* is distinctive. To my ears, the correct sound lies somewhere between the English *b*, *v*, *w*, and *m*: for instance, *abuelo* is "avwwayloh." If this is too confusing for you, you can try pronouncing both *b* and *v* like the English *v* in "Victoria" and "velvet" (as some Chileans do) until your ear becomes more attuned to the actual sound.

Cultura Latina
A common spelling error made by some Spanish-speakers is to confuse the letters *b* and *v*: "*se bende*" is *se vende*; "*vurro*" is *burro*. So you see, even native Spanish-speakers are sometimes confused by their language.

c

As in English, this letter can sound like *k*, as in *car*, and *s*, as in *city*. When the letter is written before *e* or *i*, it is pronounced like *s*. Thus, in Latin America, *ciudad* is "see oo dahd," and *césped* (lawn) is "say spehd." When *c* is written before *a*, *o*, or *u*, it is hard like *k*, as in *cantar* and *coco*.

As I mentioned in the last chapter, in Spain most people (but not all) pronounce *c* like the "th" in "think" and "fifth" when written before *e* and *i*. So in Europe, *ciudad* is "thee oo dad." One advantage to pronouncing the *c* (and *z*) this way is that some spelling errors can be avoided. Otherwise you may have to ask, "Is that spelled with an *s*, *z*, or *c*?" In Latin America the verbs *casar* ("to marry") and *cazar* ("to hunt") sound exactly the same, for example.

d

The Spanish *d* sounds almost the same as in English, but it's a bit softer and closer to the "th" in "that" and "these," as in *dado* ("dah thoh"). The hard English *d* in words such as "dandy" and "dime" sounds like *t* to Spanish-speakers. Try to soften your *d* in Spanish.

g

Like the letter *c*, *g* has two sounds. Before *a*, *o*, and *u* it is hard, as in "gate," "gone," and "gun." But before *i* and *e* (and rarely, *y*) it is soft and sounds like a raspy *h* from the back of your throat. So *gente* ("people") sounds like "hehn tay," but *gato* sounds like "gah toh." The letter *g* never makes the English *j* sound, as in "gentleman" or "Ginger Rogers."

q

Spanish could have lived without this letter. It sounds exactly the same as the *k* in "kite" and is always followed by *u* (same as English). The letter *q* is not pronounced like "kw," as in "quick" and "quack." The word *queso* (cheese) is pronounced "kay soh," never "kway soh." Spanish uses the letters *qu* to indicate a hard *k* sound before the vowels *i* and *e*—that's its main job. The letter *q* is not written before other vowels. The letter *c* is used for that: *cuidado* is "kwee dah doh."

r

The Spanish *r* is trilled (rolled), as in Scotland—but not too much when the letter is by itself. Just a wee bit. At the beginning of a word, you can flap your tongue more if you like, but be careful not to overdo it. Save that for the next sound.

rr

See the previous section (now you may overdo it).

s

In most of the Spanish-speaking world, the letter *s* sounds exactly as it does in English. In Spain, however, it has a bit of a whistle to it. If you're in Spain, try to imitate the locals. Otherwise, stick to the same old *s* sound that you use now (as in "silver" and "stress"), and you'll be fine. Spaniards will have no problem understanding you either way.

> **Acuérdate**
>
> The combinations of letters *ll* and *ch* were once considered to be one letter, but now they are usually dealt with as two separate letters that make one sound. As a consequence, older dictionaries have a *ch* and an *ll* section. However, when breaking up a word into syllables (more on that in the next chapter), the *ch* and *ll* still stay together: *ma cho* and *va lle*.

w

Used only in foreign words, the *w* usually maintains the same pronunciation as the original word. Thus, "Washington" and "William" have the same pronunciation in Spanish as they do in English. But "Wagner" (Richard) and "Wilhelm" (Schmidt) may maintain the German *v* sound.

x

Knowing how to pronounce the *x* can be tricky because its sound can vary (as it can in English: "xylophone"). Basically, *x* usually sounds like the "ks" sound that we have in "excellent" and "axe." It almost never sounds like the *gz* sound in "examine."

Until the letter *j* was invented (yes, it was invented around 1400), Spanish used *x* to represent the *h* sound. That's why we see *México* ("Meh hee koh") instead of *Méjico*. However, in Spain, you see the word spelled *Méjico*, which irritates the Mexicans to no end. This is also why the name *Javier* can sometimes be seen written as *Xavier*.

When the Spanish arrived in the New World, *x* was used to represent certain indigenous sounds (with varying degrees of success). For example, *x* sounds like *s* in *Xochimilco* ("Soh chee meel koh"), the water gardens in Mexico City. In Mayan regions, *x* sounds like our *sh* in "shell": *Uxmal* ("oosh mahl"). Elsewhere, ask the locals.

y

Pronounce this like the *y* you grew up with: "yes," "yellow." Be aware, however, that its pronunciation varies within the Spanish-speaking world. In Argentina and Uruguay especially, the letter *y* sounds like the "zh" sound in "trea*s*ure." It can even sound like "sh" in some speakers.

The letter *y* may also act as a vowel in words that came from Greek, such as *gymnasio* (gymnasium) and *gynecólogo* (gynecologist), where it sounds the same as its Latin cousin *i*. There is a tendency now, however, to replace this with the letter "i." It also makes this sound when standing alone, at the end of a word, or in certain older spellings of words (mostly names) when it comes at the beginning of a word and is followed by a consonant: *Ysleta* ("ees leh tah"), *Ybarra* ("ee bah rah").

Acuérdate _____

Both Latin and Greek gave Spanish a letter called *ee*. To differentiate between them, *y* was called the "Greek *I*." It's important to distinguish between *y* and *i*. If you just say *ee*, people will assume that you mean *i*, but some names can be spelled with either letter, so you should always say *Y griega* ("ee gree ay gah") when you mean *y*.

z

The Spanish *z* sounds the same as *s* (*zapato* is "sah pah toh"). Try not to pronounce it like the *z* in "zebra" (a mistake I even make when I'm not paying attention). In Spain, it sounds like the "th" in *with*. The letter *z* is rarely written before *i* and *e*; the letter *c* is used for that.

The parts of Spain where the *c* and *z* are pronounced like "th" are known as *ceceo* regions. The areas where they are pronounced like "ss" are called *seseo* regions. The *seseo* region included Seville, a major port city of the sixteenth century. Many of the Spaniards who colonized the New World spent time in Seville before embarking, and locals comprised many of the seamen and other hands on the ships. So it should not be surprising that Latin Americans speak a dialect derived, in large part, from the language of Seville.

Letters That Don't Play Fair ...

Finally, let's look at the consonants that behave very differently from their English cousins.

h

This letter is never, never, never pronounced. No sound. Zip, zilch, *nada*. If you really feel the urge to make an *h* sound, please see *j*, *g*, or even *x*.

j

This is pronounced like a raspy "hchhhh" (same as the soft *g*). Think "Loch" or even *"Achtung,"* in German. The raspy "hchhhh" sound of *j* is mainly heard in Spain. If you find it difficult to make this sound, you may pronounce both the *j* and the soft *g* just like the English *h* in "Hillary" and "help," and people will understand you. Many people in Central America and the Caribbean say it that way naturally, so you can, too. The letter *j* spends most of its time written before *a*, *o*, and *u*, while *g* (when sounding like an *h*) is found before *e* and *i*.

ll

This combination is usually pronounced like the letter *y* in English: *llama* ("yah mah"). In some regions (Spain, Colombia, Paraguay, Bolivia, and among purists), this letter is pronounced like the *l* + *y* sound in "million" and "Will you." You can pronounce it this way if you like, but it's not necessary. As with letter *y*, you may hear some Puerto Ricans pronounce this with a "j" sound. In Argentina and Uruguay, *ll* sounds like the "zh" sound in "trea*s*ure."

ñ

Don't let this one throw you off. It's just the Spanish way of writing the *n* + *y* together in one letter, as in "onion," "canyon," and "dominion." Remember *el Niño*?

What They Didn't Tell You About Spanish Pronunciation When You Were a Beginner

Just as English is not always spoken perfectly, Spanish-speakers don't always follow the pronunciation rules *al pie de la letra* ("to the letter"—there's a pun in there somewhere). In fact, the textbook pronunciation of Spanish can be quite different from the way many people really pronounce the language. Here are some tips to help you understand people when they don't apply the rules.

La Sinalefa

When the last vowel of a word is followed by a word that begins with a vowel, a very interesting phenomenon called *sinalefa* ("elision" in English, but I prefer to use the Spanish word) may often occur. For example, consider the following sentence:

> *La casa de Eduardo Ortíz se va a vender a Ana Álvarez.*
> Eduardo Ortíz's house will be sold to Ana Álvarez.

In rapid speech, the *e*'s between *de* and *Eduardo*, the *o*'s between *Eduardo* and *Ortíz*, and the *a*'s between *va* and *a*, *a* and *Ana*, and *Ana* and *Álvarez*, may be "sinalefized" into one sound instead of two distinct sounds: *La casa deduardortiz se va vender analvarez.*

So if someone in a store asks you "*¿Quiere destos?*" that person is not asking you if you want any "*destos*," but rather *de estos* (of these). It may take some time before your ear gets used to separating these "welded" vowels.

The Swallowed *s*

In many regions of Latin America, as well as in southern Spain, people tend to drop or "swallow" the letter *s*, especially at the end of words. This phenomenon is most common in the Caribbean, Central America, coastal Ecuador, the Southern Cone (Argentina, Uruguay, and Chile), and in other coastal areas throughout the New World. In some speakers, a slight *h* sound can be detected where the *s* is supposed to be. This *h* sound can even find itself attached to the beginning of the next word.

Following are some examples of things that you might hear from a Spanish-speaker who comes from an area where the *ss* sounds are dropped.

Not pronouncing the *s*

What They Say	What They Mean
uno, doh, treh	*uno, dos, tres*
tú tieneh seih zapatoh	*tú tienes seis zapatos*
loh tre hamigoh	*los tres amigos*
¿Cuál eh tu nombre?	*¿Cuál es tu nombre?*
nohotroh sabemoh	*nosotros sabemos*

You need to be aware of this "dropped *s*" phenomenon. Otherwise, you'll start seriously doubting your abilities to understand Spanish. Don't worry, it isn't you.

Cultura Latina

If your local broadcaster or cable TV company offers *Univisión*, *Galavisión*, or *Telemundo*, try to catch some shows that are produced in Puerto Rico, Venezuela, or even Florida. You'll hear people swallowing their *s*'s left and right. Sometimes it seems like the letter *s* never quite made it to Miami.

Dropped Initial v, m, and s in Rural Mexico

Some Mexicans, especially those who live in rural areas, may drop an initial *v*, *m*, or *s* from certain words. This isn't a major issue, but it can throw you off if you're not aware of it. Here are some of the most common examples:

"*ámonos*"   *vámonos*

"*irá*"   *mirá*

"*heñora*"   *señora*

"*í*"   *sí*

ue → u

In rapid speech, some Spanish-speakers may not fully pronounce the diphthong *ue* in short words. Again, this is not a big deal, but if you've never been exposed to it, you might waste a lot of time looking up words in your dictionary that don't exist. Take a look at the following sentences:

Mi hermano fu a la tienda a comprar pan.
My brother went to the store to buy bread. (The *fu* is really *fue*.)

Pos, yo no podo ir hasta mañana.
Well, I can't go until tomorrow. (The *pos* is really *pues*, and the *podo* is really *puedo*.)

Para → Pa'

As you know, the word *para* means "for." Some Spanish-speakers shorten *para* to *pa'* Thus, you may hear phrases such as *Esto es pa' ti*, for *Esto es para ti*.

This *pa'* phenomenon gets even more interesting because the *a* can now form a *sinalefa* with other *a*'s that begin the following words:

pal   para el (*Es pal niño*)

pallá   para allá (*Vamos pa'llá*)

patrás   para atrás (*Echale patrás*)

pa'ella   para ella (not the Spanish seafood dish)

Cultura Latina

In Puerto Rico, final *r*'s are often pronounced as *l*'s. So you'll hear "*hablal*" instead of *hablar*. Also, at the beginning or in the middle of a word, the *rrr* sound may be sounded in the back of the throat. Therefore, some *puertorriqueños* pronounce words like *arroz* as "agggggoz."

Está → 'ta

You may hear *está* shortened to simply *'ta*, especially in the Caribbean and in Uruguay:

'Ta bien (should be *está*)

Los niños 'tan jugando (should be *están*)

Lost d and –ado → ao

Some speakers swallow the *d* at the end of words or between final vowels, especially in rapid speech. So, you may hear "*usté*" for *usted*, and "*paré*" for *pared* (wall). You may also hear the *d* drop out of the ending *–ado*: *¿Ha hablao con Juan?* means *¿Ha hablado con Juan?*; *To' 'ta bien* means *Todo está bien*.

Punctuation

Generally, the punctuation marks in Spanish are the same as in English, but there *are* some differences. Let's take a quick look at the basics:

♦ Spanish places a ¿ before a question: *¿Muerde su perro?* ("Does your dog bite?")

♦ Commas can be used very much the same way that they can in English: *No, no muerde mi perro.* ("No, my dog does not bite.")

♦ In Spanish, the ¿ is rather handy, letting you know before you speak that what follows is a question. It can be placed before the interrogative part of a sentence, without having to start a new sentence: *Si no le importa, ¿puedo acariciar su perro?* ("If you don't mind, may I pet your dog?")

◆ The ¡ is placed before an interjection: *¡Ay! ¡Pensaba que no mordía su perro!* ("Ouch! I thought your dog didn't bite!")

◆ Both Spanish and English use the same period at the end of a statement. Spanish sometimes uses dashes to indicate dialogue (you'll see those later). However, when a word at the end of a sentence is enclosed by quotation marks, the period must be written outside of the quotation marks: *"Ése no es mi perro"*. ("That's not my dog.")

Algo Nuevo

Even though you might not sound like a native speaker just yet, at this point you should be reasonably familiar with the sounds made by the Spanish alphabet. So you won't need any more of those phonetic spellings like "ah bloh ehs pahn yohl." From now on, you'll be doing it *solo*. Review the information in this chapter as often as you need to.

Capitalization

Capitalization in Spanish is much less confusing than it is in English (as are most things). If a word starts a sentence or is the proper name of a person or place, it is capitalized. But months, days of the week, nationalities, languages, and many other nouns that we capitalize in English begin with a lowercase letter in Spanish. Even professional titles start with a lowercase letter, unless they are written with the name of the person. So, *el Presidente Jorge Washington* is capitalized, but when there is no last name, it is not: *El presidente durmió aquí.* When in doubt, if the word isn't a proper name, don't capitalize it unless it is at the beginning of a sentence. You'll be right most of the time.

The Least You Need to Know

◆ The spelling of a Spanish word always indicates its pronunciation.

◆ Spanish-speakers don't always pronounce everything perfectly.

◆ Punctuation in Spanish is similar to English, except for ¿ and ¡ and a few other minor markings.

◆ Far fewer words are capitalized in Spanish than in English.

Chapter 3

Accéntuating the Pósitive

In This Chapter

- ◆ The secrets of those darn áccent márks, revealed at last
- ◆ The Spanish syllable
- ◆ What happens when the rules are broken
- ◆ *Tildes* to distinguish similar words

Even the most advanced students of Spanish can have trouble understanding how to use those accent marks (from now on, called *tildes*). And even if you know what to do when you read one, many students are often unsure when to write one, when not to write one, and why the silly thing needs to be written in the first place. Well, I'm gonna tell you, so you don't have to stress about them anymore (pun intended).

Truth be told, these little *tildes* (*á, é, í, ó, ú,* and *ü*) actually make sense if you know the rules. The problem is that many textbooks and Spanish teachers have traditionally been unable to adequately explain the logic behind why and when these marks are needed. I promise that I am about to establish a new tradition.

Esteban's "No Stress" Method to Spanish Accentuation

I am now going to outline the rules of Spanish stress and accentuation. DO NOT SKIP THIS SECTION. You may even need to read it a few times. I know that this stuff can be dry, but trust me—learning it is well worth the effort.

Acuérdate _____

The *tilde* in Spanish always goes the same way: é. That other accent mark that the French use, è, is never seen (except in French, of course).

What Is Accentuation?

Accentuation simply refers to the part of a word that sounds the loudest. We say that the stress or accent falls on this or that syllable. We do it in English all the time. Often, stress in English falls on the first syllable of a word:

TELephone

CANdle

BAby

CATegory

ADequate

COMfortable

ELephant

APple

Sometimes the stress falls on an internal syllable:

com**PU**ter

re**UN**ion

hippo**POT**amus

in**STINC**tive

anthro**POL**ogy

Stress in English doesn't often fall on the last syllable, but it does happen:

enDOW

reMAIN

reBOOT

reVIEW

acQUIRE

Okay; so far, so good. Now for some rules about stress in Spanish.

The Spanish Syllable

First, let's define what constitutes a syllable in Spanish. A Spanish syllable is formed by the combination of a consonant (or consonant cluster) and a vowel (or diphthong). Here are a few examples of simple consonant + vowel Spanish syllables (I'll discuss diphthongs in a minute):

ba

pe

chu

que

ño

ru

do

re

mi

fa

so

la

ti

You probably know that Spanish and English share many cognates—words that are similar, or even the same. One thing to remember is that Spanish words rarely need a double consonant. Where you would see *tt*, *ss*, *mm*, and other such combinations in English, you will almost always see only one of these letters in the Spanish word: communication = *comunicación*; committee = *comité*.

Consonant pairs or "clusters" such as *pr*, *pl*, *br*, *bl*, *fr*, *fl*, *tr*, *dr*, *cr*, *cl*, *gr*, and *gl* stick together and begin a single syllable:

primo   pri mo

broma   bro ma

clavo   cla vo

gripe   gri pe

fruta   fru ta

extremo   ex tre mo

tri go   tri go

progreso   pro gre so

But if the vowel or diphthong is followed by two consonants other than the clusters just mentioned, the first consonant will stick with the first syllable; and the second will latch on to the second:

pasta   pas ta

diente   dien te

presto   pres to

glenda   glen da

triste   tris te

trampa   tram pa

estrógeno   es tro ge no (*s* and *t* separate; *tr* together)

If a vowel or vowel sound begins a word, it is usually considered a syllable by itself if followed by a either a single consonant, a cluster, or a consonant sound such as *ch* or *ll*:

amigo   a mi go

achicar   a chi car

allende   a llen de

hugo   hu go (watch that silent *h*)

hico   hi co

atrever   a tre ver

jugo   ju go

ocampo   o cam po

In one-syllable words, the syllable may end in a consonant:

dan

sin

mis

pez

mil

sol

pum

tras

Spanish Diphthongs

A diphthong consists of two vowels together, as in "soil" and "boil." The following diphthongs in Spanish count as part of one syllable (unless you see a *tilde* written over one of them ... more on those later): *ia, ai, ei, ue, ie, io, oi, iu, ua,* and *au*. All of these are one-syllable diphthong combinations.

This means that *pue, cie, fei, pia, troi,* and so on count as one syllable, not two. In other words, with respect to accentuation, most diphthongs are treated as if they were a single vowel, not two distinct vowels (yes, I'll elaborate on the diphthongs that do not follow this rule in a moment).

puente   puen te

cielo   cie lo

afeitar   a fei tar

austral   aus tral

farmacia   far ma cia

coima   coi ma

ausente   au sen te

guano   gua no

Great. Now, hold on to your *sombrero* ….

Acuérdate

Occasionally you will see dots written over *u*, as in *ü*. These dots allow the *u* to be pronounced after the letter *g* before *i* or *e* as in *bilingüe* ("bee ling gway") and *pingüino* ("peen gwee noh"). Otherwise, the *u* would be silent and these words would be "bee ling gay" and "peen gee noh."

Doing What Comes Naturally

In Spanish, when the stress in a word is falling where it is supposed to, there is no need to write a *tilde*. It's only when the rules are broken that *tildes* need to be written. So, let's start with the rules.

In order for you to fully understand how this all works, you *must* come to believe the following rules with all your heart and soul.

Esteban's Rule No. 1

The stress in *every* Spanish word that ends in the following letters falls on the *penultimate* (that is to say, the second-to-last) syllable:

◆ A vowel (or one of the one-syllable diphthongs listed previously)

◆ The letters *n* or *s*

This is a very important rule in Spanish. It *does not* matter what kind of word it is, what form of a word it is, or how many syllables the word contains. It doesn't matter if it's a conjugated verb, either. If the word has 10 syllables, the rule applies. If the word has two syllables, this rule still applies because the first syllable of a two-syllable word is *still* the second to the last.

Notice that *n* and *s* are special. They are the only two consonants that will never change the expected placement of the stress in a Spanish word. It is no accident that these two letters are also very common when conjugating verbs or when making nouns plural.
If you need to add an *n* or *s* to the end of a word for grammatical reasons, it will not change the stress of that word.

In the following examples, the stress must always fall on the second-to-last syllable. Because the rules are being followed in these examples, you won't see any *tildes:*

> **SA**po
>
> **CA**rro
>
> e**STA**ba
>
> e**STA**ban (the *–n* doesn't change anything)
>
> e**STE**ban
>
> ele**FAN**te
>
> **MU**cho
>
> com**PREN**do
>
> yo **HA**blo
>
> tú **HA**blas (the *–s* at the end makes no difference)
>
> ellos **HA**blan (the *–n* doesn't change anything)
>
> congre**SIS**ta
>
> presi**DEN**te
>
> presi**DEN**tes (the *–s* at the end makes no difference)
>
> mexi**CA**no
>
> mexi**CA**nos (the *–s* at the end makes no difference)
>
> intere**SAN**tes (the *–s* at the end makes no difference)

This takes care of words ending in a vowel, in a one-syllable diphthong, in *n*, or in *s*. But wait, there's more ….

Acuérdate _____

When adding an object pronoun to an infinitive, there will be no need to write a *tilde* because no accentuation rules are broken: *hablarme, sentirla, quererse,* and so on. The stress falls on the penultimate syllable. However, you will need to write a *tilde* when two pronouns are added, as in *decírselo.* More on this later.

Esteban's Rule No. 2

If a word ends in a consonant other than *–n* or *–s*, the stress *always* falls on the last syllable.

In the following list, no *tildes* are written because everything is happening just as it should:

> habl**AR**
>
> be**BER**
>
> condu**CIR**
>
> entreten**ER**
>
> comuni**DAD**
>
> ciu**DAD**
>
> re**LOJ**
>
> man**TEL**
>
> Para**GUAY**
>
> ri**GOR**
>
> fu**GAZ**
>
> manzan**AL**

Okay. Now, keep holding on to your *sombrero* because here's where you need to stretch your brain a little ....

Exceptions to Esteban's Rules

Every time the pronunciation of a particular word does not follow Rules No. 1 and/or No. 2, a *tilde* will be required to show that the rules have been broken.

To illustrate the previous point, read on:

- Let's say that you know the Spanish word for "number" is *numero*. According to the rules of Spanish stress, this word ends in a vowel, so it should be pronounced "noo MEH roh," with the stress falling on the penultimate (second-to-last) syllable. However, let's say you also know that the correct pronunciation for this word is "NOO meh roh," with the stress on a syllable other than the one on which it is supposed to fall. So to indicate that the rules have been broken, a *tilde* must be written over the *u*. Thus, the word is written as *número*.

- The name of the country you're writing is *Peru*. If you check the rules, it ends in a vowel. So this word, as it stands, would be "PEH roo" because the stress is obligated to fall on the second-to-last syllable (which, in *Peru*'s case, also happens to be the first of the word). But you know that this country's name is really "peh ROO," and so the *tilde* must be written on the *u*: *Perú*.

  If a *tilde* appears on the last syllable of a noun ending in a consonant (such as –*ón*), it will disappear when you add a plural –*es* ending. The syllable with the *tilde* has just become the penultimate (second to last) and thus no longer requires a special mark: *balcón* → *balcones*. The –*ón* now gets stressed automatically.

- A person who studies human activities is called an anthropologist. This word in Spanish is *antropologo*. If we follow the rules, this word, which ends in a vowel, should be pronounced "ahn troh pohl OH goh" with the stress falling on the penultimate syllable. But that isn't how this word is pronounced. Esteban's cherished rules have been broken. So a *tilde* must be written to indicate this fact: *antropólogo*.

- The surname *Calderon* ends in an *n*. The letters *n* and *s* at the end of a word still require the stress to fall on the penultimate syllable: "Kahl DEH ron." But we know that this person's name is pronounced "Kahl deh ROHN," with the stress on the last syllable. So we need to put an accent mark on the final *o*: *Calderón*.

- The word *alcazar* ("castle") ends in a consonant. We checked it out, and, no, it's not *n* or *s*. This means that the stress must fall on the last syllable, "ahl kah SAHR." But the word that we are trying to write is actually pronounced "ahl KAH sahr." Therefore, we must write a *tilde* over the middle *a* to show that the rules have been broken and the stress really falls in the middle: *alcázar*.

> ### Cultura Latina
>
> Even native speakers mess up a *tilde* now and then. Some e-mail programs don't send *tildes* very well, so some Spanish speakers leave them out on purpose when sending e-mails. I have done my best to make sure that the *tildes* in this book are correct, but hey, even here you may find one missing or misplaced somewhere. Don't worry: if you forget the *tilde*, people will still understand what you've written.

Back to Those Diphthongs

I told you not to stress over the diphthongs. But there's one final thing I need to mention before this all comes together: as it turns out, not all Spanish diphthongs are created equal. Here's why: the vowels *i* and *u* (and occasionally *y*) are considered weak with respect to accentuation. The others (*o*, *a*, and *e*) are strong. Any combination of vowels that consists of a weak + weak (*iu*, *ui*) or a weak + strong (*au*, *ei*, and so on) will form a one-syllable diphthong, as you saw previously.

On the other hand, when both vowels are strong (*oa*, *ea*, *eo*, and so on), they must be dealt with as two separate syllables: *ae* = "ah eh"; *oe* = "oh eh"; *eo* = "eh oh"; *oa* = "oh ah."

When we need a diphthong that consists of two weak vowels (or of one weak vowel and one strong vowel) *not* to form a one-syllable diphthong (which is what it will *naturally* do), we must write a *tilde* on one of them to prevent this from happening. Usually it's the first vowel that gets the *tilde*. Take a look at the following examples:

♦ As you know, the surname *García* is pronounced "Gahr SEE ah." Without the *tilde* over the *í*, this person's name would have only two syllables: GAHR syah.

♦ The name *María* is pronounced "Mah REE ah." It would sound like "MAH rya" without the *tilde*.

♦ The word *cortesía* ("courtesy") is pronounced "kohr teh SEE ah." Without the *tilde*, it would be "kohr TEH syah."

♦ The word *baúl* ("trunk," "chest") needs that *tilde* over the *u*; otherwise, it would sound like a one-syllable "bahwl" instead of the correct two-syllable "bah OOL." Same thing with the name *Raúl*.

But remember that two strong vowels will be separated naturally into two distinct syllables:

maestro   mah EH stroh

poema   poh EH mah

paella   pah EH yah

proa   PROH ah

Algo Nuevo

Spanish calls words that are stressed on the penultimate syllable *palabras graves* (or *llanas*). Words with the stress on the last syllable are called *palabras agudas*. Words that are stressed on the third-to-last syllable are called *palabras esdrújulas*. There are even *palabras sobresedrújulas*, which are stressed on the first syllable among four: *cómpreselo*. You don't need to memorize these terms to understand how this all works. But don't let anyone say that Esteban never told you.

Tildes and Other Words

Occasionally a *tilde* must be written simply to distinguish one word from another word that looks exactly the same. These *tildes* have nothing to do with accentuation; they are simply a way for Spanish speakers to tell two identically written words apart.

Using Tildes

Word	No Tilde	With Tilde	Example
el	article	pronoun	*él es el hombre*
de	"of"	verb *dar*	*dé una caja de tres*
se	pronoun	verb *saber*	*se sabe que yo sé*
te	pronoun	tea	*te gusta tomar el té*
mi	"my"	pronoun	*mi taco es para mí*
si	"if"	"yes"	*si Juan dice que sí*
tu	pronoun	"your"	*tú quieres tu taco*
mas	but/plus	more	*tengo más, mas no las vendo*

The Least You Need to Know

◆ Spanish follows very logical rules as to where the stress in a word is expected to fall.

◆ Whenever the rules are broken, a *tilde* must be written over the vowel.

◆ A few little words have *tildes* just to make them look different.

Chapter 4

Caminos Hacia el Español (Roads to Spanish)

In This Chapter

◆ Suggestions to help you learn

◆ About dictionaries

◆ Using the Internet as a learning tool

◆ Ideas for effective practice

Learning a new language is like going to the doctor: it's always a good idea to get a second opinion. No book can teach you everything—not even this one—and the more information you have at your disposal, the better. Sometimes you just need to hear the same stuff explained in a different way before it all makes sense. This chapter will give you some ideas for further study so that you'll have as many second opinions as possible.

Gathering Your Tools

Even though *The Complete Idiot's Guide to Intermediate Spanish, Second Edition*, should be your tool *número uno* right now, let's start by going over some additional resources that you should have at your disposal.

The Bilingual Dictionary

If nothing else, you must have a decent Spanish/English dictionary. *The Complete Idiot's Guide to Intermediate Spanish, Second Edition,* is not designed to give you all the vocabulary or definitions that you'll ever need—that would be impossible. Every language student must feel comfortable using his or her dictionary.

Not only will your dictionary help you to learn new words, it can also show you new ways to use words that you already know. For example, you know that *gato* means "cat." But I'll bet you didn't know that this same word also means the "jack" you use to lift up your car to change a flat. With a good dictionary, you can indeed learn something new every day.

To get the most out of your dictionary, make sure that it is relatively new (no more than 10 years old). This really *does* make a difference; if you have an older dictionary, I'd advise you to replace it with something more up-to-date. There are many Spanish/English dictionaries on the market. Some are definitely better (and more expensive) than others. You don't have to spend a lot of money to get something decent, though; you can always buy that gold-plated $250 hardback dictionary with a CD-ROM and action figures later. I recommend some possibilities in Appendix B.

Ten Cuidado

Yes, your dictionary can be your best friend—but not always. Sometimes it will offer you little or no guidance when giving definitions, especially for cognates. You might look up a word such as *translimitación* and get "translimitation" as a definition, as if that really helps! My motto: dictionaries are wonderful, but they are *guides*, not *gods*.

The Internet

Outside of actually living in a Spanish-speaking country, the World Wide Web is now the best place to find up-to-date Spanish. The Internet will allow you free access to an endless number of Spanish texts, chat-lines, and tutorials. If your computer has audio and video capability, you can even watch and listen to programming in Spanish. Anything and everything you ever wanted to know about the Spanish language and Latin culture is as close as a click on your *ratón* (believe it or not, *el mouse* is also used to refer to your computer's mouse). The number of websites in Spanish is enormous; bookmark the sites that strike your fancy, and visit them often.

Books, Magazines, and Newspapers

In cities with large Spanish-speaking populations, you should have no trouble finding books or newspapers in Spanish. There may even be a *librería latina* in the area. Check your local telephone directory under the Bookstores heading.

In addition to the many lesser-known Spanish-language *revistas*, *Newsweek* and *Readers' Digest* have been publishing Spanish versions of their magazines for years (*Newsweek en Español* and *Selecciones de Readers' Digest*). Many other "mainstream" magazines such as *Cosmopolitan* and *People* also have begun to publish in Spanish. If you'd like to subscribe, contact the publishers to find out more.

Many university libraries stock Spanish-language newspapers as well. Ask the librarian if you can take home a few older editions that might otherwise be headed for the recycle bin. If you're interested in receiving newspapers by mail, you may be able to subscribe to a Spanish daily or weekly paper from a city with a large Hispanic population, such as Los Angeles, Miami, or New York. Your local public library may also have a Spanish section.

Before you spend any more money on additional books or tapes, see what's available for free at the library. You may find books and instructional tapes or videos in Spanish on the shelves. Libraries run by colleges and universities certainly will have books in Spanish.

Cassettes, CDs, DVDs, and Videos

Most bookstores sell "teach-yourself" tapes and video courses for Spanish and other languages. The in-flight magazine of your favorite airline probably advertises similar products. You can also purchase these packages through the Internet.

Some of these courses are excellent; others are not. The problem is that it can be difficult to learn the language from CDs or DVDs alone. Some programs merely throw a lot of words at you without any grammar or context. But these can still be an excellent way to hear the language pronounced correctly. They can also help you to expand your vocabulary. Before you spend any money, see if your local library has Spanish instructional tapes, CDs, DVDs, or videos that you can check out for free.

Other Books About Spanish

In the spirit of my "get a second opinion" approach, you may find it useful to look at some other books about Spanish in addition to *The Complete Idiot's Guide to Intermediate Spanish, Second Edition*. Although I might like to think otherwise, there really isn't anything new under *el sol* when it comes to Spanish grammar. Still, you may find it helpful to hear the same material explained in a different way. Just remember to check out what's free before you spend money (of course, you can always buy as many copies of my book as you like).

Watch Spanish-Language TV and Films

Check to see what Spanish-language programming is offered in your area. In the United States, *Univisión, Telemundo, Galavisión*, and local Spanish-language broadcasters may already be on your TV. Most cable companies offer at least one of these stations as part of their expanded basic cable service. If you have a satellite dish, you definitely have Spanish TV at your disposal. If you're not sure, call your cable company or satellite provider.

Univisión, Telemundo, and *Galavisión* have quality news programs every evening. Or you could start with something easier, such as PBS's *Plaza Sésamo,* the Spanish-language version of *Sesame Street.* For a more "mature" approach, try getting hooked on a Latin American soap opera (*telenovela*).

Your local video rental store or library should carry a few movies in Spanish. Although the selection may be limited, only the best foreign language films tend to make it to the mainstream English market. So the Spanish-language movie you choose will probably be reasonably good (there are exceptions). Read the jacket to make sure that the movie is subtitled and not dubbed into English.

Having your own copy of at least one film in Spanish can be a great way to work on your language skills, because it gives you the opportunity to watch the same movie over and over whenever you want. Each time you see it, you'll pick out and understand new words and phrases. Have your dictionary and notebook on hand, and keep your finger on the pause button to give yourself a moment to write things down.

Lastly, don't forget to look through your own DVD collection. You will find that many Hollywood films on DVD have a Spanish language track. Select Spanish from the main menu, and you can watch your favorite movies in Spanish. For best results, watch the same movie over and over. You'll learn more each time.

Speak Spanish as Much as You Can

Hooking up with a native Spanish-speaker can be very helpful to you. A native speaker can guide you in your pronunciation and vocabulary, and you'll feel encouraged each time this person understands something you've said in Spanish.

If you don't know any native Spanish-speakers who can help you with your studies, ask around to see if there is someone who speaks Spanish in your area. If this doesn't work, consider one of the following ideas:

◆ Mexican restaurants are a good place to start (although I once came upon a Mexican restaurant that was owned by a Chinese family who didn't speak a word of Spanish—go figure).

◆ How about a retirement home? You may meet a Spanish-speaking senior citizen who would greatly appreciate your company.

Ten Cuidado

You can get the addresses of many pen pal organizations over the Internet. Just search for "pen friends" or "pen pals." But be careful—some of these organizations are actually fronts for mail-order marriage services.

◆ Call the local Catholic church or diocese. They'll probably know if there are any Spanish-speakers in the area.

◆ Put up posters on public bulletin boards and at colleges with a number where you can be reached: *Quiero practicar mi español con usted* ("I want to practice my Spanish with you"). You may get some good leads. Offer English lessons in exchange for help with your Spanish.

◆ See if there are any charitable organizations working with Spanish-speakers that are looking for volunteers.

Still no luck? Well, desperate times may call for desperate measures. Open the phone book and look under last names such as García, González, Hernández, López, and Martínez, and start calling around. You may find that someone out there would love to help you with your Spanish. It's a bold step, but if you're really stuck, it's worth a try.

Write in Spanish

Finding Spanish-speaking "e-pals" is easy. Visit www.mundolatino.org to start your search. Another possibility is www.latin-chat.com. America Online, Yahoo!, and other Internet service providers are also good places to hook up with Spanish-speaking "virtual *amigos.*"

Take Classes

Find out what Spanish classes are being offered at your local community college or adult learning center. Tuition is usually pretty reasonable, and there might be both day and night classes to fit your schedule.

Listen to Spanish Radio

Spend a few minutes roaming through the FM and AM bands of your radio. Depending on your location, you may be able to find Spanish-language programs on the radio. Many major U.S. cities, as well as Toronto and Vancouver, have at least one station that broadcasts in Spanish. Listening to the radio can be a great way to keep your Spanish active. A great way to take advantage of the radio is to record an hour or so of a Spanish-language program that appeals to you. You should try to record some music, an announcer, and maybe even the news. Listen to the tape over and over until you practically have it memorized. I promise that it will do wonders for your Spanish.

If you have a broadband Internet connection, there are many programs you can listen to live (streaming audio) or download.

Ten Cuidado

While some instructional computer programs may seem reasonably priced, you must be careful. Far too many students have purchased a cheap "Teach Yourself Spanish" software package only to discover that it's practically useless because of its dull and uninspired format. Read the box carefully before you open your wallet, and make sure that the program's presentation really appeals to you.

More Things You Can Do

If you can't actually *be* an exchange student, you may be able to invite a Spanish-speaking student into your home. The International Rotary Club, American Field Service, and other exchange organizations place foreign students with host families. Contact AFS at www.afs.org and the Rotary Club at www.rotary.com.

Or, try talking to yourself. We all think about things. Sometimes we think too much. Ever have one of those days when your mind just won't shut up? Well, why not harness some of that energy and put it to good use by privately translating your thoughts into Spanish? When you look at your watch, say the time to yourself in Spanish. If you suddenly remember that you need to take out the garbage and put out the cat, think *basura* and *gato*—even if you don't know how to say "to take out" or "to put out."

Of course, you could always marry or date someone who speaks Spanish. There's no doubt about it; if you do form a romantic relationship with someone who speaks Spanish, you'll get lots of practice. Now, I'm not saying that falling in love with someone just because you can practice your Spanish with him or her is a strong foundation for a long-term relationship. But, hey, who am I to stand in the way of *el amor?* If you're already married, this option is definitely out. Sorry.

Algo Nuevo

Whenever I have trouble falling asleep, it's usually because my mind is working overtime reviewing the day's events, planning for the next day, or analyzing some childhood memory. If you find yourself doing too many mental gymnastics at night, try thinking your thoughts in Spanish instead of English. Even if your vocabulary is limited, you can still fill in Spanish here and there. At least this activity might put you to sleep a little faster.

The Least You Need to Know

♦ You must have a good bilingual dictionary.

♦ The Internet is a great place to find and learn about Spanish.

♦ You can do many things to improve your Spanish without ever having to leave your house.

Part 2

Getting to Know the Spanish-Speaking World

Get ready to learn about the various countries that make up *el mundo latino*. This part introduces you to your first *lecturas*. Each *lectura* discusses some aspect of a country or region where Spanish is spoken. The grammar sections go into greater detail about the building blocks of Spanish, such as nouns, adjectives, and verbs. Even if you feel that you know this stuff, taking another look with a new perspective may help you to fill in any gaps. *¡Adelante!*

Chapter **5**

Espaňa: Where It All Began

In This Chapter

- ◆ Your first *lectura*
- ◆ Statistics about Spain
- ◆ The Spanish noun
- ◆ Your first *Risa del Día*

When it comes right down to it, it's really all Spain's fault. Even if your focus is strictly on Latin America, Spain is where the language started: no Spain, no *Complete Idiot's Guide to Intermediate Spanish, Second Edition*. And then where would we be?

Spain is as diverse culturally as it is geographically. Its topography ranges from the Pyrenees Mountains in the north, to the dry Meseta plain, to a coastline that stretches from the Atlantic Ocean to the Mediterranean Sea. The Spanish economy relies on agriculture, heavy industry, and tourism. Each year, more than 50 million people visit the country that financed Christopher Columbus's voyage to what would become the Americas and Spain's colonial empire.

So, get ready to sink your *dientes* into some real Spanish! This chapter begins with your first reading, or *lectura*. You'll have a short vocabulary list, an analysis of the juicy parts of the text, and a grammar section about nouns. Not to worry—I'll keep it all as painless as possible.

Cultura Latina

Spain shares the Iberian Peninsula with Portugal. In Roman times, this region was called Iberia, hence the name we use today. *Castellano*, the Spanish spoken in Madrid and surrounding areas, comes from Castilla, one of Spain's most populous *autonomías*. But not everyone in Spain speaks *castellano*.

Lectura: La Geografía de España

For your first *lectura*, read this brief geographic description of Spain. Go through it a few times if you need to, and don't get bogged down if you can't understand a particular word or phrase. If you don't understand something, skip it for now. Refer to the *Vocabulario Útil* section and your dictionary for any new words. *No te alarmes* ("Don't panic"); you'll do just fine. We'll analyze the passage in detail afterward.

España está situada al suroeste de Europa, en la Península Ibérica. Comparte este territorio con Portugal, ocupando un 80 por ciento del mismo. Incluye también las islas Baleares (Ibiza, Mallorca, y Menorca), en el mar Mediterráneo, las Islas Canarias en el Océano Atlántico, al suroeste de la península, frente a la costa de Marruecos, y en el norte de África cuenta con las ciudades de Ceuta y Melilla. Es el 3° país europeo en extensión y el 5° en población. Al norte limita con Francia y Andorra, encontrando su frontera natural en los Pirineos.

Geográficamente posee cinco grandes cadenas montañosas que la atraviesan y casi un 40 por ciento de su territorio se asienta sobre mesetas. Sus costas están bañadas por el mar Mediterráneo, en el Este, desde los Pirineos hasta el Estrecho de Gibraltar, por el Océano Atlántico en su costa Oeste, y en su costa Norte por el mar Cantábrico.

Great! You survived. Now, let's take a closer look at what you just read. First, some vocabulary:

Vocabulario Útil

> *suroeste*   southwest
>
> *situar*   to situate
>
> *compartir*   to share
>
> *incluir*   to include
>
> *frente a*   facing; in front of
>
> *limitar*   to share a border with

por ciento   percent

atravesar   to go across

asentarse   to sit; to lie (in a topographical context)

meseta   plateau

extensión   size

contar con   literally "to count on"; here, "to have"

los Pirineos   the Pyrenees Mountains

Marruecos   Morocco

frontera   border

Análisis del Texto

Now let's take a closer look at the juicy parts of the text:

España está situada al suroeste de Europa.   *España* is feminine. So, *está situada* is in the feminine. *Situada* is a past participle being used as an adjective, and the *-a* ending tells us it's feminine.

Note also the use of *al* meaning "to the" southwest. When you want to state the cardinal direction (*norte, sur, este, oeste*) in which something is located, use *al* (*a* + *el*). North, south, east, and west are all masculine in Spanish.

Comparte este territorio …   *Compartir* means "to share." Notice that *España* is understood to be the subject here, so there is no need to say *España comparte*. *Este* means "this" and is a demonstrative adjective (more on those later).

… *ocupando un 80 por ciento del mismo.*   *Ocupar* is cognate with "to occupy." Here *ocupando* is in the present participle *–ing* form. *Mismo* means "same" and refers back to *territorio*.

Es el 3° país europeo …   The little ° makes the number 3 into an ordinal number (first, second, third, and so on). It would be read as *tercero*. If the noun had been feminine rather than the masculine *país*, there would have been a little *a* there instead.

Sus costas están bañadas …   Literally, "Its coasts are bathed." Use your imagination.

Cultura Latina

People in Galicia, the northwestern part of Spain, speak *el gallego*. This dialect is actually closer to Portuguese than to *castellano*. But you won't have any trouble making yourself understood by speaking regular old Spanish in Galicia. In Barcelona, many people speak *el catalán*. Catalan shares some words and grammatical constructions with Spanish, but it is definitely a distinct language. Most Barcelonans, however, also speak or understand Spanish.

Vista Panorámica de España

Now learn a few more geographical and demographic statistics about Spain. There are many cognates in this section. If you read a word and can guess what it means by the way it sounds, you'll do fine. There's a lot of great vocabulary here:

Nombre official: *Reino* (kingdom) *de España*

Gobierno: *Monarquía constitucional con 17 autonomías*

Capital: Madrid

Ciudades principales (major cities):

Madrid
Barcelona
Valencia
Bilbao
Sevilla
Málaga
Zaragoza

Tamaño (size): *504.783 kilómetros cuadrados*

Población (population): *Aproximadamente 40 millones; 77 por ciento urbana, 23 por ciento rural*

Divisa (currency): *Peseta (Pta.)*

Forma adjetival (adjectival form): *Español/española*

Recursos naturales (natural resources): *Carbón, hierro* (iron)*, uranio, mercurio, yeso* (lime)*, cinc, plomo, tungsteno, cobre, energía hidroeléctrica, otros*

Industrias: *Textiles, calzado* (footwear)*, acero* (steel)*, automóbiles, alimentos preparados* (prepared foods)*, aparatos electrónicos* (electronic devices)*, bienes de consumo* (consumer goods)*, turismo, otras, trigo* (wheat)*, arroz* (rice)

Industrias agropecuarias (agricultural industries): *Frutas (cítricas y uvas), granos, verduras, aceitunas, aceite de oliva, otros*

Remember that *el* is the masculine definite article and *la* is the feminine. These correspond to *the* in English. The indefinite articles are *un* and *una*; these correspond to *a* or *an*. The plurals of *el* and *la* are *los* and *las*, while the plurals of *un* and *una* are *unos* and *unas*. Don't you love it when people tell you things that you already know?

Gramática: Los Sustantivos (Nouns)

Now we'll begin to focus on fundamental grammar. Even though you may have studied much of this already, a quick review with a new perspective can't hurt (or can it?).

Boy Meets Girl? Not Exactly ...

You know that nouns are people, places, things, ideas, and beliefs. You also know that there are both abstract nouns (such as progress, freedom, and destiny) and concrete nouns (such as houses, dogs, trees, and, well, concrete).

Spanish nouns are classified as being either masculine or feminine. In general terms, Spanish nouns that end in *–a* are feminine, while those that end in *–o* are masculine. There is no neuter gender for Spanish nouns, so your "fixed" cat is still a *gato*, even though he may not be quite as *macho* as he once was.

Many living things have both a masculine and a feminine form. Usually, the final letter is the only difference between the two forms.

Nouns and Their Genders

English	Masculine	Feminine
teacher	*maestro*	*maestra*
neighbor	*vecino*	*vecina*
child	*niño*	*niña*
friend	*amigo*	*amiga*
boyfriend/girlfriend	*novio*	*novia*
cat	*gato* (tomcat)	*gata* (female cat)
dog	*perro* ("tom" dog)	*perra* (female dog)

You probably have come to accept by now that Spanish indicates girls with –*a* and boys with –*o*. But the concept of masculine and feminine words still confounds many English speakers. While we can accept the idea of gender when it comes to living things, inanimate nouns (money, patriotism, mud, doornails, and so on) are obviously neither girls nor boys. So what's the deal?

Well, those words are also either masculine or feminine, and the –*a* and –*o* rules apply just the same. But try not to think of nonliving Spanish nouns as male or female, per se. If the masculine/feminine thing doesn't work for you, consider all inanimate Spanish nouns as belonging to one of two grammatical categories: "A" class words and "O" class words—sort of like blood types. Usually it's just the spelling of the word, rather than any latent masculine or feminine qualities, that determines the gender of inanimate nouns.

Unlike animates, nonliving nouns usually do not have an equivalent in the opposite gender. For example, the Spanish word for beer is *cerveza*. There is no such thing as *cervezo*. It doesn't matter if a man or a woman is drinking it—the word *cerveza* never changes. It ends in –*a*, so it's feminine (or A class, if you prefer).

Algo Nuevo

Yes, Spanish nouns are classified as either masculine or feminine. But before you start to criticize those silly Spaniards for their folly, you should know that centuries ago, English also had masculine and feminine nouns. It was only due to historical events that inanimate gendered nouns in English were discarded. Had Britain not been settled (invaded?) by so many different peoples over the centuries, each noun that we write today in English might well have been masculine, feminine, or even neuter.

Spanish uses all this gender stuff to help hold the language together once you start building sentences. Usually "maleness" and "femaleness" have nothing to do with it. For example, in the second sentence of the *lectura*, you read the following:

> *Comparte este territorio con Portugal, ocupando un 80 por ciento del mismo.*

This *del mismo* literally means "of the same" and is serving as a pronoun. But there's more here than meets the *ojo*. It refers back to *territorio*. How do I know this? Because *mismo* is displaying the same masculine gender of *territorio*; their gender is linking the two words together. We could have repeated the word *territorio* here as well ("it shares this territory … occupying 80 percent of the same territory"), but to make the passage sound better, *mismo* functions as a pronoun for *territorio* to avoid repetition. We'll study more of this "gender-linking" in subsequent chapters.

Nouns with Other Endings

The bad news, of course, is that not all Spanish nouns end in *–a* or *–o*. But even so, there are many useful guidelines that can help you know what the gender of a word is without having to look it up in your dictionary.

Nouns ending in consonants such as *r, l, s, z, j,* and *n* tend to be masculine, as do words that end in the vowels *i* and *u* (not too many of these). And words that end in an accented vowel (as in *el bongó*) also tend to be masculine. Those that end in *–e* can go either way (although *–ie* tends to be feminine).

Fortunately, you'll usually learn the gender of a new word when you hear or read it in a sentence. But if you come across a word by chance or out of context, it may be a good idea to check your dictionary just to be sure:

un reloj   a watch

el árbol   the tree

un balcón   a balcony

el pañal   the diaper

un imbésil   an unintelligent person

el francés   French (language)

el alemán   German (language)

un sofá   a couch, divan, sofa

un hotel   one hotel

el café   coffee

el esquí   the ski; skiing

el maní   peanut (in parts of Latin America)

un restaurante   a place to eat

el bote   small boat; tin can (in Mexico)

el Perú   a South American country

But ...

la flor   the flower

la gente   the people

una nube   a cloud

Nouns ending in *–dad*, *–tad*, *–tud*, *–ción*, and *–sión* are abstract nouns and are all feminine. Always! No extra guesswork is required. Words ending in *–umbre* (*costumbre* means habit) and *–ie* (*serie* means series) are nearly always feminine.

Occasionally there can be two versions of the same inanimate word, one masculine and one feminine. For example, both *cesto* and *cesta* mean "basket." There's also *bolsa* and *bolso*, which both mean "bag." Don't let this trouble you. Such words usually have approximately the same meaning. Sometimes one is just larger than the other; the usage may be simply a matter of personal or regional preference.

"Wrong-Ending" Words

Some words that end in *–a* are actually masculine. Most nouns that end in *–ama*, *–ema*, *–ota*, and *–eta* are masculine:

el planeta   the planet

un mapa   a map

el programa   the program

el problema   the problem

el clima   the climate

But not always …

la forma   the form; the manner

la paleta   the Popsicle (in Mexico)

Some nouns simply change the article to indicate male or female:

un/la idiota   a male/female idiot

un/una estudiante   a male/female student

un/una paciente   a male/female patient

un/una joven   a male/female young person

un/una modelo   a male/female fashion model

Nouns that end with the suffix *–ista* (cognate with *–ist* in English) also fall into this category. When the word refers to a man, it's *el*, but it takes *la* when referring to a woman.

    un socialista   a socialist (a man)

    el capitalista   the capitalist

    un sandinista   a Nicaraguan left-wing party member

    un turista   a male tourist

But …

    una capitalista   a female capitalist

    una turista   a female tourist

A few nouns do not change, regardless of the gender of the person or people in question:

    la persona   the person (never becomes *el persona*)

    la víctima   the victim (never becomes *el víctima*)

    la gente   could be a group of men

The good news about all these irregular nouns is that after a while, even the exceptions seem to make sense and follow a logical pattern. You'll eventually see that such words aren't really exceptions at all, but are just following the beat of their own *conga*. With a little practice, you'll be able to guess the gender of a word from its ending (and be right about 95 percent of the time).

Ten Cuidado

Words beginning with a stressed *a* (or *a* sound, as in *hacha*) take a masculine article in the singular, even though the words are really feminine and need feminine adjectives. The most common is *agua*: you must say *el agua*. The idea is that *la agua* would create an undesired *sinalefa* and be hard to say. *Las aguas* is fine. In the *lectura*, you saw the word *África*, which also works this way.

Plurals

In English, we put an *–s* on the end of a word to indicate plurality: one car, two cars; one telephone, two telephones; one house, two houses; one mouse, two mouses (okay, not always). Spanish also uses the *–s* at the end of a word to indicate "more than one."

Pluralizing Nouns That End in a Vowel

English	Singular	Plural
the hat(s)	*el sombrero*	*los sombreros*
the shirt(s)	*la camisa*	*las camisas*

For words that end in a vowel (such as the previous examples), all we need to do is add an *–s* at the end. If the word ends in a consonant (including *y*), *–es* is added.

Pluralizing Nouns That End in a Consonant

English	Singular	Plural
the rumor(s)	*el rumor*	*los rumores*
the mouse (mice)	*el ratón*	*los ratones*
the diaper(s)	*el pañal*	*los pañales*
the option(s)	*la opción*	*las opciones*
the king(s)	*el rey*	*los reyes*

When a noun ends in *–z*, the *z* becomes *c* in the plural.

Pluralizing Nouns That End in *–z*

English	Singular	Plural
the voice(s)	*la voz*	*las voces*
the ostrich(es)	*el avestruz*	*los avestruces*

If a noun or family name already ends in *–es* or *–z* in the singular, there is no change in the plural, except for the article.

Pluralizing Nouns Ending in *–es* and Family Names Ending in *–z*

English	Singular	Plural
Monday	*el lunes*	*los lunes*
the Gonzalez family	n/a	*los González*

You may add a number before the plural article to indicate a specific quantity:

    los tres amigos   the three friends

    las cuatro hermanas   the four sisters

    los cuarenta ladrones   the 40 thieves

    las noventa y nueve botellas de cerveza   the 99 bottles of beer

In this construction, the indefinite articles are really acting like adjectives.

Un and *una* may also take a plural: *unos* and *unas.* Although the idea of a "pluralized singular" may seem like an oxymoron, it's how Spanish expresses the concept of "some," as in "there are some X's here":

    unos amigos   some friends

    unas nubes   some clouds

    unos problemas   a few problems

Don't forget that gender does not change a cardinal number. So *cuatro* doesn't change to "*cuatra*" just because the noun is feminine. However, when the number is 1, you must use *un* or *una* according to the gender of the noun, and in the hundreds, *cientos* must change to *cientas* for feminine nouns.

El Web

To find out more about Spain, visit one of the following websites: www.sispain.com, www.andalucia.com, or www.gae.unican.es. You can find hundreds of other great websites by doing a simple search for "Spain" or "*España.*"

Risa del Día

Let's get away from grammar for a moment. It's time for a joke—not a good joke, but a joke nonetheless.

Humor is one of the hardest things to translate from one language to another. In fact, many jokes simply cannot be translated because the punch line usually contains a pun or play on words that won't work in another language. For your first *Risa del día*, I will keep it very simple.

¿Por qué cruzó el pollo la calle?

Para llegar al otro lado.

Vocabulario Útil:

cruzar   to cross

pollo   chicken

calle   road

llegar a   to get to

otro lado   other side

Cultura Latina

What we would call a "dirty" or "off-color" joke in English is known as *un chiste verde* (green joke) or *un chiste colorado* (red joke) in Spanish, depending on what country you're in. There is most certainly no shortage of *chistes verdes*. I find it interesting that such jokes are "off-color" in English, but full of color in Spanish. Go figure.

The Least You Need to Know

◆ Spain is where Spanish started (big surprise).

◆ Spanish nouns are either masculine or feminine.

◆ Inanimate nouns are also masculine or feminine, but "maleness" and "femaleness" have nothing to do with it.

◆ Some nouns take an unexpected gender, but after a while even these make sense.

◆ Plural endings are –s and –es.

Chapter 6

México: Pyramids, Politics, and Playas

In This Chapter

- *Lectura:* Lázaro Cárdenas
- Statistics for Mexico
- The Spanish verb revisited

In Mexico, Aztec and Mayan ruins coexist with modern tourist resorts, untamed jungles, and vast desert landscapes. Mexico City competes with Tokyo as the most densely populated city in the world. The country is well-known for its bright textiles, festivals, *picante* food, and liquor. Modern Mexico is also known for its volatile economy and politics.

Mexico has strengthened its economic ties with the United States and Canada with the enactment of the North American Free Trade Agreement (NAFTA, which, by the way, means "gasoline" in Argentina). It has the largest Spanish-speaking population in the world and is the Latin American country most visited by American and Canadian tourists. Sharing a 2,000 mile-long border with the United States, Mexico's history is greatly interwoven with that of its *vecino al norte*.

In this chapter, we'll read a *lectura* about Lázaro Cárdenas, check out some basic statistics about Mexico, and, most importantly, take an in-depth look at the Spanish verb.

Cultura Latina

Mexico and the United States have not always been the good neighbors that they are today. In addition to the Mexican/American war of the 1840s, the U.S. military has invaded Mexican territory on numerous occasions. On March 9, 1916, Pancho Villa's men crossed the Mexican border and destroyed the American town of Columbus, New Mexico, killing several townspeople. Of course, things have greatly improved since those days.

Lectura: Lázaro Cárdenas

Lázaro Cárdenas was one of Mexico's most popular presidents. This reading briefly discusses Cárdenas and the situation in Mexico during his presidency:

Lázaro Cárdenas llegó a la presidencia el 1° de diciembre de 1934. En su gobierno, se propuso cumplir algunas de las promesas de la Revolución. El problema de los campesinos fue el que más le preocupó y durante su régimen se expropiaron grandes latifundios para repartir esa tierra entre quienes la trabajaban; se fundaron ejidos y se dedicó más dinero para atender al campo. Cárdenas se preocupó por multiplicar las escuelas, sobre todo rurales, y por impulsar la enseñanza técnica. Amplió la red de carreteras y dio facilidades para que creciera la industria nacional.

Los años treinta fueron difíciles. Para mejorar la economía de México, el gobierno impulsó la formación de industrias. Se abrió un banco para prestar dinero a los campesinos y se fundó el Instituto Politécnico Nacional para mejorar la enseñanza técnica.

En España, la rebelión de una parte del ejército contra el gobierno de la república provocó la Guerra Civil (1936–1939) y obligó a miles de españoles a salir de su país Muchos de ellos fueron recibidos por México y enriquecieron la vida del país, sobre todo en el terreno de la educación, la ciencia y las artes.

Vocabulario Útil:

ejército   army

enriquecer   to enrich; to make richer

promesa   promise; vow

terreno   land; terrain

enseñanza   education; teaching

campesinos   country people; peasants

multiplicar   to increase the number of; to multiply

prestar dinero   to lend money

proponer   to propose

régimen   administration; government; regime

latifundios   large landholdings

repartir   to distribute

ejido   communal land farmed by *campesinos*

campo   rural land

red   network (feminine)

carretera   highway; roadway

provocar   to provoke

Análisis del Texto

Now let's analyze some of the more interesting parts of the text:

llegó a la presidencia   Literally, this means "arrived at the presidency." A better translation would be "came to the presidency" or even just "became president."

En su gobierno, se propuso cumplir ….   *Proponer* means "to propose." It has *poner* in it, so it acts like *poner.* Notice the *se propuso,* which means "he or she intended or set out to do."

El problema de los campesinos fue el que ….   Notice the *fue el que.* This *el* is standing in for *el problema.* The masculine gender links *el* to *el problema.* The phrase literally translates as: "the problem of the rural peasants was the one that …."

Cárdenas se preocupó por multiplicar ….   The *se* here is reflexive: *preocuparse,* which in this context means "to be concerned about." Notice that *procuparse por* must be followed by an infinitive (*multiplicar*). In English, it would have been followed by an *–ing* form of the verb: "concerned about increasing." We'll review *por* and *para* later.

entre quienes   This simply means "among the people who" (or "among those who"). It could also have been written, somewhat less eloquently, as *entre las personas que.*

los años treinta "The Thirties." When you want to talk about years in terms of a particular decade—the Roaring Twenties, the Boring Eighties—say *los años* plus the corresponding decade.

obligó a miles de españoles a salir This could also have been expressed with a subjunctive construction: *obligó a que 'salieran' miles de españoles.* Certain verbs that by nature require a subjunctive (*obligar* is "to obligate") can sometimes take an infinitive to express the same thing. More on the subjunctive later.

I have included literal English translations of some Spanish phrases simply to explain certain constructions. If you're really trying to translate something, you'll want to stay away from a "word-for-word" translation because that rarely sounds natural. Instead of translating, try to understand the Spanish without thinking of the English equivalents.

Vista Panorámica de México

Nombre oficial: *Estados Unidos Mexicanos*

Gobierno: *República Federal de 31 estados y un Distrito Federal*

Capital: *México, D.F. (con aprox. 23 millones de habitantes)*

Ciudades principales:

México, Distrito Federal
Chihuahua
Tijuana
Monterrey
Mazatlán
Tampico
Veracruz
Guadalajara
Coatzacoalcos
Puebla
Ciudad Juárez
Acapulco

Tamaño: *1.958.201 kilómetros cuadrados*

Forma adjetival: *Mexicano/mexicana; also mejicano/mejicana*

Población: *Aproximadamente 105 millones; 70 por ciento urbana, 30 por ciento rural*

Divisa: *Nuevo peso mexicano*

Grupos étnicos: *Mestizo* (mixed race), *60 por ciento; indígena, 25 por ciento; blanco europeo, 15 por ciento*

Recursos naturales: *Petróleo, cobre, plata, oro, plomo, cinc, maderas*

Industrias: *Petróleo y sus derivados, productos químicos, productos eléctricos, textiles, minería, hule* (rubber), *bebidas, turismo*

Industrias agropecuarias: *Maíz, frijol, café, algodón, azúcar, verduras y frutas tropicales*

Transportes: *Buen sistema de carreteras, ferrocarriles, y 78 aeropuertos con servicio nacional e internacional*

Gramática: The Spanish Verb

Spanish verbs are listed in the dictionary in what is known as the *infinitive* form. As you already know, all verbs in this form end in *–ar, –er,* or *–ir.* Though these endings come at the end of the verb (as most endings do), the *–ar, –er,* and *–ir* parts roughly correspond to the "to" part of an English verb. So, while you could take it literally as "go to," "eat to," and so on, it really means "*to* go," "*to* eat," "*to* love," "*to* sleep," "*to* be" or "not *to* be," and so on:

hablar	"speak-to"	to speak
trabajar	"work-to"	to work
comer	"eat-to"	to eat
entender	"understand-to"	to understand
sentir	"feel-to"	to feel

There's not much you can do with an infinitive all by itself. Sometimes an infinitive can be used as a very insistent command, usually when you're trying to boss someone around. I wouldn't recommend using it, however, because it can be a bit harsh. When used as a command, the infinitive may be preceded by *a:*

¡A trabajar!   Get to work!

¡A callarte!   Be quiet!

¡Escribir!   Write! (Start writing!)

Algo Nuevo

You'll hear the terms "regular verb" and "irregular verb" tossed about. These descriptions may in fact be misnomers; even the irregular verbs are logical once you understand the patterns. When we say that a verb is "regular," this means that there are no surprises when it is conjugated and that everything follows the rules. An "irregular" verb simply belongs to a class of verbs that follows a different set of rules. Don't automatically assume that every "irregular" verb is an island unto itself. Who knows, maybe the "irregular" verbs just need to eat more fiber?

As in English, an infinitive can be used as the object of another verb. For example, look at *Yo quiero* (I want). If you follow this phrase with an infinitive verb, you are saying that you "want to X." Other similar verbs, such as *necesitar, preferir, poder,* and *desear* (just to mention a few) do the same thing. Just remember that the pronouns included in this list are optional:

Yo quiero bailar.
I want to dance.

Yo no necesito ir.
I don't need to go.

Puedo cantar.
I can sing.

No quiero pagar.
I don't want to pay.

Prefiero comer aquí.
I prefer to eat here.

No quiero tener problemas.
I don't want to have (any) problems.

Yo no quiero trabajar.
I don't want to work.

The present indicative can also be used colloquially to indicate what someone is willing to do or intends to do in the near future. In this case, a future time must be specified or implied: *Lo hago mañana* means "I'll do it tomorrow."

Conjugation 101

Conjugating a verb means that you are changing the verb's form to indicate when, how long, and who or what does, did, would, or will perform the action. By conjugating the verb, you are committing it to actually doing something, where before you just had an infinitive suggesting some general action. So, the English verb "to go" is not conjugated, whereas "John *goes*" or "John *went*" is.

Conjugating a Spanish verb usually means that you remove the *ar/er/ir* part of the infinitive and add some different ending. This ending will indicate who is doing the action of the verb. When you remove the infinitive ending, the part left behind is called the stem. So the stem of *hablar* is *habl–*, and the stem of *comer* is *com–*.

The English word tense comes from the Latin word *tempus*, which means "time." The tense of a verb tells you when something occurred and whether the action has been completed. The first tense that you learned was probably the present indicative: *Yo hablo.* It's used to express the idea of "now and in general, but not necessarily at this very minute."

Now, look at the following sentences. They are all examples of regularly conjugated verbs in the present indicative tense:

> *Yo hablo el inglés.*
> I speak English.

> *¿Es usted mexicano?*
> Are you Mexican?

> *¿Habláis con Héctor cada semana?*
> Do you all speak with Hector every week?

> *Tú hablas un poco del español.*
> You speak a little Spanish.

> *Ella canta, pero él no.*
> She sings, but he doesn't.

Nosotros vamos cada día a la tienda.
Every day we go to the store.

Ellos tocan música guatemalteca.
They play Guatemalan music.

¿Viajan ustedes en avión cada año a Mazatlán?
Do you all travel to Mazatlán by airplane every year?

Mi esposo come muchas tortillas de maíz.
My husband eats a lot of corn tortillas.

El niño sabe muchas cosas.
The child knows a lot of things.

Algo Nuevo

When asking a question, you should place the pronoun after the conjugated verb: *¿Habla usted el español?* But you'll also find that some Spanish-speakers don't always follow this pattern. Often, a rising tone is all that's required to indicate a question. Thus, you may hear *¿Usted habla el español?* In the Caribbean, especially in Puerto Rico, you may be asked *"¿De dónde tú eres?"* instead of the more usual *"¿De dónde eres tú?"*

Stem-Changing Verbs

Now that you've reviewed some regular verbs, let's look at some not-so-regular verbs. The most common irregularity occurs in stem-changing verbs, where there is an actual change within the stem when the verbs are conjugated. You may have heard of these verbs referred to affectionately as "shoe verbs." If this helps you, great. Personally, I've never quite bought into the idea of these verbs having anything to do with shoes, but whatever floats your *barco*.

These are the various changes that can occur in the stem of a stem-changing verb:

Infinitive	Present Tense (First Person)	What Happens
contar	*cuento*	$o \rightarrow ue$
poder	*puedo*	$o \rightarrow ue$
jugar	*juego*	$u \rightarrow ue$
querer	*quiero*	$e \rightarrow ie$
pensar	*pienso*	$e \rightarrow ie$
pedir	*pido*	$e \rightarrow i$

The Stem Just Can't Take the Pressure

Rather than shoes, I like to think of stem-changing verbs as weak verbs with vowels in their stems that can't handle the added stress that lands on them when conjugated. If you will recall the rules for accentuation, infinitive verbs are all stressed naturally on the last syllable (*haBLAR, coMER, peDIR*) because they end in a consonant other than *n* or *s*. However, conjugation shifts the stress back to the penultimate syllable, and sometimes the vowel in that syllable is "too weak" to handle all that stress by itself. So, it turns into a diphthong or a more stable vowel.

Let's look at the verb *poder* ("to be able"):

(Yo) puedo.   I can.

(Tú) puedes.   You can.

(Él) puede.   He can.

The verb *poder* has an *o* in its stem. When conjugated in the present indicative tense, the stress shifts from the final syllable of the infinitive (*poDER*) back to the penultimate *o: POdo.* But this little *o* is too emotionally fragile to carry all that stress, so it changes into a more stable diphthong: *ue.*

In the *nosotros/nosotras* form, however, the syllable with the *o* is no longer the penultimate syllable and is off the hook here. Now the *e* of the *–emos* ending is sitting in the penultimate spot (same for *–amos* and *–imos* endings in other verbs). For *vosotros/vosotras*, the stress is on the last syllable, and the *o* still gets a break:

nosotros/nosotras   podemos

vosotros/vosotras   podéis

In the second and third person plural (*ellos/ustedes*) the stress falls back on the poor *o:*

pueden   They can.

When a stem ends in a vowel, add a *tilde* on the *nosotros/nosotras* ending to prevent the formation of a diphthong. For example, with the verb *sonreír* ("to smile"), the stem is *sonre–.* When you add the *–imos* ending, you get *sonreimos.* But the *ei* combo would form a one-syllable diphthong and sound like sohn RAY mohs. You must add the *tilde* to prevent that from happening: *sonreímos* (sohn ray EE mos).

Your dictionary should indicate stem-changing verbs with a (*o → ue*) or (*e → ie*) or (*e → i*) after the verb. It may also refer to another common verb that is conjugated in the exact same way as the verb you're looking up. Check your dictionary to see how it indicates verbs that are stem-changing. If it doesn't, consider buying a better dictionary.

The Verb Haber and the Past Participle

The verb *haber* means "to have." But its role in Spanish is mostly confined to that of a helping verb. It performs the same function as the "have" in the following sentence: "I have written this book and you have paid too much for it." You probably remember the present indicative of *haber* from your beginning text: *he, has, ha, hemos, habéis, han.*

And just what is a past participle? Well, participles are made from verbs, but they are not conjugated. In fact, they are actually used as adjectives. For example, English words such as *opened, closed, finished,* and *defeated* are all participles because they are adjectives formed from verbs. Most English past participles are formed by adding *–ed* or *–en* to the verb.

Formation and Use of the Past Participle

With most verbs, just drop the infinitive ending and add the past participle ending. For *–ar* verbs, add *–ado.* For verbs ending in *–er* and *–ir,* add *–ido.* It doesn't matter whether the verb is stem-changing in the present indicative—it's the same deal.

The tense formed by *haber* + past participle is known as the present perfect tense. It tells of an action that occurred at an indefinite time in the past.

> *Yo he cantado la canción.*
> I have sung the song.
>
> *Hemos comprado los boletos.*
> We have bought the tickets.
>
> *Ustedes han aprendido muy bien el español.*
> You all have learned Spanish very well.
>
> *Quiero haber terminado el trabajo.*
> I want to have the work finished.
>
> *No hemos estado en Puerto Vallarta todavía.*
> We haven't been to Puerto Vallarta yet.

Later, we'll see other uses of *haber* + past participle.

Acuérdate _____

There are also a number of irregular past participles, such as *escrito, hecho,* and *puesto.* You should have seen them in your beginning textbook. If you need to review, you'll find a list of irregular past participles on the reference card at the beginning of this book.

The Verb Ir

You should already know this verb (*voy, vas, va*, and so on). It's pronounced like those things on the sides of your head that you hear with.

Take a look at the following sentences. They demonstrate some of the principal uses of this versatile little verb. You may wish to consult your dictionary under *ir* for even more examples:

Voy a la playa.
I'm going to the beach.

Vamos al centro a ver el desfile.
We're going (Let's go) downtown to see the parade.

El camino va por la costa.
The road goes along the coast.

La cerveza no va bien con el helado.
Beer and ice cream don't go well together.

Los turistas van en autobús a las ruinas.
The tourists go to the ruins by bus.

Me gusta el ir y venir de la gente por la calle.
I like the comings and goings of the people on the street.

A eso voy.
I am getting to that (issue).

Esta vez, va en serio.
This time, he (she) means business (is serious).

Voy a ir de payaso a la fiesta.
I'm going to the party (dressed) as a clown.

Algo Nuevo

Although technically a present tense construction, the present perfect is a great way to express a past tense aspect for actions that have been completed. It should be fairly easy for you, given its similarities with the English "I have done it" construction. In fact, if you don't feel comfortable with the preterit tense yet, you should consider this as your past tense until the preterit flows more naturally for you.

The Ir + a + Infinitive Future Tense

If you put an infinitive verb after the *a*, you can express a future tense—very much like the English "I'm going to …." This form of the future tense is very common in daily speech and should come somewhat naturally to you because it follows the same pattern as English:

> *Voy a viajar a Bolivia en barco.*
> I'm going to travel to Bolivia by boat. (Good luck!)

> *Vamos a ver.*
> Let's (we will) see.

> *¿Vas a poder pagar la cuenta o no?*
> Are you going to be able to pay the bill or not?

> *No van a querer pelear conmigo.*
> They aren't going to want to fight with me.

> *Vamos a tratar de llegar temprano a la reunión.*
> We are going to try to arrive at the meeting early.

> *Vais a tener que comprar un nuevo coche.*
> You all are going to have to buy a new car. (Spain)

> *Y ahora, la Sra. Esperanza Cano va a hablar con ustedes.*
> And now, Mrs. Esperanza Cano will talk with (to) you.

When *ir* + *a* + infinitive itself is the object of a verb (more on objects later), it translates as "for the purpose of" or "in order to":

> *Quiero ir a jugar al tenis ahora.*
> I want to go and (in order to) play tennis now.

Piensan ir a conocer las ruinas aztecas.
They are thinking of going and getting to know the Aztec ruins.

No puedo ir a ver los mariachis hoy.
I can't go and see the mariachis today.

Ten Cuidado

When used with forms of *haber*, the past participle is always left in the masculine form. Don't change words such as *abierto* to *abierta* when used with *haber*, even if you or the person doing the action is female, or the object of the action is a feminine noun. You'll see *abierta* in other constructions with *estar*, rather than *haber*.

The verbs *ser*, *estar*, *ir*, and *dar* ("to give") have an *–oy* ending in the first person singular: *Yo soy, estoy, voy, doy*. Because these verbs are so short, it was probably a good idea to give them a slightly longer ending in the *yo* form. Otherwise they would have been "*so, esto, vo,* and *do*."

Passive Constructions with Se

The most common way in Spanish to form a passive (something "is done," "is said," "is known," and so on) is to use *se* in combination with the third-person conjugation of the verb. The subject of these constructions may be a nonspecific *it*, as in "It is spoken" and "It is done here."

The trick to recognizing these passive constructions is to look for a verb in the third-person singular or plural conjugation next to *se*. You will never see phrases such as *se hablas* or *se sabemos*. Study the following examples:

Se habla español.
Spanish is spoken.

Se vende este terreno.
This land is for sale ("is being sold").

El español no se usa en Brazil.
Spanish is not used in Brazil.

¿Cómo se dice eso en el inglés?
How do you say that in English? (How is that said?)

No se sabe si lo van a cambiar o no.
It isn't known whether they will change it or not.

¿Aquí se compran libros usados?
Do you buy used books here?

Sí, se compran.
Yes, we do. (They are bought.)

Acuérdate

If you want to say "I'm on my way" or "I'm coming" when someone calls for you, say *Voy*. Literally, *voy* does mean "I'm going," but in the context of telling someone that you are on your way (to answer the door, going to a meeting, and so on), it means "I'm headed in that direction."

El Web

Learn more about Mexico by visiting www.knowmexico.com or www.mexonline.com. You can also do a general search for "Mexico" and find hundreds of other great websites about art, history, culture, and tourism.

Risa del Día

Too much grammar? I agree. Here's your second joke. At least it's a step up from the chicken joke you got in the previous chapter:

> *Doctor, ¡me he fracturado el brazo en varios lugares!*

> *Bueno, entonces no regrese a esos lugares.*

Vocabulario Útil:

fracturar   to fracture; to break

brazo   arm

varios   various; several

lugares   places

bueno   "Well …"

entonces   then; so

regresar   return

esos   those (masculine plural)

The Least You Need to Know

♦ Population-wise, Mexico is the largest Spanish-speaking country.

♦ Verbs in Spanish conjugate to show time, aspect, and subject.

♦ You don't always need to say *yo, tú, él*, and similar pronouns.

♦ Some verbs also change in the stem when conjugated.

El Cono Sur: South America's Southern Cone

In This Chapter

◆ *Lectura:* El Festival Nacional de la Tonada

◆ Overview of the *Cono Sur*

◆ Reviewing adjectives

◆ Demonstrative adjectives and pronouns

Chile, Argentina, Uruguay, and Paraguay are known collectively as *el Cono Sur*, or South America's Southern Cone. I suppose that the area is rather cone-shaped. Let's take a quick look at the diverse countries that make up this region.

Chile

Chile is unique for its very long (2,650 miles) and comparatively narrow (maximum 250 miles) shape, and for the great variety of its natural features. The country's northern region near the Peruvian border is one of the driest areas in the world, while Chile's southern regions are among the wettest in South America. The country shares the Andean mountains (known by the locals as *la cordillera*) with its eastern neighbor, Argentina.

Chilean democracy is still recovering from the dictatorship of General Augusto Pinochet, who came to power in 1973 after a military coup (*golpe de estado*). However, in its economy and public services, Chile is one of the most developed countries in Latin America. Exports of wine, produce, and even high-tech components have been steadily on the rise.

Argentina

Although Argentina declared its independence from Spain in 1816, the culture in South America's largest Spanish-speaking country is still greatly influenced by Europe. Much of the national identity centers on its sophisticated capital, Buenos Aires. Argentina was home to legendary first lady Eva Peron, who was the inspiration for the musical *Evita*. Decades of military control, which included a lengthy "Dirty War" against leftists that resulted in thousands dead, ended in 1983. Since then, Argentina has enjoyed a modest economic recovery by privatizing many government-owned industries and by checking the hyperinflation it endured during the early 1990s. The economy continues to go through good and bad periods, but all in all, things are currently better in Argentina than they have been for many years.

Paraguay

Ninety-five percent of Paraguayans are of mixed Spanish and Guarani Indian heritage. Between 1865 and 1870, more than half of Paraguay's population died in the brutal War of the Triple Alliance that Paraguay waged against neighboring Brazil, Argentina, and Uruguay. In the years that followed, Paraguay suffered a series of short-lived and often oppressive governments. A new constitution established in 1992 has helped the country move toward democracy. Paraguay held its first free elections in 1993.

Cultura Latina

Buenos Aires and Montevideo are both located on the *Río de la Plata*, or River Plate. People from Buenos Aires are known as *porteños*, which means "people from the port." The Spanish spoken in both Montevideo and Buenos Aires has been greatly influenced by Italian immigrants. Argentines are often referred to as *Ché* because they are known to say *"ché"* a lot. The Marxist leader of the Cuban revolution Ché Guevara got that name because he was actually from Argentina.

Uruguay

The first inhabitants of what we now call Uruguay were a small tribe of Native Americans know as the *Charrúas*, a nickname used for Uruguayans to this day. These *Charrúas* were a tough bunch. When Spanish explorer Juan Díaz de Solís landed in 1516, he was promptly dispatched (that is, killed). Their stubborn resistance, combined with the lack of valuable natural resources in the area, kept European settlers out until 1624.

Today, Uruguay is one of the most urbanized countries in the world, with 44.5 percent of the population living in its capital, Montevideo. Sometimes called the "Switzerland of South America," the country has had a long history of democracy. The political climate took a downturn in the 1970s and 1980s however, after a military takeover. With the return of democratic elections in the mid '80s, though, Uruguay's future looks brighter than ever.

Both Argentina and Uruguay have a long history of raising cattle. Cattle are called *ganado*, and cowboys in Argentina and Uruguay are called *gauchos*. To say that someone is *muy gaucho* is a compliment, implying honesty, courteousness, and strength of character. In Chile, the word for a cowboy is *huaso*. Both words are originally from the Quechua language.

Lectura: El Festival Nacional de la Tonada

The *tonada* is an Argentine form of folk ballad. Each year, a music festival in celebration of *la tonada* is held near Mendoza, the largest city in Argentina's Andean region. This isn't really a big deal on a national level, but it makes a good *lectura*. Here are some details:

En el departamento de Tunuyán, ubicado a 80 kilómetros al sur de la Ciudad de Mendoza, se realiza todos los años, en los primeros días del mes de febrero, el acontecimiento de la música popular más importante de la Argentina: "El Festival Nacional de la Tonada".

Músicos consagrados de todas las latitudes del territorio argentino y del Mercosur no quieren perderse este megaevento que, en la XVIII edición, en febrero de 1999, convocó en el Anfiteatro Ciudad de Tunuyán a más de 200 mil personas en cuatro jornadas. El Festival Nacional de la Tonada es una fiesta popular y a los analistas del género folklórico les resulta difícil comprender cómo en un departamento de sólo 38 mil habitantes no haya noche tonadera con asistencia inferior a los 50 mil espectadores.

El festival será transmitido por Internet los días 3, 4, 5, y 6 de febrero del 2001.

Vocabulario Útil:

realizarse   to happen; to take place; to make real

ubicar   to locate

acontecimiento   event; occurrence

consagrado   sacred; here, well respected

latitudes   latitudes; places; parts

Mercosur   trade agreement among several South American countries

perderse   to miss (not show up)

megaevento   big event

convocar   to call or bring together

jornada   24-hour period; day

género   kind; type

resultar   to be (after some effort); to turn out

tonadera   having to do with *tonadas*

inferior   less than; inferior

asistencia   attendance (false cognate)

espectador   spectator

Análisis del Texto

Now let's take a closer look at the more interesting parts of the text:

se realiza todos los años   The *se* makes this a passive construction. The verb *realizar* is almost a false cognate because it doesn't mean "to realize" in the sense of "I just realized that someone has stolen my wallet." Rather, it means "to make real" or "to make happen." It is, however, a cognate with the word *realize* in "to realize your dreams."

de todas las latitudes del territorio argentino   Try not to let this sort of thing throw you off. This is just an elegant way of saying "from every part of Argentina."

Mercosur   The countries of the Southern Cone (including Brazil) have a trade agreement called *Mercosur*. The author is just trying to be clever and save himself some time by not mentioning all of the countries in the region by name.

Algo Nuevo
In written Spanish, you often will come across a literary device known as "elegant variation." We also use this device in English. For example: the President of the United States; the Leader of the Free World; the Commander-in-Chief; the Resident of the White House. All of these refer to the same person. In a Spanish text, it is even more common to find the same subject referred to in a multitude of ways. Don't let this confuse you.

en la XVIII edición   Here it means "the eighteenth time they've held the festival." It's not an edition like a book. Sometimes you need to stretch your imagination to understand what is being talked about.

a los analistas del género folklórico les resulta difícil comprender   The a ("to") at the beginning of this phrase lets us know that there is an object around somewhere. Later we find *les*, which points us back to *analistas del género*. So now we know who the object is. The verb *resultar* is just an elegant way of saying "is," as in *A mí me resulta difícil hablar* ("It is hard for me to speak"). So this phrase means "It is difficult for the analysts of (people who study/follow) the genre to understand."

Vista Panorámica del Cono Sur

Nombres oficiales de los países: *República Argentina; República Oriental del Uruguay; República del Paraguay; República de Chile*

Gobiernos: *Argentina: república de 22 provincias; Uruguay: república de 19 departamentos; Paraguay: república de 19 departamentos; Chile: república de 12 regiones*

Capitales:

Buenos Aires (Argentina)
Montevideo (Uruguay)
Asunción (Paraguay)
Santiago (Chile)

Tamaños: *Argentina: 2.780.399 kilómetros cuadrados; Uruguay: 176.215 kilómetros cuadrados; Paraguay: 406.752 kilómetros cuadrados; Chile: 756.626 kilómetros cuadrados*

Poblaciones: *Argentina: 37 millones; Uruguay: 3 millones; Paraguay: 5 millones; Chile: 15 millones*

Divisas: *Argentina: peso; Uruguay: nuevo peso uruguayo; Paraguay: el guaraní; Chile: peso chileno*

Formas adjetivales: *argentino; uruguayo; paraguayo; chileno*

Recursos naturales de la región: *Tierras fértiles, petróleo, gas natural, mineral de hierro, uranio, plata, cinc, plomo, bosque, potencia hidroeléctrica, otros*

Industrias: *Carne, lana, pieles, productos de cuero, metales, textiles, comida, cemento, vinos, azúcar, madera, productos químicos, maquinaria*

Industrias agropecuarias: *Granos, semillas oleaginosas* (oil seeds), *caña de azúcar, trigo, remolacha, jugos de naranja, arroz, uva, maíz, soja, algodón, otros*

Gramática: Los Adjetivos

Adjectives modify or describe nouns: *tall* tree, *big* mistake, *heavy* load, *red* brick, *angry* bear, *annoying* insect, and so on. Yes, you knew this already.

You also know that in Spanish, adjectives *must* agree in number and gender with the nouns they modify. This means that if the noun is feminine, the adjective modifying it also takes a feminine ending. If it's masculine, you need a masculine ending. And if the noun is plural, the adjective must be pluralized:

> *hombre viejo*   old man
>
> *mujer alta*   tall woman
>
> *hombres viejos*   old men
>
> *mujeres altas*   tall women

In Spanish, descriptive adjectives are usually placed *after* the noun they modify. This is the opposite of what you are used to in English:

> *gato bueno*   Looks like "cat good," but means "good cat"
>
> *perro malo*   Looks like "dog bad," but means "bad dog"

Remember all the grief you suffered as a kid when you used a double negative such as "I don't got nothing"? Well, Spanish is your lucky language. Double negatives are a must in Spanish: *Él no hace nada* is the correct way to say "He doesn't do anything." Yes, the argument can be made that "if he doesn't do nothing, then he must be doing something." But not in Spanish! Get used to double negatives.

> **Acuérdate** _____
>
> Remember that whenever you're talking about a group of nouns, whether animate or inanimate, the adjectives always take the plural masculine form unless every noun or person in the group is feminine. No, I suppose it's not politically correct, but in Spanish it is grammatically correct. Sorry.

Adjectives with Other Endings

Not all adjectives end in –*o* or –*a*. In fact, many adjectives end in –*e* or in a consonant such as –*l*, –*r*, –*s* or –*z*. But the good news is that this actually makes things easier. Most adjectives that end in a letter other than –*o* or –*a* are said to be "invariable" (they do not change) with respect to gender. So, you can use the same form of the adjective with both masculine and feminine nouns:

un hombre inteligente   an intelligent man

una mujer inteligente   an intelligent woman

un vaso grande   a large glass (for drinking)

las fiestas grandes   the big parties

una reunión urgente   an urgent meeting

un caso urgente   an urgent case

los muchachos felices   the happy boys

la muchacha feliz   the happy girl

> **Ten Cuidado** _____
>
> Don't be thrown off if the noun ends in a letter other than –*o* or –*a*; the adjective must match the gender of the noun *only*. Use the article as your guide.

However, even though there may be no change for gender, all adjectives must add –*s* (or –*es*, when they end in a consonant) if they modify plural nouns: *ocho mujeres inteligentes* is "eight intelligent women."

There is an exception to the previously stated rule: adjectives referring to nationality, religion, or geographical division will take an –*a* if they end in a consonant:

un turista alemán   a male German tourist

una turista alemana   a female German tourist

Hakim es musulmán.   Hakim is a Muslim.

Fátima es musulmana.   Fatima is a Muslim.

un señor español   a Spanish gentleman

las canciones españolas   the Spanish songs

el pan francés   the French bread

la sopa francesa   the French soup

Acuérdate

When *de* comes before the definite article *el*, the contraction *del* is formed. This contraction is not optional. However, you should use *de el* if the *el* is part of a proper name: *la ciudad de El Paso, Texas.*

Remember that *de* plus a noun can also help you construct an adjectival relationship:

la camisa de algodón   the cotton shirt

el monitor de computadora   the computer monitor

la puerta de madera   the wooden door

el viaje de placer   the pleasure trip

el boleto de avión   the airplane ticket

Dumb, Dumber, Dumbest: Comparisons and Superlatives

We often use adjectives to draw comparisons between two or more things. This is known as (get ready for this one) a *comparative:* "I run *faster* than he does." And if we want to indicate which noun (or nouns) among several possesses the most or least of a specific quality, we call that a *superlative:* "I'm the *fastest* runner in the world."

In English, many adjectives follow the "fast, faster, fastest" pattern. But Spanish follows the "difficult, more difficult, most difficult" pattern.

Comparatives

Let's start with some basic comparisons:

un hombre alto   a tall man

un hombre más alto   a man more tall (taller)

una mujer menos alta   a woman less tall (shorter)

To indicate what's being compared to what, que is needed:

hombre más alto que …   taller man than …

Marco es más inteligente que José.   Marco is more intelligent that José.

José es menos inteligente que Marco.   José is less intelligent than Marco.

Superlatives

To say "the most" or "the least," or "the best" or "the worst" of something, we need to introduce the definite article *el, la, los, las* back into the picture:

> *el hombre más rico*   the richest (most rich) man
>
> *los más caros de la tienda*   the most expensive (ones) in the store
>
> *el turista menos inteligente del mundo*   the least intelligent tourist in the world

The little word *de* works with superlatives to indicate the group from which the subject is the most/least of the quality indicated:

> *Yo soy la menos rica del pueblo.*
> I'm the least rich (woman) in town (of the town).
>
> *Yo no soy el autor más famoso del mundo.*
> I'm not the most famous author in the world.
>
> *El edificio es el más alto de la ciudad.*
> The building is the city's tallest (tallest of the city).

Algo Nuevo

Adjectives can easily be changed into nouns simply by adding an article: *un chileno* is "a male Chilean person"; *una argentina* is "a female Argentine person"; *los uruguayos no, pero los paraguayos sí* means "Uruguayans don't, but Paraguayans do." By using the definite article (*el, la, los, las*) with the adjective, we can express the idea of "the X one," as in *No quiero el rojo, sino el amarillo* ("I don't want the red one, but rather the yellow one"). Also, *Quiero los nuevos* means "I want the new ones."

Adjectives That Don't Follow the Rules

A small group of common adjectives does not use *más* when making a comparative or superlative. They are invariable for gender.

Adjectives That Don't Follow the Rules

Adjective	Comparison	Superlative
bueno	*mejor* (never *más bueno*)	*el/la mejor*

continues

Adjectives That Don't Follow the Rules   (continued)

Adjective	Comparison	Superlative
malo	*peor* (not *más malo*)	*el/la peor*
grande	*mayor* ("older") (referring to age, usually)	*el/la mayor*

Here are a few examples of the adjectives in the previous table and how they would be used:

> *La comida del restaurante es la peor del mundo.*
> The restaurant's food is the worst in the world.

> *Pedro es el mejor estudiante de la clase.*
> Pedro is the best student in (of) the class.

> *Soy el mayor de la familia.*
> I'm the oldest in the family.

The plurals of the irregular comparatives are logical: *las mejores, los peores, los mayores,* and so on.

Bueno, Malo, Grande

A small group of adjectives have a shorter form that must be used before any masculine *singular* noun. *Grande* becomes *gran* before any singular noun, masculine or feminine. Some of these you have seen before, while others may be new. I will explain their placement in the next section.

Adjectives and Singular Nouns

Adjective	with Singular Noun	Means ...
bueno (good)	*buen hombre*	good man
malo (bad)	*mal hombre*	bad man
alguno (some)	*algún hombre*	some man
ninguno (no, none)	*ningún hombre*	no man
primero (first)	*primer hombre*	first man

tercero (third)	*tercer hombre*	third man
uno (one)	*un hombre*	a man
santo (holy, saint)	San Pablo	Saint Paul
grande (big, great)	*un gran día*	a great day
	una gran idea	a great idea

The Last Word on the Placement of Adjectives

By now you have accepted the idea that adjectives are placed after the nouns they modify. However, some adjectives have a different meaning depending on whether they are placed in front of the noun or after it.

Adjectives Before and After

Adjective	Before Noun	After Noun
antiguo	former	ancient
cierto	some	definite
diferente	unlike	various
nuevo	another	new
grande	great; grand	large
pobre	pitiable	not rich
varios	several	varied; different
viejo	long-standing	old (age)

Here are a few examples:

una casa nueva   a new house (built recently)

una nueva casa   a new house (a different one)

un amigo viejo   an old friend (in age)

un viejo amigo   an old friend (known him a long time)

un hombre grande   a large man

un gran hombre   a great man (not necessarily big)

el autor pobre   the destitute writer (no money)

el pobre autor   the poor writer (feel pity for him)

Acuérdate _____

Colors are usually adjectives, but sometimes they are used as nouns. When this is the case, colors take a masculine article: *el blanco de los ojos* means "the white of the eyes."

While adjectives in Spanish do spend most of their time after the nouns they modify, descriptive adjectives may also be placed in front of a noun to emphasize the quality of the characteristic being described. This is extremely common in writing:

los malos sueños de Eduardo Eduardo's bad dreams

los bellos ojos de Marta Marta's beautiful eyes

las verdes plantas de la selva the green plants of the jungle (if it were *plantas verdes* it would imply that there are a lot of nongreen plants in the jungle)

Pointing Words: Este, Ese, Esta, Esa, Aquel, and So On

Spanish recognizes three levels of proximity. First we have the things that are really close to us. For these we use *este, esta, estos,* and *estas.* Then there are the things that are not so close, but are not necessarily out of reach. For those we need *ese, esa, esos,* and *esas.* Finally, we have the things that are quite far away. For those you'll use *aquel, aquella, aquellos,* and *aquellas.* You probably knew this already. But let's take a quick look at these pointing words one more time.

Demonstrative Adjectives

The demonstrative adjectives always appear together with the nouns they modify. There are no *tildes* on these. They must match the gender and number of the thing(s) they are pointing or referring to. Study these examples:

Queremos comprar estas cosas.
We want to buy these things.

¿Cuánto cuestan estos juguetes cada uno?
How much do these toys cost each?

Aquellos tres turistas ya no tienen dinero.
Those three tourists over there don't have any money left.

Aquel hombre es vendedor de recuerdos típicos.
That man over there is a seller of typical souvenirs.

Este regalo será para mi abuela. Ese regalo será para Enrique.
This gift is (will be) for my grandmother. That gift is (will be) for Enrique.

Acuérdate

There are two classes of demonstratives in Spanish: adjectives and pronouns. Both must match the gender and number of the noun or nouns being modified. While this may take you a while to get used to, the good news is that the words for the adjectives and pronouns are the same. The only difference is that the pronouns are written with *tildes*, and the adjectives are not.

Demonstrative Pronouns

These are the same words that you just learned—only now they're written with *tildes*. Demonstrative adjectives modify nouns, but the demonstrative pronouns actually stand in for nouns (the added responsibility means that they get to wear the *tilde*).

The gender and number of the demonstrative pronoun will link it to the noun or nouns in question, so there is no need to mention the nouns specifically. You can often translate these as "this one," "that one," and even "these ones."

Study the following examples to see how they differ in usage from the demonstrative adjectives. Again, the noun or nouns being referenced won't actually be mentioned. The pronouns are here to give the real nouns a break:

Queremos comprar éstas.
We want to buy these (feminine things).

Éste cuesta dos mil pesos, y ése cuesta mil cuatro cientos.
This one costs 2,000 pesos, and that one costs 1,400 (pesos).

Aquéllos no son baratos.
Those over there aren't cheap.

¿Cuál es el precio de éste?
What is the price of this one?

Éste será para mi abuelo, y ése será para Juan.
This one is for my grandfather, and that one is for Juan.

Neuter Demonstrative Pronouns: Esto, Eso, Aquello, Ello

Yes, both the demonstrative adjectives and pronouns must match the gender and number of the nouns being modified or substituted. But there are other times when the "this" or "that" you are referring to is not a specific or quantifiable noun, but rather an idea, an event, a series of things, or something you don't know the name of yet.

Ten Cuidado

Be careful not to place a *tilde* on the neuter pronouns *eso, esos,* and *aquello;* they don't need one. There is no equivalent neuter adjective in Spanish. We don't need to write a *tilde* because there is only one kind of neuter demonstrative, and thus there's no similar-looking demonstrative adjective to distinguish it from. Smart, huh?

When you say, "This is great" or "That's a shame," you're referring to an idea or situation in general. And if you ask "What is that?" you won't know the gender of the noun because you don't know what the thing *is.* That's why you asked.

In such situations, the neuter demonstrative pronouns *eso, esto,* and *aquello* can save the day. If you don't know the name (much less the gender) of the thing you're referring to, these are the words for you.

Don't stress too much over the *ese* versus *aquel* issue at this point. Many native speakers use ese, esa, and *eso* for "that" when technically *aquel, aquella,* or *aquello* should be used. In fact, *aquel* and its permutations are slowly disappearing from the daily speech of certain Latin American regions, especially the Caribbean. It will always be understood, however, and you might as well use it properly.

Read the following examples to see the neuter demonstratives in action:

> *¿Qué es esto?*
> What is this? (This could be an unknown noun or a situation.)

> *¿Cómo se llama esto?*
> What do you call this?

> *Esto no es justo.*
> This isn't fair.

> *No queremos comprar esto, queremos comprar eso.*
> We don't want to buy this (stuff), we want to buy that (stuff).

Aquello es otro tema.
That's another issue.

Eso es una buena idea.
That's a good idea.

Finally, there is *ello*, which you won't come across much except occasionally in writing, where it basically means "that issue."

El Web

For more information about the countries of the Southern Cone, visit the following websites: www.uruguay.com, www.paraguay.com, www.visit-chile.org, and www.argentina.com. You can also do a general search and find many more great websites.

Risa del Día

A popular form for humor in Spanish is the *Jaimito* or *Pepito* joke. *Jaimito* is a mischievous little kid who is always in trouble at school or saying crazy things to his parents. Many of the words that come out of his mouth are not fit for chaste ears. The following joke is rather tame. See if you get it:

Jaimito vuelve de la escuela:

Papá, papá, ¡hoy casi me saqué un 10!

¡Bárbaro! … pero ¿por qué "casi"?

Porque se lo pusieron al nene del banco de al lado.

Vocabulario Útil:

volver   to return

casi   almost

sacar   to get; to come out with

un 10   a perfect score; an "A"

¡Bárbaro!   wonderful!; great!

se lo   "to him it" ("it" being *un 10*)

pusieron   preterite form of *poner*

nene   kid; boy

de al lado   at the side; next to (me)

The Least You Need to Know

♦ The *–o* and *–a* endings work with adjectives, too.

♦ All adjectives must match the gender of the noun.

♦ All adjectives must match the singular and plural form of the noun they modify.

♦ Demonstrative pronouns take a *tilde;* the adjectives and neuters don't.

Chapter 8

Los Países Andinos: The Land of the Incas

In This Chapter

◆ *Lectura:* Machu Picchu

◆ *Datos sobre los países andinos*

◆ Everything you ever wanted to know about *ser* and *estar*

◆ *Hay*—it ain't just for horses

The northern Andes were once the cradle of an advanced and powerful indigenous civilization: the Incas (and a few others before they rose to power). Today, the descendents of this vast nation, together with immigrants from various parts of the world, live in one of the most culturally rich areas in Latin America.

Perú

Peru (which can also be written as *el Perú*), the largest of the Andean countries, was the focus of Spanish colonial domination for well over 200 years. What remains of pre-Columbian America with regard to people, culture, and settlements is perhaps better represented in Peru than in any other nation. Thus, it is no surprise that the country has seen a dramatic increase in tourism over the last few decades. Unfortunately, political insurgency has plagued Peru for many years, and the government has spent countless resources fighting rebel groups such as Tupac Amaru and the Shining Path. Though great progress has been made on these fronts, the fighting is not completely over yet.

Bolivia

Bolivia, the only landlocked Andean country, also has a largely indigenous Indian population that has preserved its native languages and much of its traditional way of life. It is South America's least developed country, and nearly two thirds of its people live in poverty. In recent years, however, there have been improvements in the Bolivian economy thanks to the government's austere economic reform measures. Most Bolivians live in the thin air of the Altiplano, a plateau along the western edge of the country that is 11,550 feet above sea level. In 2006, the country elected Evo Morales, the country's first indigenous head of state since the Spanish Conquest.

El Ecuador

As its name suggests, Ecuador extends over both sides of the equator. It is the smallest of the Andean countries, but has the highest average population density in South America. Interestingly, Ecuador's two largest cities share few things in common. Quito, the capital, is situated high in the Andes. Guayaquil, the country's largest city, is at sea level and is a major port on the Pacific. The Galapagos Islands form Ecuador's Colón province. Charles Darwin visited the islands in 1830, where he conducted the major portion of his observations that led to his theories on evolution. Scientists continue to carry out research on the islands, and the Galapagos have become a popular destination for eco-tourists.

Cultura Latina

The music of the Andean countries has become very popular recently. The panpipes played by Andean musicians are known as *quenas*. Andean musicians also play a small mandolin-like instrument called a *charrango,* which is usually made from the body of an armadillo. A party or small concert of this kind of music is known as a *peña.* You also can find Andean music online by searching for "Traditional Andean Music."

Colombia

Colombia is the only South American country with ports on both the Atlantic and Pacific oceans. People living on the coasts share more in common with the neighboring Caribbean countries than with their Andean neighbors. However, much of the mountainous interior of the country is definitely Andean in culture and climate. Colombia's main exports include oil and coffee, but the country is equally renowned as the world's largest producer of cocaine. Regional drug cartels also deal in heroin and marijuana. Colombia has had a violent history, including bloody civil wars at the beginning of the twentieth century and again in the 1940s and 1950s. Drug-related killings plagued the country in the 1980s but have declined since the death of Medellin Cartel leader Pablo Escobar in 1993.

Cultura Latina
Two main native languages are spoken in this region: Quechua and Aymará. Quechua-speakers can be found from Peru to southern Colombia. Aymará is spoken mainly in Bolivia and along Peru's southern border. The two languages are not mutually intelligible. If you want to learn more about these languages, a simple Internet search should do the trick.

Lectura: Machu Picchu

This text describes Peru's most popular archeological attraction. It's a little longer than some of the previous *lecturas*. Don't worry if you need to read the passage more than once.

Descubierta en 1911 por Hiram Bingham (profesor de la Universidad de Yale, EE.UU.), Machu Picchu viene a ser el atractivo arqueológico más importante de América del Sur.

Se podría decir que con el tiempo, este lugar se ha ido convirtiendo en el símbolo de todo lo que fue la vida y el esplendor prehispánico de los Andes. Su ubicación geográfica y el entorno físico hacen de Machu Picchu un espacio de ensueño y de rara belleza comparable a los más bellos paisajes creados por la naturaleza y adornados por la vida del hombre.

No se sabe a ciencia cierta cuándo fueron construidos los edificios prehispánicos. Afirman las más recientes investigaciones que las primeras construcciones pueden ser atribuidas al famoso Inca Pachacuti, el organizador del Imperio.

Debido a la gran cantidad de esqueletos de mujeres encontrados, se piensa que fue un lugar donde vivían las mujeres del Inca o un refugio de mujeres durante la época de la conquista. De lo que sí no hay duda es que Machu Picchu representa un extraordinario ejemplo de arquitectura e ingeniería.

Por lo general un tour a Machu Picchu dura un día entero. Empezando temprano por la mañana se toma el tren en Cuzco.

Después de 3 horas se llega a Aguas Calientes (la ciudadela de Machu Picchu se encuentra en la cima de una montaña a la cual se llega mediante pequeños autobuses). Una vez en las ruinas empieza el recorrido guiado, finalizando con un almuerzo en el hotel. Después del almuerzo hay tiempo para sacar fotos o hacer un breve recorrido por su cuenta.

Vocabulario Útil:

descubrir   to discover

debido a   due to

atractivo   attraction

convertirse   to become; to be converted into

esplendor   splendor

ubicación   location

edificio   building

espacio de ensueño   place of dreams; fairy-tale land

entorno   environment

raro   rare (adjective before noun)

afirmar   to affirm; to assert; to state

imperio   empire

esqueleto   skeleton

refugio   refuge

duda   doubt

ingeniería   engineering

durar   to last

entero   whole; entire; complete

ciudadela   citadel

cima   top

recorrido   a trip; a round

por su cuenta   on your own; by yourself

belleza   beauty

paisaje   landscape; view

adornado   decorated; adorned

sacar fotos   to take pictures

arqueológico   archeological

Análisis del Texto

This text has a lot of goodies to teach us. Let's take a closer look:

viene a ser   *Venir a ser* really just means "to be" here, with the idea that Machu Picchu is "coming to be" the most important archeological site in South America. *Venir* has many idiomatic uses apart from its basic meaning of "to come." For example, we can use *venir* to say that something *ha venido a menos* which loosely translated means "it isn't what (as good as) it used to be." Check your dictionary for more uses of this versatile little verb.

este lugar se ha ido convirtiendo   This is a tough one. The subject is *este lugar* ("this place"), which is really just standing in for Machu Picchu. The *se* is a third person reflexive and actually goes with *convirtiendo*, the present progressive *–ing* form of *convertirse* (to convert oneself into, to change oneself into, to become). *Ha*, naturally, is from *haber* and means "has," and *ido* is the irregular past participle of *ir* and means "gone." So, literally, we have "this place itself has gone becoming." Of course, this makes no sense. A better translation might be "Machu Picchu has, over a period of time, been in the process of becoming …."

los más bellos paisajes creados por la naturaleza   Notice that the adjective *bellos* is placed before the modified noun *paisajes*. This adjective might also have come after the noun, as most adjectives in Spanish tend to do: *Los paisajes más bellos* …. But there is a difference between the two placements, albeit a subtle one. With the adjective coming before the noun, the beauty of the landscapes is emphasized ("the most beautiful landscapes"). With the adjective after the noun (*paisajes bellos*), the emphasis is more on the landscapes ("the landscapes that happen to be beautiful"), suggesting that there might also be a lot of ugly landscapes around that aren't being considered.

a ciencia cierta   Literally "by certain science," this idiomatic phrase just means "with certainty."

se piensa que   The *se* makes it passive: "it is thought that." There are several passive *se* constructions in this text.

De lo que sí no hay duda es que Machu Picchu   This construction would normally be a lot simpler: *No hay duda que Machu Picchu* …. However, because the previous sentence casts some doubt as to what Machu Picchu was used for, this sentence, as a contrast to the uncertainty of the previous statement, starts off by telling the reader what we really do know for a fact. The *de lo que* literally means "of that which." The *sí* is an intensifier for what is being said. So a better translation: "What there really is no doubt about is that …."

la cima de una montaña a la cual se llega mediante pequeños autobuses   The *a la cual* means "to which." The *la* refers to *cima* because both words are feminine. Literal translation: "The top of a mountain to which (feminine) it is arrived by way of small buses." Better translation: "You get to the top of the mountain on small buses."

por su cuenta   Literally, "by your account." A better translation: "on your own" or even "by yourself."

Vista Panorámica de los Países Andinos

Países de la región: *República de Bolivia; República del Perú; República del Ecuador; República de Colombia*

Gobiernos: *Bolivia: república de 9 departamentos; el Perú: república de 23 departamentos y una provincia; el Ecuador: república de 20 provincias; Colombia: república de 23 departamentos, tres intendencias, y cinco comisarías*

Capitales: *Bolivia: La Paz (administrativa), Sucre: (constitucional); Perú: Lima; Ecuador: Quito; Colombia: Santa Fé de Bogotá*

Tamaños: *Bolivia: 1.098.581 km. cuadrados; Perú: 1.285.000 km. cuadrados; Ecuador: 269.178 km. cuadrados; Colombia: 1.141.748 km. cuadrados*

Poblaciones: *Bolivia: 10 millones; Perú: 29 millones; Ecuador: 13 millones; Colombia: 36 millones*

Divisas: *Bolivia: boliviano; Perú: nuevo peso peruano; Ecuador: el sucre; Colombia: peso colombiano*

Formas adjetivales: *Boliviano; peruano; ecuatoriano; colombiano*

Recursos naturales: *Carbón, petróleo, gas natural, esmeraldas* (emeralds)*, hierro, plomo, oro, piedra, madera, metales, minerales, pesca, estaño* (tin)*, plata, arroz, tungsteno, cinc, otros*

Industrias: *Comida y bebidas, minería, textiles, productos químicos, procesamiento de minerales, harina de pescado, ensamblaje de autos, productos farmacéuticos, cemento, plásticos, otras*

Industrias agropecuarias: *Café, bananas, flores, algodón, azúcar, tabaco, papas, soja, sorgo* (sorgum)*, maíz, cacao, mariscos, ganadería, lana, trigo, otros*

Cultura Latina

The food in this region is very diverse, varying with altitude and the local agricultural conditions. *Cuy* (roasted guinea pig) is popular in the mountainous areas. There is a great variety of fresh fruit available, particularly at lower altitudes. Seafood is popular on the coast. Shrimp is a favorite, as is *ceviche*, a raw, marinated fish dish. A popular street food in Ecuador is potatoes served with pig blood. Sounds yummy (or not).

Gramática: Ser vs. Estar

As you know, two Spanish verbs translate as "to be" in English: *ser* and *estar*. Each has its own special uses. This phenomenon often causes confusion among students of Spanish. This section tries to better explain the differences in usage of these two verbs.

Ser and Estar with Nouns

Ser is used to indicate where things come from, their relationship to one another, and the groups to which they belong. *Ser* describes who owns a noun or what it's made of. *Ser* usually speaks to a quality that is unchanging and static. Please note the following:

- **Profession:** *Mi tío es médico.* My uncle is a doctor.
- **Origin:** *Soy de Lima.* I am from Lima.
- **Nationality:** *Mi abuela es colombiana.* My grandmother is Colombian.
- **Material:** *La casa es de madera y ladrillo.* The house is made from wood and brick.
- **Ownership:** *El libro es de Oscar.* The book is Oscar's.
- **Relationship:** *Esta llama no es mía.* This llama is not mine.
- **Religion:** *Cecilia es católica.* Cecilia is Catholic.

When used with nouns, the verb *estar* refers to location and position:

◆ **Location:** *Mi esposo siempre está en el trabajo.* My husband is always at work.

◆ **Position:** *El baño está al lado de la puerta.* The bathroom is next to the door.

Ser and Estar with Adjectives

Ser is used to express characteristics that are not expected to change any time soon. Use *ser* when you wish to be objective about the state or appearance of something. *Ser* is used to define things at their core.

Ten Cuidado _____

Although you'll almost always use *estar* to indicate where someone or something is located, you must use *ser* for the location of an event: *¿Dónde es la fiesta?* "Where's the party?"

Estar, on the other hand, is used to indicate characteristics or situations (how things are at the present time). Use *estar* when you want to express a more subjective opinion about something. *Estar* is used more for descriptions than for definitions. Read the following examples carefully:

Soy guapo.   I am good looking. (I always have been.)

Estoy guapo.   I am looking good. (Usually I look terrible, but *today* I look great!)

Juana es loca.   Juana is crazy. (She suffers from a mental disorder and may need psychiatric treatment).

Juana está loca.   Juana is acting crazy. (She's behaving odd or silly at this moment, but usually she's got both feet on the ground.)

Antonio es gordo.   Anthony is fat. (Anthony is a large man. He has always been that way and is expected to remain so.)

Antonio está gordo.   Anthony is (looking) fat. (He has been eating too much lately and has developed a paunch. He'll probably go back to normal after the holidays.)

Take another look at the last two examples. Let's say that Antonio is tired of everyone saying "*Es gordo.*" So he goes on a diet. Once he is visibly thinner, people will start saying "*Antonio está delgado*" ("Anthony is looking thin"). This means that although he usually isn't thin, he appears so now. He could gain the weight back at any time. But if he remains thinner for an extended period, sooner or later people will start saying

"*Antonio es delgado*" ("Anthony is a thin man"). The change from *estar* to *ser* indicates that people are no longer thinking of him as *gordo*.

Ser and Estar with the Past Participle

For *ser*, the same rules apply to past participles as for all other adjectives. You can use *ser* if the past participle describes some characteristic. You probably won't find yourself using *ser* with past participles very often when speaking the language. Its use is more common in the written language:

> *Julio es un hombre muy bien conocido.*
> Julio is a very well-known man.

> *Es comprado por los turistas.*
> It is bought by tourists.

> *Es sabido por todos.*
> It is known by everyone.

> *Marcelo es una persona muy fría.*
> Marcelo is a cold (unfeeling) individual.

Algo Nuevo

Take another look at this phrase from the reading: *Afirman las más recientes investigaciones que ….* Notice the word order here. A literal translation would be, "They substantiate the most recent investigations that …." In Spanish, because the verb indicates the subject by its conjugated form, there is more flexibility in terms of subject placement. So I can say either *Juan lo compró* ("John bought it") or *Lo compró Juan* ("Bought it John"). It makes no difference. Don't let this throw you off.

However, unlike *ser*, you'll be using *estar* with past participles all the time. Use *estar* with a past participle to describe the condition of a noun without considering who made it that way: *La tienda está cerrada* means "The store is closed." Here are a few good examples:

> *El mercado está abierto, pero las tiendas están cerradas.*
> The market is open, but the stores are closed.

> *Estoy perdido.*
> I'm lost.

Estás equivocado.
You're wrong.

Estamos perdidos.
We're lost.

El agua está hervida.
The water has boiled. (Remember: *agua* is feminine but takes *el*.)

Ellas están muy preocupadas.
They (women) are very worried.

> **Ten Cuidado** _____
>
> Now and then you'll come across an expression that doesn't quite follow the rules. For example, *Ramón está muerto* means "Ramón is dead," even though most people would consider his death to be rather permanent. Sometimes both *ser* and *estar* can be used to express the same concept. For example, to say that you are married, you can say *Estoy casado/a* or *Soy casado/a*.

Hay—Not Just for Caballos

You know that the word *hay* (rhymes with the English *pie* and *sky*) means "there is" or "there are." Technically, it's a verb form derived from *haber*; but unlike all other verbs, it doesn't change with respect to singular or plural. Use *hay* when you want to state that (or ask if) something (or things) exists:

Hay mucha gente en el mundo.
There are a lot of people in the world.

Señor, disculpe. ¿Hay agua? ¿Hay comida?
Excuse me, sir. Is there (do you have) any water? Food?

Hay muchos problemas aquí.
There are a lot of problems here.

No hay bananas.
We have no bananas.

Hay also works with *que* plus an infinitive to say "we need to" or "one must" or "you gotta." *Hay que* is more general and less specific to a single person or persons than *tener que*.

¿Hay que pagar antes o después?
Do I/we have to pay before or after?
(in general)

Hay que comer para vivir.
One must eat to live. ("You gotta eat
to live.")

Hay que tener paciencia.
We need to be patient. ("You gotta have patience.")

Hay que trabajar para ganar dinero.
People need to work to earn money. ("You gotta work ....")

Acuérdate _____

You can use *Sí hay* and *No hay* to respond to *¿Hay "X"?* questions: *¿Hay pan? Sí, hay. ¿Hay tiempo? No, no hay.*

A Word About Adverbs

And now for something completely different .... Let's talk about adverbs. Adverbs modify verbs, adjectives, or other adverbs. English words that end in *–ly* such as *quickly*, *happily*, and *unfortunately* are adverbs. Other adverbs are shorter, such as *right* and *well*.

Spanish adverbs work in a similar way. Some are formed by adding an ending to an adjective, while many of the more common adjectives are simply short little words with no special ending. Unlike adjectives, Spanish adverbs do not take *–a* or *–o* as endings, and are never affected by gender, even when they modify an adjective that is gender-specific.

The equivalent ending for *–ly* in Spanish is *–mente*. Spanish adverbs can be formed by adding *–mente* to the feminine form of the adjective. If the adjective is invariable and ends in *–e* or with a consonant, *–mente* may still be added:

Adjectives to Adverbs

Masculine Adjective	Feminine Adjective	Adverb	English
rápido	*rápida*	*rápidamente*	quickly
honesto	*honesta*	*honestamente*	honestly
básico	*básica*	*básicamente*	basically
natural	(no change)	*naturalmente*	naturally
urgente	(no change)	*urgentemente*	urgently

Here are a few examples:

◆ *Los colombianos me han tratado muy cordialmente:* The Colombians have treated me very cordially.

◆ *Están casados felizmente:* They are happily married.

◆ *Probablemente, no sabe Juan cómo se llega a Arequipa:* Probably, Juan doesn't know how to get to Arequipa.

Ten Cuidado

A few –*mente* adverbs are false cognates:

Últimamente means "recently," not "ultimately."

Casualmente means "by chance," not "casually."

Eventualmente means "possibly," not "eventually."

Absolutamente should only be used negatively, as in "absolutely not."

Although it's good to know how to use the –*mente* ending, you'll find that most of the more common adverbs you'll use on a daily basis won't use –*mente*.

Here are some common "non –*mente*" adverbs. A few are also adjectives:

◆ *bien* (well); *hablar bien* (to speak well)

◆ *más* (more); *más fácil* (easier)

◆ *menos* (less); *menos fácil* (less easy)

◆ *mejor* (better); *hablar mejor* (to speak better)

◆ *peor* (worse); *cantar peor* (to sing worse)

◆ *mal* (poorly); *hablar mal* (to speak poorly)

◆ *jamás* (never ever); *hablar jamás* (to never speak)

◆ *nunca* (never); *nunca cantar* (to never sing)

◆ *casi* (almost); *casi hecho* (almost done)

◆ *muy* (very); *muy fácil* (very easy)

◆ *siempre* (always); *siempre habla* (always talks)

◆ *también* (also); *también canta* (sings, too)

◆ *tampoco* ("either"); *tampoco baila* (doesn't dance, either)

◆ *todavía* (still); *todavía está* (is still here)

◆ *ya* (already, now); *ya está aquí* (it's already here)

Just a few examples should do the trick:

Es muy difícil leer el chino.
It is very difficult to read Chinese.

Tampoco no es fácil pronunciar el chino.
It's not easy to pronounce Chinese, either.

Mi suegra todavía está aquí con nosotros.
My mother-in-law is still here with us.

El bebé siempre llora.
The baby always cries.

El rey es tan rico.
The king is so rich.

Las montañas son tan grandes.
The mountains are so big.

Acuérdate _____

Some adjectives can't take the *–mente* ending. Adjectives denoting physical appearance, origin, nationality, and religion usually do not take *–mente* to make adverbs, although there are a few exceptions.

Acuérdate _____

The adverb *tampoco* is the negative form of *también*. Because *también* means "also," *tampoco* means "not also" or "either," as in *No hablo el holandés, y tampoco no hablo el alemán*: "I don't speak Dutch, and I don't speak German, either." Be careful not to say "*también no.*"

Ya means "already." It can also mean "now." When used with "no," it means "anymore": *Ya no toco la guitarra* means "I don't play the guitar anymore."

The con + Noun Adverb Construction

You can also use nouns as adverbs by putting the word *con* in front of the noun. I call this the "Night Before Christmas" construction, as in: "The stockings were hung by the chimney *with care*." Observe:

El maestro siempre lee el diario con cuidado.
The teacher always reads the newspaper with care (same as "carefully").

Vamos a esperar con paciencia.
We are going to wait patiently (with patience).

Alejandro habla de su madre con mucho amor.
Alejandro speaks lovingly of his mother (with much love).

El Web

Here are some great websites about the countries of the northern Andes: www.bolivia.com or www.boliviaweb.com, www.colombia.com, www.ecuador.com, and www.peru.com.

Risa del Día

I think that this joke is rather international:

> *En la oficina:*
>
> *¡Sr. Perez! ¿No sabe usted que está prohibido beber durante las horas de trabajo?*
>
> *No se preocupe jefe, ¡no estoy trabajando!*

Vocabulario Útil:

estar prohibido   to be prohibited

beber   to drink (here, something with alcohol)

horas de trabajo   working hours

preocuparse   to worry

trabajando   present participle: working

The Least You Need to Know

- Both *ser* and *estar* mean "to be" but have very different uses.
- *Ser* is generally for inherent qualities; *estar* is generally for conditions.
- *Hay* means both "there is" and "there are"; singular and plural don't matter.
- The Spanish adverbial ending is *–mente*, but many shorter adverbs won't need this ending.

Chapter 9

Los Países del Caribe

In This Chapter

- ◆ *Lectura:* La República Dominicana
- ◆ *Datos sobre los países caribeños*
- ◆ Objects and object pronouns

When Cristóbal Colón (a.k.a. Christopher Columbus) discovered the Americas, it was to the islands of the Caribbean that he first came. So it's no wonder that he (and many other Europeans after him) kept coming back. When I think of a tropical paradise, this is the place. If it weren't for the economic and political instabilities of the region, as well as the occasional hurricane, the Caribbean islands would indeed be a heaven on Earth.

Come to the Islands

Santo Domingo, the capital of the Dominican Republic, was the first permanent Spanish settlement in the Americas. It was founded in 1496, four years after Columbus landed. The Dominican Republic has had a turbulent political history. The country was occupied twice by Haiti in the 1800s and by the U.S. Marines from 1916 to 1924. President Johnson sent the Marines back in 1965 to prevent a civil war. Since then, the political climate has settled down, making the country a popular spot for beachgoers, retirees, and eco-tourists.

> ### Cultura Latina
>
> Okay, so Venezuela isn't an island. But because the majority of the country's population lives along the Caribbean coast, the culture, speech, and lifestyle of most Venezuelans are similar to those of the other Spanish-speaking island nations in the region. That is why I have included the country in this chapter.

What we now call Puerto Rico was once called *Borinquen* by the Taíno Indians who originally inhabited the island. Today, Puerto Ricans often refer to themselves and their language as *boricua*. The United States took possession of Puerto Rico at the end of the Spanish-American War. The Commonwealth of Puerto Rico has a "Free Associated State" relationship with the United States. Puerto Ricans have the same rights as all U.S. citizens, and many Puerto Ricans have left the island to live "on the continent," especially in the state of New Jersey and in New York City.

Venezuela is home to both the world's highest waterfall, the 3,212-foot Angel Falls; and the anaconda, the world's longest snake. (The two seem unrelated, however.) Venezuelans revere nineteenth-century hero Simón Bolívar, who led a decade-long revolution to oust the Spanish from much of South America. The country's currency bears his name. Indian languages are spoken by about 200,000 Amer-indians in the remote interior of the country. This oil-rich country has held democratic elections since 1958. However, the political situation has taken an interesting turn recently, as its current president, Hugo Chavéz, continually thumbs his *nariz* at the United States.

The birthplace of the *rumba*, *mambo*, and the *cha cha*, Cuba is the largest island in the Caribbean. It endures as one of the last bastions of communism. The country is ruled by Fidel Castro, who took power in 1959 with popular support. Cuba suffered an economic blow in 1989 when its European Communist trading partners began falling apart. Since Castro's revolution, many Cubans have left the island for political and economic reasons. From 1959 through the 1990s, almost 1 million Cubans immigrated to the United States, many of whom now live in Miami, Florida. Cuba also has a rich literary tradition.

Lectura: La República Dominicana

This *lectura* discusses some important facts about the Dominican Republic.

La República Dominicana, con una extensión de 48.442 km2, ocupa las dos terceras partes de la superficie de la Zona Este de la Isla de Hispañola. El lado Oeste lo ocupa la República de Haití.

Clima:

El clima que impera en la zona costera es cálido, como propio del trópico. En la región central, las temperaturas son más frescas. El promedio de la temperatura a lo largo del año es de 29 grados centígrados (84 grados F). En la zona montañosa, y principalmente en invierno, se registran muy bajas temperaturas, en ocasiones a menos de 0 grados C (32 grados F), principalmente en Valle Nuevo, Constanza y el Pico Duarte. El mes de agosto es el más caluroso del año y enero el más fresco. La mayor temporada de lluvias se produce entre mayo y agosto y la menor en los meses de noviembre y diciembre.

Divisa:

La moneda nacional es el peso. El valor real del peso dominicano fluctúa frente al dólar americano y su valor está sujeto a las leyes de la oferta y la demanda. El peso está dividido en cien unidades.

Religión:

La mayoría de los dominicanos y de las dominicanas profesan la religión católica, apostólica y romana.

Tránsito:

En Santo Domingo se conduce a la derecha. Los visitantes con licencia de conducir vigente pueden usarla durante un período máximo de 90 días, sin necesidad de ningún trámite adicional. El máximo de velocidad permitida en las autopistas es de 80 kilómetros por hora; en zonas suburbanas, 60 kilómetros y 40 kilómetros por hora en las ciudades, salvo que haya señalización específica.

Acuérdate

The words for certain foods often change significantly from place to place. In the Caribbean, the word for banana is *guineo*. *Los plátanos* are the larger plantains that are fried. But in Mexico, a *plátano* is your regular old banana.

Vocabulario Útil:

superficie surface

ocupar to occupy

velocidad speed

autopista highway

imperar to prevail

promedio   average

trámite   procedure; paperwork

principalmente   principally

temporada   season; time of year

profesar   to profess

fluctuar   to fluctuate; to vary

estar sujeto a   to be subject to

fresco   cool

costero   coastal

cálido   hot

caluroso   warm

vigente   valid; in force

unidad   unit; measurement

señalización   signs; signage

específico   specific

Análisis del Texto

Now let's study some words and phrases from the text:

48.442 km2   Read this number as *cuarenta y ocho mil, cuatro cientos cuarenta y dos kiló-metros cuadrados.* In English: "square kilometers."

las dos terceras partes   This means "two thirds"; literally, "the two thirds parts."

Algo Nuevo
Many common words sometimes have secondary meanings that you may not be aware of. Take, for example, the word *bajo*. Depending on the context, this little word can mean "low," "vulgar," "short," "under," "during," "the first floor of a building," "the hem of a dress," "the cuff of a shirt," "the underside of a vehicle," "a bass (instrument)," and more. If you come across a word that you are already familiar with, but in a context that doesn't make sense, you may need to look up the word again to see if it has any secondary meanings.

como propio del trópico   You may have learned *propio* as meaning "own," as in *Quiero tener me propia casa*: "I want to have my own house." In the previous phrase, *propio de* has another meaning and translates as "usual for" or "characteristic of."

La mayor temporada de lluvias se produce   *Producir* does indeed mean "to produce," and *se produce* could be translated as "is produced." But that really wouldn't sound right for this phrase: "The greatest season of rains is produced ...." In reality, *se produce* is just being used as an alternative to the verb "to happen" or "to occur" in order to make the text sound more interesting.

y la menor en los meses de   The *la* is standing in for *temporada*, which was mentioned in the earlier part of the sentence. We know this because *la* is feminine and *temporada* is also feminine; the two words are linked by gender.

las leyes de la oferta y la demanda   This phrase means "the laws of supply and demand."

salvo que haya señalización específica   *Haya* is the subjunctive form of *hay*. We need subjunctive because *salvo que*, which means "unless," always requires a subjunctive.

Vista Panorámica de los Países Caribeños

Países de la región: *República de Cuba; República de Venezuela; Estado Libre Asociado de Puerto Rico; República Dominicana*

Gobiernos: *Cuba: república socialista de catorce provincias; Venezuela: república federal de veinte estados, un distrito federal y dos territorios nacionales; Puerto Rico: estado libre asociado de los EE.UU., con dos cámaras legislativas, un gobernador elegido. Tiene representantes en el Congreso de los EE.UU., pero no pueden votar; República Dominicana: república democrática de treinta provincias*

Capitales: *Cuba: la Habana; República Dominicana: Santo Domingo; Venezuela: Caracas; Puerto Rico: San Juan*

Tamaños: *Cuba: 110.860 km cuadrados; República Dominicana: 48.442 km. cuadrados; Venezuela: 912.050 km. cuadrados; Puerto Rico: 9.104 km. cuadrados*

Población: *Cuba: 11 millones, sin incluir a los cubanos que viven en los EE.UU.; República Dominicana: 7.5 millones; Venezuela: 24 millones; Puerto Rico: 3 millones, sin incluir a los puertorriqueños que viven en los EE.UU.*

Divisas: *Cuba: peso cubano; República Dominicana: peso dominicano; Venezuela: bolívar; Puerto Rico: dólar estadounidense*

Recursos naturales de la región: *Níquel, oro, plata, madera, cobalto, hierro, cobre, manganeso, sal, pesca, petróleo, azufre, gas natural, carbón, diamantes, turismo*

Industrias de la región: *Industria petrolero (Venezuela), cemento, industria tabacalera* (tobacco), *refinamiento de azúcar, textiles, minería de piedra, arena, grava* (gravel), *café*

Industrias agropecuarias: *café, cacao, azúcar de caña, piñas, naranjas, guineos* (bananas), *flores, leche, vegetales, tabacos, aves de corral, otros*

Gramática: Direct and Indirect Object Pronouns

To speak Spanish with any level of fluency, you must have complete hegemony over the pronouns. There's no way around them. This is something you've just gotta get.

Your beginning Spanish text probably covered the object pronouns. But many students of Spanish seem to have trouble using them correctly, so I think it would be a good idea to review these guys and give you my own perspective on how this all works.

Transitive and Intransitive Verbs

As you probably already know, there are two kinds of verbs: those that pass on their action to something else and those that seem to just sit there. For example, in the sentence "I throw a stone," the verb "to throw" requires that I throw *something*. The stone is the object of my throwing. This kind of verb is called a transitive verb. So the stone, as the thing being thrown, is the "direct object" of this verb.

Acuérdate

Sometimes the direct object of a transitive verb is not actually in the sentence but is merely understood. In the sentence "He threw from the infield," the object of his throwing is still a baseball, even though the baseball is not mentioned. So the verb is still transitive. However, "He throws with his left arm" is intransitive, because there is no direct object.

Here are a few more examples of direct objects with transitive verbs. The direct objects are in italics:

I see *Juan.*

Elvira is learning *Spanish.*

Alejandro answered *the telephone.*

Juana sent *an e-mail.*

The dog bit *the man.*

The man bit *the dog.*

In each of the previous sentences, we could substitute the word *what* or *it* for the direct object, and the sentence would still make sense: "Juana sent it."

Verbs that don't or can't take a direct object are called "intransitive." They pretty much just "are":

> The telephone *rang*.
>
> Problems *exist*.
>
> The story *evolved*.
>
> I *think*, therefore I *am*. (Descartes)

Many verbs can be used both transitively and intransitively, depending on whether they are taking an object:

> Cindy eats every two hours. (intransitive)
>
> Cindy eats *cake* every two hours. (transitive)
>
> Our baby weighs 20 pounds. (intransitive)
>
> The butcher weighs *meat* on a scale. (transitive)

The Direct Object Pronouns (DOPs)

The object pronouns are not the same as the subject pronouns you learned for conjugating verbs (*yo, tú, él, ella*, and so on). But they do perform a similar function because they also stand in for nouns so that you don't have to repeat them (note clever use of direct object pronoun here). To use the direct object pronouns—DOPs, for short—the noun for which the pronoun is substituting must be the direct object of a transitive verb. In other words, to avoid always having to restate the object of the verb ("I see the ball; I want to buy the ball; I like the ball; Give me the ball"), we use the DOP ("I see *it*; I want to buy *it*").

In English, we use *me, you, it, him, her, us,* and *them*. Look at these:

> He hit *me*.
>
> I love *you* and *them*.
>
> We eat *it*.
>
> The dog bit *him, her,* and *us*.

Naturally, you'll need to do the same kinds of substitutions in Spanish. You probably learned these before:

Spanish DOP	English DOP
me	me
te	you
lo/la	him/her/you (must match gender)
nos	us
os	you all (Spain)
los/las	them/you all (must match gender)

Ten Cuidado

When you are going to use a third-person DOP (*he/she/it/they*), remember that the noun must already have been stated or at least be understood. Otherwise, no one will know what the DOP stands for.

The direct object (I mean the *real* noun, not the pronoun) of a transitive Spanish verb usually ends up in the same place that it does in an English sentence: *Yo compro leche* means "I buy milk."

But when a Spanish direct object *pronoun* is used with a *conjugated* transitive verb, it must come before the verb, not after it. This can be tricky for English-speakers because the structure is very different from what we are used to. In English, we say, "I see you." In Spanish, it's "I *you* see."

Let's look at the *Yo compro leche* sentence again. To substitute a pronoun for *leche*, I need to put the DOP that means "it" before the conjugated verb: *Yo la compro* ("I it buy") really means "I buy it." The *la* stands in for *leche*. We need *la* (and not *lo*) because *leche* is feminine. Once again, gender is linking words and concepts together. Take a look at these examples:

¿Habla usted el español?
Sí, lo hablo. ("Yes, I it speak.")

¿Quién tiene los zapatos?
Yo los tengo. ("I them have.")

¿Ves las montañas?
No, no las veo. ("No, I don't them see.")

¿Sabe usted la letra del himno nacional?
No, en realidad, no la sé. (No, actually, I don't.)

The DOP, when used in a phrase containing an infinitive, may be affixed to the end of the infinitive verb. The DOP also may be placed before the conjugated verb. There's no change in meaning between these two forms. Only the placement of the DOP has changed.

Moving the DOP Doesn't Change Meaning

This ...	Or This ...	Still Means This ...
Puedo verte.	*Te puedo ver.*	I can see you.
¿Quieres verme?	*¿Me quieres ver?*	Do you want to see me?
Necesitamos pagarlo.	*Lo necesitamos pagar.*	We need to pay it.
Ella quiere llamarnos.	*Ella nos quiere llamar.*	She wants to call us.
Vamos a hacerlo mañana.	*Lo vamos a hacer mañana.*	We'll do it tomorrow.
No puedo entenderla.	*No la puedo entender.*	I can't understand her.
Tienes que decirlos.	*Los tienes que decir.*	You must say them.
¿No vas a besarme?	*¿No me vas a besar?*	Aren't you going to kiss me?

Acuérdate

Remember that *lo/la* and *los/las* are gender-specific; the others aren't. For the third person (*he/she/it/they/those*, and so on), you must match the gender of the pronoun to the gender of the person or thing for which you are substituting. This is where gender helps link things together. Simply by matching the DOP with the gender of the word you have in mind, you can avoid repeating the noun again and again.

The Indirect Object Pronouns (INDOPs)

The indirect object of a sentence is the final destination of a transitive verb's direct object. In other words, this is where the direct object ultimately ends up. It isn't *what* is given, but *who* gets it: "to whom." For example, in the sentence "I gave Julio my bicycle," the object is *bicycle* and *Julio* is the indirect object because he was the recipient of my giving. In the sentence "I throw stones at my neighbor's house," the object is *stones*, and the indirect object is *my neighbor's house*.

The best way to explain indirect objects is by example. The indirect objects in the following sentences are italicized:

I gave the ball *to Jorge*.

I gave *Jorge* the ball.

He told *Alberto* the story.

The police gave *Roberto* a hard time.

John sold *Esteban* some Arizona beachfront property.

Ten Cuidado

When the direct object of a verb is a person or pet, a must come before it: *Veo a Juan* ("I see Juan"); and *Amo a mi perro Fido* ("I love my dog Fido"); but *Veo el avión* ("I see the airplane"). This is known as the "personal *a*."

Notice that the placement of the indirect object in English can vary from sentence to sentence. If it's at the end, we need to put a *to* there to indicate what follows is the indirect object: "to Jorge."

The Spanish indirect object pronouns, or INDOPs, look pretty much the same as the DOPs. In fact, the only difference between them is in the third person. The good news is that these guys are not gender-specific, only *person*-specific.

Indirect Object Pronoun Table

Spanish DOP	English DOP
me	to me
te	to you
le	to him/her (and *usted*)
nos	to us
os	to you all (Spain)
les	to them (and *ustedes*)

Study the following Spanish examples:

> *María nunca le dice la verdad.*
> Maria never tells him (her, *usted*) the truth.

> *¡Háblame!*
> Talk to me! (Commands always put DOPS and INDOPS at end.)

> *Te doy mi número de teléfono.*
> I'll give you my phone number.

> *¿Me vas a dar un beso o no?*
> Are you going to give me a kiss or not? (*Vas a darme …*)

> *Os van a llamar a las cinco.*
> They are going to call you all at five. (Spain) *Van a llamaros …*)

> *Ellos no pueden darles mucha información.*
> They can't give them (or *ustedes*) a lot of information. (*No les pueden dar …*)

Note that the INDOP can also indicate "for someone," not just "to someone." In the sentence *¿Me puedes hacer un favor?* the idea is more "Can you do a favor *for* me?" than "Can you do a favor *to* me?" Also remember that it's the verb that indicates "who" is doing, "what" they're doing, and "when" they are doing it (by virtue of the tense). The DOP indicates the "object" of their doing, and the INDOP indicates "who" or "what" is receiving the object or action.

Getting the DOP and the INDOP Together

Except for third person combinations, getting the DOP and the INDOP together is no sweat. The INDOP always comes first. And, as before, you have some choices. If there is an infinitive, you may stick the two together at the end. If there is a conjugated verb only, the INDOP and the DOP must go first.

When placed before a conjugated verb, the INDOP and the DOP are written separately: *te lo*, *me los*, and so on. But if they are stuck to the end of an infinitive, they are written together. Watch for *tildes*—they may be needed to preserve correct stress:

> *Me los dan.*
> They give them to me.

> *Te lo digo.*
> I'll tell it to you.

> *Te las envío mañana.*
> I'll send them to you tomorrow.

> *Me lo van a dar el lunes.*
> They're going to give it to me on Monday. (*Van a dármelo …*)

> *Puede decírtelos.*
> He/She can tell you them. (also, *Te los puede decir …*)

> *Voy a comprártela el jueves.*
> I'm going to buy it (feminine noun) for you on Thursday. (or, *Te la voy a comprar …*)

As you can see from the examples, the INDOP comes first, followed by the DOP. When attached to an infinitive, the INDOP and DOP are stuck together, and *tildes* will appear to maintain correct stress.

Third-Person DOP Meets Third-Person INDOP

You may be thinking that if you put the third-person DOP and the third-person INDOP together, you'd get *lelo, lela, leslo, lesla, leslos*. And you're also no doubt thinking that the following examples should be entirely correct: *dárlelo, decírlela, comprárlesla, comprárlelos, le los compro* ("I buy them for him/her/you"), *les las doy* ("I give them to them"), and so on. Seems logical to me, too. Unfortunately, all of these examples are very *wrong!*

Whenever a third-person DOP and a third-person INDOP are put together in a sentence, no matter if the objects are singular or plural, the INDOP always turns into *se*. For example, when you want to say "give it to him," it would logically be *dar + le* (or *les*) + *lo* (or *la, los, las*), but the *le* or *les* needs to be replaced by *se*.

In other words, take the sentence *Se lo doy*. Here the little word *se* is standing in for *le*, which is standing in for "to a person we know." The *lo* indicates that the thing given is a singular masculine noun, and the *doy* indicates "I give." If the *lo* weren't there, the *le* wouldn't have to change to *se*.

Here are some more examples:

> **Ten Cuidado** _____
>
> Never say *lelo, leslos,* and other variations of this sort. Just saying it feels funny. Always remember to use *se* for the INDOP when you mean "to a third person" whenever a DOP is present. If there's no DOP, *le* and *les* don't change. Both singular and plural INDOPs change to *se* in combination with a DOP.

Se las mando.
I'll send them to him (her/*usted*).

Se los van a enviar mañana.
They're going to send them to him (her/*usted*) tomorrow. (*Van a dárselos …*)

Voy a comprársela mañana.
I'm going to buy it for them (or *ustedes*) tomorrow. (*Se las voy a comprar …*)

Se lo va a dar algún día.
He's (She's) going to give it to him/her/*usted* someday.

Avoiding Confusion

In most cases, you'll find that the context makes it pretty clear which noun a DOP is referring to. The gender also is a clue because it always links the DOP to the object being substituted.

However, the third-person INDOP can be a little tricky because *le* can mean "to him," "to her," "to it," or "to *usted*," and *les* can mean "to them" or "to *ustedes*." And when DOPs and third-person INDOPs get together, confusion may arise because the *se* can be singular or plural, and can refer to a man, a woman, both, or to one or more inanimate nouns.

Whenever the possibility for confusion exists, or when you wish to emphasize just who is actually involved, you can clarify the indirect object (and sometimes the object, if no indirect object is present) by adding an *a* plus the person, persons, or things:

a él to him	*a ellas* to them (women)
a ella to her	*a los hombres* to the men
a Juan to Juan	*a ustedes* to "you all"
a María to Maria	*al señor* to the gentleman
a usted to you, Sir/Madam	*a las organizaciones* to the organizations
a ellos to them	

And so on ...

Se lo voy a decir a él.
I'm going to tell it to him.

Ya se lo he dado a Juan.
I've already given it to Juan.

Le voy a dar un peso a María.
I am going to give Maria a peso.

María nunca le dice la verdad a Hector.
Maria never tells Hector the truth.

Acuérdate

The *a* in phrases such as *a él* and *a ella* looks like the personal *a* I mentioned before. This *a* is actually called the "dative *a*." You don't need to worry about its name, but you need to add it before these pronouns when you want to clarify that the action is going "to someone."

Remember that when adding both DOPs and INDOPs to an infinitive, a *tilde* will appear over the last syllable of the infinitive to preserve the stress: *dárselo, decírselos,* and so on. Otherwise, it would be *darSElo* and *decirSElos.*

El Web

You can find some great websites about the countries of the Caribbean. Learn more about each country at www.dominicanrepublic.com, www.venezuela.com, www.cuba.com, and www.puertorico.com.

Also, if you enjoy reading jokes in Spanish, visit www.chistes.com. You can really learn a lot of Spanish from reading these *chistes*.

Risa del Día

Here's another *Jaimito/Pepito* joke. As with many of these, this one takes place at school. I hope you get it:

En una escuelita rural, todos los alumnos llegan tarde a clase. La maestra les pregunta:

A ver Jorgito, ¿por que llegaste tarde?

Y, porque cuando venía mi burro se tropezó con una piedra y se cayó y tuve que venir caminando.

¿Y tú, Pedrito?

Y, yo venía en el burro y apareció una piedra y …

¿Y tú Miguelito?

Lo mismo, señorita.

¿Y tú, Pepito?, y no me digas esa historia del burro porque yo sé que tú no tienes burro.

No, señorita, a mí me trajo mi papá en auto, pero con tantos burros tirados por el camino ….

Vocabulario Útil:

escuelita little school

a ver let's see; "Tell me."

Y, Here, this means "Well …"

tropezarse to trip

caerse to fall down

traer (trajo) to bring (brought)

historia story

tirar to throw; "thrown all over"

The Least You Need to Know

♦ Direct objects receive the action of a verb.

♦ Indirect objects receive the direct objects.

♦ The Spanish third-person DOPs must match gender and number of the direct object.

♦ Never say *lelo* or *lesla*, or similar combos. Use *se* to replace *le* and *les* with a third-person INDOP + DOP.

♦ Use *a él*, *a Juan*, *a ustedes*, and so on for clarification when *se* leaves room for doubt.

10

Centroamérica

In This Chapter

◆ *Lectura:* Reunión militar

◆ *Datos sobre América Central*

◆ The past tenses

◆ Future and conditional

Central America is a land of volcanoes, rain forests, exotic wildlife, and ancient cultures. The Central American isthmus forms a bridge between North and South America, and is among the most diverse ecological areas in the world. For example, there are three distinct temperature zones in the region. The hot country, or *tierra caliente*, extends from sea level to about 900 meters (about 3,000 feet) and has average yearly temperatures of 24° C (75° F) or more. The temperate country, known as *la tierra templada*, begins at about 900 meters and extends to 1,800 meters (about 3,000 to 6,000 feet).Here the average temperatures range from 18° to 24° C (65° to 75° F). Finally, there's the *tierra fría* (yes, it can get cold in Central America), from about 1,800 meters to 3,050 meters (about 6,000 to 10,000 feet). In this region the average yearly temperatures range between 13° to 18° C (55° to 65° F).

Los Países de Centroamérica

There are six Central American countries. English is the official language of Belize (once known as British Honduras). The other five are Spanish-speaking.

El Salvador

The smallest country of the five, El Salvador is also the region's most densely populated. Named after "the Savior," El Salvador has been plagued by civil war since it gained independence from Spain in 1821. Political turmoil dominated the country until 1992, when El Salvador finally resolved its 12-year civil war with the signing of a U.S.-sponsored peace agreement. In recent years, there has been a great deal of investment in the country by Salvadorians living in the United States. El Salvador's economy is based almost entirely on its coffee crop, although tourism is slowly emerging as a new moneymaker.

Nicaragua

Nicaragua is Central America's largest country. Like El Salvador, for centuries Nicaragua has been plagued by internal power struggles and foreign invasions. In 1979, the rebel *Sandinistas* seized power and formed the country's first leftist government, only to be undermined by U.S.-backed Contras. Political instabilities have only recently begun to subside after a free election system was established in 1990.

Guatemala

Guatemala is Central America's most populous country. More than 50 percent of Guatemalans are direct descendants of the Mayans, and the country has retained many Native American languages and traditions in its small fishing and agricultural villages. Guatemala has suffered greatly during three decades of civil war. In 1996, President Alvaro Arzú brokered a peace treaty among all parties involved in the conflict, formally ending the war. But sporadic incidents of violence, some aimed at tourists, continue in several regions of the country, including the capital, Guatemala City, where crime has risen steadily over the last several years.

Cultura Latina

Many Guatemalans do not speak Spanish. Approximately 30 different Indian languages are spoken in the country, and the principal dialect is known as Quiché. However, even in the most remote villages, there will always be someone who understands some Spanish.

Honduras

Honduras has also endured its share of uprisings, civil wars, and unpopular changes in government. Until the middle of the twentieth century, U.S. companies virtually controlled the economy through ownership of banana plantations along the northern coast. The military ceded formal power in 1981, and its role in the country has shrunk in recent years. It has also become a more popular tourist destination.

Costa Rica

Costa Rica's heavily European culture is unique in Central America. Anticipating vast mineral wealth, Spanish settlers in the early 1500s named this country "rich coast." But Costa Rica's riches are found aboveground in its fertile landscape, lush with rain forests and dotted with volcanoes. After a civil war in the 1940s, Costa Rica adopted a new constitution that prohibits the country from maintaining an armed force. Today, eco-tourism is fast becoming one of the country's principal industries.

Cultura Latina
Central Americans actually have nicknames for each other: Guatemalans are known as *chapines*, El Salvadorians are known as *guanacos*, Hondurans are *catrachos*, Nicaraguans are *nicas*, and Costa Ricans are *ticos*. No offense is meant or taken when using these nicknames.

El Panamá

Panama was once a province of Colombia. The country is bisected by the 51-mile-long Panama Canal, built by U.S. military engineers between 1904 and 1914. The project was actually begun by the French, but abandoned due to a malaria epidemic. The canal provides strategic passage between the Atlantic and Pacific oceans, and generates nearly half of the country's income. Control of the canal has reverted back to Panama, and there is talk of making additional improvements to the system.

Lectura: Reunión Militar

Your *lecturas* have been getting progressively longer. This time I'm giving you a break. This short reading is a news flash about a meeting in Guatemala. The style of writing is typical for news headlines and communiqués. So, although the reading is short, it's still pretty challenging:

Los ministros de defensa y comandantes de las fuerzas armadas de El Salvador, Guatemala, Honduras, y Nicaragua se reunieron el 9 de junio, en Guatemala para profundizar la integración de los ejércitos de la zona. Los jefes militares pasaron revista a las nuevas amenazas comunes que conforman su nueva agenda de seguridad, relacionadas con la nueva época de paz, narcotráfico, robo de vehículos, tráfico de ilegales, contrabando y otros ilíticos que están bajo el control de mafias organizadas del área.

Vocabulario Útil:

ministro   minister (not religious)

defensa   defense

comandante   commander

fuerzas armadas   armed forces

reunirse   to meet; to get together

ejército   army

profundizar   to deepen; to go into depth

integración   integration

jefe   leader; "boss"

pasar revista a   to review; to look over

amenaza   threat

común   common

conformar   to constitute; to make up

seguridad   security

narcotráfico   drug trafficking

época   period; time (not as grand as "epoch")

ilegales   illegals (probably people)

ilícitos   illegal activities

relacionado   related to

Análisis del Texto

All right. Let's see what this little *lectura* has to offer:

se reunieron el 9 de junio   Notice that there is no need for any additional preposition, such as *en* for "on." This would still be translated as "met on June 9," even though the "on" isn't needed in the Spanish. When discussing a date on which something occurred, it's usually not necessary to add any prepositions. If it's in the future, you may use *para* if you want.

jefes militares pasaron revista   *Pasar revista* is a compound verbal phrase. Many such compounds use a common helping verb, such as *hacer*, *tener*, *pasar*, or *dar*. The verb *revisar* also could have been used here.

relacionadas con la nueva época de paz   The participle *relacionadas* is linked to *amenazas* because it shares the feminine gender. Need I say more?

del areárea   The word *área* is feminine but takes a masculine article in the singular because of the stressed *a* sound at the beginning.

Vista Panorámica de Centroamérica

Nombres oficiales: *República de Guatemala; República de El Salvador; República de Honduras; República de Nicaragua; República de Costa Rica; República del Panamá*

Gobiernos: *Guatemala: república de 22 departamentos; El Salvador: república de 14 departamentos; Honduras: república de 18 departamentos; Nicaragua: república federal de 16 departamentos; Costa Rica: república democrática de 7 provincias; Panamá: república centralizada en la que el presidente tiene el poder ejecutivo*

Capitales: *Guatemala: Ciudad Guatemala; El Salvador: San Salvador; Honduras: Tegucigalpa; Nicaragua: Managua; Costa Rica: San José; Panamá: Ciudad de Panamá*

Tamaños: *Guatemala: 108.780 km. cuadrados; El Salvador: 21.476 km. cuadrados; Honduras: 112.088 km. cuadrados; Nicaragua: 148.100 km. cuadrados; Costa Rica: 50.900 km. cuadrados; Panamá: 78.046 km. cuadrados*

Poblaciones: *Guatemala: 12 millones; El Salvador: 6 millones; Honduras: 6 millones; Nicaragua: 6 millones; Costa Rica: 3.5 millones; Panamá: 2.8 millones*

Formas Adjetivales: *Guatemalteco; salvadoreño; hondureño; nicaragüense; costaricense; panameño*

Divisas: *Guatemala: el quezal; El Salvador: el colón; Honduras: el lempira; Nicaragua: el nuevo córdoba; Costa Rica: el colón; Panamá: el balboa (dólar de EE.UU.)*

Recursos naturales de la región: *Agricultura, bosque, pesca, energía hidroeléctrica, oro, lugar geográfico estratégico, cobre, otros*

Industrias: *Comida procesada, bebidas, textiles, maquinaria, materiales para construcción, procesamiento del café y del cacao, fertilizantes, calzado, productos químicos y petrolíferos, cigarros, llantas* (tires), *turismo, otras*

Industrias agropecuarias: *Frutas tropicales, azúcar, arroz, frijol, maíz, algodón, ganado, café, otros*

Cultura Latina

The U.S. dollar is legal tender in Panama. Panama currently does not print a paper currency of its own, but it does have coins. The coins all have Vasco Núñez de Balboa on the face and are inscribed *diez centésimos de balboa, un cuarto de balboa,* and *medio balboa.* These coins are used very commonly and are interchangeable with the American-equivalent coins, which are also used in Panama.

Gramática: The Other Tenses

You are now officially ready to revisit the rest of the verb tenses. Once again, if this is all review for you, that's great. But I would still encourage you to carefully read this section, just to see if anything new comes your way.

The Preterit: I Did It, and It's Over

The preterit past tense is used to indicate a past action or occurrence that both began in the past and finished in the past. Concepts expressed with the preterit are not thought of as having a strong influence on the present—they are over and done with. Usually, the preterit tells of something that occurred only once. It may also express a past action or series of actions that occurred several times if they are considered to be related and finished as a group.

If you need to review the formation of the preterit tense, consult your beginning Spanish textbook or look in Appendix A. Now, here are some examples to help you better understand the uses of the preterit tense:

Ten Cuidado

The preterit forms for *ir* and *ser* are the same: *fui, fuiste, fue, fuimos, fuisteis, fueron.* But don't worry; confusion between the two is practically impossible. The context will make it clear whether the verb is "to be" or "to go."

Mario fue al mercado de Chichicastenango a comprar regalos.
Mario went to the Chichicastenango market to buy gifts.

Hablé con el guía sobre la ruta a Petén.
I spoke to the guide about the route to Petén.

Anoche no pude dormir.
I couldn't sleep last night.

Compró una nueva mochila.
He/She bought a new backpack.

Me gustaron todas las obras de Orozco y Rivera.
I liked all of the works by Orozco and Rivera.

Los indígenas de aquella época abandonaron el uso de esa técnica.
The indigenous people of that period abandoned the use of that technique.

María tuvo que comprar una tarjeta postal.
Maria had to buy a postcard.

Cristóbal Colón descubrió las Américas.
Christopher Columbus discovered the Americas.

Ayer estuve bien, pero hoy estoy mal.
Yesterday I was fine, but today I'm not well.

Acuérdate

In regular *–ar* verbs, the *nosotros* form of the preterit is the same as the *nosotros* form in the present indicative. Thus, *hablamos* can mean "we talk" or "we talked." The context usually indicates whether the statement is in the past or present. If necessary, you may indicate "when" with words such as *ahora*, *ayer*, or *el año pasado* to avoid misunderstandings.

The Imperfect Tense: I Used to Do It Often

The other past tense is called the imperfect tense. But there's absolutely nothing wrong with it. These are the *–aba*, *–abas*, *–aba* and *–ía*, *–ías*, *–ía* endings. If you need a review, consult your beginning text or Appendix A.

The difference between the preterit and the imperfect is that the imperfect is used to express or describe past actions or events that occurred over an extended period of time, while the preterit tells of events that only occurred once (or are thought of as having occurred as a unit). Use the imperfect to describe conditions in the past or to tell of actions done often or habitually.

You may have noticed that the first-person and third-person singular forms look the same. The context usually makes it clear what's going on, but pronouns and names may also be added for clarity.

Luckily, only three common verbs take an irregular imperfect form: *ser*, *ir*, and *ver* ("to see"). You'll need these right away, though, so you should learn them now.

Acuérdate

Express a recent past action by using *acabar* + *de* + infinitive: *Acabo de salir de la biblioteca* translates as "I just left the library"; *Acaban de ver la película* means "They just saw the movie." *Acabar* can also be used in the imperfect tense: *Juan acababa de estudiar el retrato cuando cerraron el museo* means "Juan had just studied the painting when they closed the museum."

Three Common Verbs That Are Irregular in the Imperfect

Verb	Conjugation
ser	*era, eras, era, éramos, erais, eran*
ir	*iba, ibas, iba, íbamos, ibais, iban*
ver	*veía, veías, veía, veíamos, veíais, veían*

Here are some examples to help you better understand the uses of the imperfect tense:

Description:

> *Era la mañana y llovía bastante.*
> It was morning, and it was raining a lot.

> *La casa estaba pintada de un color gris.*
> The house was painted a gray color.

> *Desde el techo se veía el mar.*
> From the roof one could see the sea.

> *Los pintores del siglo veinte eran todos muy extraños.*
> The painters of the twentieth century were all very strange.

Habitual action:

> *El pintor asistía a la escuela de arte cuando era niño.*
> The painter attended art school when he was a child.

> *Íbamos al mercado cada día cuando vivíamos en Managua.*
> We used to go to the market every day when we lived in Managua.

> *Mi papá compraba muchos coches.*
> My dad used to buy a lot of cars. (When and how many are not important.)

Algo Nuevo

In the sentence *Compré diez coches el año pasado*, which means "I bought 10 automobiles last year," the preterit form of *comprar* is used, even though the transactions may have taken place at different times during the course of the year. There are no implications that this action will impact this year or next. The purchase of the vehicles is over and done with. Because these actions are being considered collectively as a group, the preterit is required here. An imperfect *Compraba muchos coches* would change the focus to "I used to buy a lot of cars," making the listener wonder what might have changed since then ("Well, are you still buying a lot of cars or not?").

The imperfect and preterit can often be used in the same sentence. This is a good way to tell of an action that was occurring when something else interrupted it. The imperfect says what was going on when something happened (preterit):

Yo estaba leyendo Don Quijote cuando sonó el teléfono.
I was reading *Don Quixote* when the phone rang.

Estábamos conduciendo hacia el volcán cuando se nos descompuso el coche.
We were driving toward the volcano when the car broke down on us.

Me dijeron que Julio estaba hablando contigo cuando sucedió.
They told me that Julio was talking with (to) you when it happened.

Acuérdate _____

The verb *querer* in the past has two different meanings in the negative: *No quiso* means "refused to do," while *no quería* means "didn't want to." So *querer* in the imperfect is not as forceful.

Remember that perfect tense from before? Well, *haber* can also be used in the imperfect (yes, an "imperfect perfect tense"!). This tense, called the past perfect, corresponds to the English "had done," "had been," "had seen," and so on. It tells of a condition that existed prior to a later past occurrence or action. Observe:

No fue la primera vez. Lo había hecho el año pasado.
It wasn't the first time. I had done it last year.

Se había casado tres veces ya cuando conoció a su cuarta esposa.
He had already been married three times when he met his fourth wife.

Ya se había renovado el edificio cuando se convirtió en museo.
The building had already been renovated when it was converted into a museum.

Algo Nuevo

There is a third form of these "sigos": *consigo* It means "with himself/herself" and is a combination of *con + sí. Está muy enojado consigo mismo* is "He's very angry with himself"; *Llevaba consigo dos pistolas grandes* is "He was carrying (with himself) two large pistols."

The Future Tense

The future tense in Spanish is similar to the "shall" future tense in English. It isn't as common in daily conversation as the *ir + a + infinitive* model that you reviewed a few chapters ago. However, when you do use it, it's as clear as a *campana*.

For most verbs, all you need to do is add the corresponding future tense ending right onto the infinitive. You can review the formation of the future tense in Appendix A if you need to. Otherwise, read on:

Hablaré con el agente de viajes mañana.
I will/shall speak with the travel agent tomorrow.

¿Bailaremos?
Shall we dance?

Estaremos en San José por un mes.
We will be in San Jose for a month.

No irás nunca jamás a la casa de Jaime.
You will never ever go to Jaime's house (again).

¿Cuántas personas serán?
How many people will you be (in your group/party)?

Veremos qué pasará.
We'll see what happens (will happen).

Servirán comida durante el vuelo.
They will serve food during the flight.

Vosotros comprenderaís todo mañana.
You all will understand everything tomorrow.

¿De veras irás a Nicaragua de vacaciones?
Are you really going to Nicaragua for vacation?

Perderás tu mochila si la dejas en el autobús.
You will lose your backpack if you leave it in the bus.

Qué será, será.
Whatever will be, will be.

Ten Cuidado

You'll notice that the *yo* form and *él/ella/usted* form are the same in the conditional and imperfect tenses. Usually, the context makes it clear who the subject of the sentence is. But you can always add the subject pronoun to your sentence to avoid any ambiguities: *yo hablaría, él hablaría, ella hablaría.*

The Conditional Tense

In daily speech, the conditional tense is more common than the future tense. I like to think of it as the *Mr. Rogers' Neighborhood* tense: "Would you be mine, could you be mine, won't you be my neighbor?" The conditional tense is used where we use the helping verbs *would* and *could* in English. As with the future tense, conditional tense endings are slapped onto the end of the infinitive. Review them as needed in Appendix A or elsewhere:

Yo hablaría con el guía, pero ahora no tengo tiempo.
I would talk with the tour guide, but I don't have time now.

Hoy me gustaría ir a la selva.
I would like to go to the jungle today.

Les gustaría viajar a las once de la noche.
They would like to go at 11:00 P.M.

Compraríamos dos boletos de tren, pero no tenemos dinero.
We would buy two train tickets, but we don't have any money.

¿No sería posible llegar a la Ciudad de Panamá a las dos?
Wouldn't it be possible to arrive in Panama City at 2:00?

Many verbs that have changes in the present indicative (such as *pensar*, with *pienso*), are quite regular in the future and conditional (*pensará*, *jugaría*). However, several common verbs do change their stem when forming the conditional and future tenses: *hacer* is *har*; *tener* is *tendr*; *saber* is *sabr*; and so on. The change is exactly the same for both tenses. You'll find a more complete list on the Reference Card in the front of this book … if you haven't lost it already!

The conditional can be used to soften a request. For example, *¿Me puede ayudar con mi equipaje?* translates as "Can you help me with my luggage?" and is a fine sentence. But you can make the request even more courteous by using the conditional: *¿Me podría decir usted si el tren llegará a las seis y media, por favor?* means "Could you please tell me if the train will arrive at 6:30?"

El Web

Here are some great websites for information on the countries of Central America:

www.panama.com	www.guatemala.com
www.elsalvador.com	www.nicaragua.com
www.honduras.com	www.visitcostarica.com

Also, you can practice your grammar skills online at www.trinity.edu/mstroud/grammar. If you need extra help with the future and conditional tenses, this is the place to get it. If this site goes under, a simple search should do the trick.

Risa del Día

Okay, this is the last joke that has anything to do with kids in school, I promise. But this joke is actually funny:

> *El padre de un niño va a la escuela a investigar por qué a su hijo le pusieron un cero en el examen.*
>
> *Lo que pasó—dijo la maestra—es que su hijo copió del examen de otro niño. Es tan claro que los dos exámenes son casi iguales.*
>
> *El padre, sintiendo su orgullo herido reclamó:*
>
> *Pero si los dos exámenes son casi iguales, pudo haber sido el otro niño que copiara de mi hijo.*
>
> *La maestra siguió explicando:*
>
> *Nos dimos cuenta que fue su hijo que copió porque en una de las preguntas, el otro niño escribió: "YO NO SÉ," y su hijo escribió: "YO TAMPOCO."*

Vocabulario Útil:

investigar   to investigate; to research

cero   zero; an F

examen   test

lo que pasó   what happened; the thing that happened

igual   the same

orgullo   pride

herido   wounded

darse cuenta   to realize

yo tampoco   neither do I; I don't either

The Least You Need to Know

◆ There are five Spanish-speaking countries in Central America.

◆ The preterit is the simple past and describes things that are over and done with.

◆ The imperfect past describes events that took place over a period of time.

◆ The future and conditional tense endings are added to the verb after the *-ar/-er/-ir* ending.

◆ Several common verbs form irregular future/conditional stems.

Chapter 11

Los Estados Unidos de América

In This Chapter

- ◆ *Lectura:* Estudios de discriminación
- ◆ *Datos sobre los EE.UU.*
- ◆ Revisiting the present subjunctive

Believe it or not, the United States of America is one of the largest Spanish-speaking countries in the world. This is not simply due to recent developments; Hispanics have had a long history in the United States.

Esteban's History Lesson (Abridged)

In 1848, Mexico lost its war with the United States, and the United States acquired nearly half of Mexico's territory. When the land known as the Mexican Cession became the American Southwest (Texas, Arizona, Nevada, California, New Mexico, Utah, and part of Colorado), the Mexicans who lived there became American citizens. As part of the Treaty of Guadalupe-Hidalgo, the new Mexican-Americans were to be guaranteed the same basic civil rights and freedoms of all citizens, including the possession of their land and the freedom to retain their cultural identity, language, and religion, without interference. However, much of this treaty was ignored, and many of the Mexicans living in these territories lost their land and eventually became second-class citizens.

During World War I, the expanding defense industry and the drafting of American men into the military created a labor shortage in agriculture. At the request of U.S. growers and industrialists, nearly 73,000 Mexicans were legally admitted to the United States to be employed in agriculture and other industries.

The demand for Mexicans ended quickly during the Great Depression. With 25 percent unemployment, the U.S. government decided that it would be less expensive to repatriate (send back) Mexicans than to include them in the public welfare programs of the New Deal. Thus, many Mexicans, some of whom had become legal residents or even U.S. citizens, were repatriated to Mexico during the 1930s.

With the coming of World War II, American growers again began to lobby the government to bring Mexican workers back to the United States to work on American farms. In 1942, Mexico and the United States signed the Bracero Agreement. Under the terms of this agreement, Mexican workers were recruited in specified centers in Mexico to work in the United States. The Bracero Program was to last for the duration of the war only, but was extended in 1951 and continued until 1964.

Agriculture quickly began to rely on undocumented Mexicans to provide cheap labor. In 1986, the Immigration Reform and Control Act (IRCA) granted amnesty to millions of undocumented aliens, many of whom spoke Spanish, and allowed them to apply for legal residence. However, even though IRCA made it a crime for businesses to hire undocumented workers, illegal immigration continues today, and immigration reform is still a very hot topic in Washington.

Cultura Latina

The term *chicano* is used by some Mexican-Americans with pride. Other Mexican-Americans feel that they are not *chicanos* and may even take offense at the word. Generally, *chicanos* are Mexican-Americans who have lived in the United States (mostly in California) for several generations. It is always best to ask if a Mexican-American considers himself or herself to be *chicano/a* before using the word. Visit www.chicano.org to learn more.

At the end of the Spanish-American War (1898), Spain lost control of Cuba and Puerto Rico. Puerto Ricans eventually became U.S. citizens. During the 1940s and 1950s, many Puerto Ricans left the island for economic reasons. Today there are almost as many Puerto Ricans living in New York City as there are in San Juan. Most are second- and third-generation *neoyorquiños*.

In 1959, Fidel Castro came to power in Cuba with popular support. The Batista regime that preceded him was indeed very corrupt and did little for the poorer people of the island. However, when Castro turned to the Soviet Union for help in his collectivization of the island's resources, many Cubans felt betrayed and fled the island for Spain or the United States. In 1980, Castro signed an agreement with the United States that allowed Cubans to legally immigrate to the United States. The next day, 120,000 Cubans met at the Port of Mariel and sailed to Florida. This event became known as the Mariel Boat Lift, and Cubans who came at that time are known as *marielitos*. Today, many Cubans still brave the waves in their attempt to flee the island for Florida.

Hispanics from other nations have also come to the United States in recent years. During the decades of civil war in Central America, many Guatemalans, Salvadorans, and Nicaraguans fled their countries as political refugees. Washington, D.C., has one of the largest Salvadoran communities outside of El Salvador.

Lectura: Estudios de Discriminación

The following reading is an opinionated editorial, written from the perspective of a Hispanic living in the United States. Of course, you are free to agree or disagree with the opinions expressed in the passage. But I think the text makes a good *lectura:*

A pesar de los esfuerzos que los gobiernos federales y estatales de los Estados Unidos han hecho para eliminar el racismo en los campos de la vida social y cultural, la discriminación racial sigue siendo una práctica constante.

Por ejemplo, se puede observar el trato que la principal fuente de noticias, entretenimiento e información de los EE.UU. le da a la minoría más numerosa del país; los latinos permanecen virtualmente invisibles en la televisión.

Algunos estudios recientes han mostrado que cuando la televisión de habla inglesa finalmente informa sobre los latinos, generalmente muestra estereotipos negativos. Evidenciaron también que en la actualidad los programas televisivos comúnmente conocidos como "programas basados en la vida real" han hecho que la situación sea aún peor, dado que solamente muestran a los pocos latinos que tienen problemas con la ley o que han cometido algún delito.

Vocabulario Útil:

esfuerzo	effort	*campo*	field; area
estatal	state (adj.)	*permanecer*	to remain
trato	treatment	*minoría*	minority
racismo	racism	*entretenimiento*	entertainment

estereotipo	stereotype	*actualidad*	at this time; these days
invisible	invisible	*comúnmente*	commonly
estudios	studies; investigations	*cometer*	to commit
evidenciar	to show evidence that	*delito*	crime (other than murder)
informar	to inform; to give news	*ley*	law

Análisis del Texto

Okay, let's take a look at some words and phrases from the *lectura*:

A pesar de This idiomatic phrase means "in spite of." It can also be seen as *a pesar de que*, when it may be followed by a subjunctive form of the verb: *a pesar de que Miguel lo sepa* means "in spite of the fact that Miguel might know it."

sigue siendo una práctica *Seguir* can take a present perfect –*ing* form of a verb. Here it means "continues to be." Remember that the *u* after the *g* is just an orthographic convenience. It makes no sound and is just there to make sure the *g* doesn't go soft and sound like an English *h*.

la principal fuente de noticias, entretenimiento e información de los EE.UU. Notice that this entire phrase just means "the television." We learn this at the end of the sentence. This is just more elegant variation.

de habla inglesa This is how you say "English-speaking" in Spanish. *Habla* is feminine but will take *el* because of the stressed *a* sound at the beginning.

Cultura Latina

I've seen far too many mistranslations of the word "crime" as *crimen*. The word *crimen* in Spanish means "murder," and *cometer un crimen* means to "commit murder." If someone commits a crime that is not murder, call it *un delito*. A traffic violation would be una *infracción*. Don't say *violación*, which means "rape."

Evidenciaron también This is a good example of how a Spanish verb can need a long translation in English. *Evidenciar* means "to show evidence of."

en la actualidad This is just a fancy way of saying "now." Remember that *actual* is a false cognate and means "present/current," not "actual." The adverb *actualmente* doesn't mean "actually," but rather "at this present time."

programas basados en la vida real Sometimes Spanish can't come up with the short buzzwords that we create in English. This means "reality-based."

han hecho que la situación sea aún peor   Notice the subjunctive *sea*, which means, "have made (that) the situation (may be) worse." There is a force being generated on another subject here (*la situación*), so a subjunctive verb form is required. More on the subjunctive in *un momento*.

Vista Panorámica de los EE.UU.

Nombre oficial: *Estados Unidos de América*

Gobierno: *República federal de 50 estados y un distrito federal*

Capital: *Washington, Distrito de Columbia*

Estados con alto porcentaje de hispano hablantes: *California, Nueva York, Florida, Texas (Tejas), Illinois, Colorado, Arizona, Nuevo México, Washington, Nuevo Jersey, otros*

Ciudades con alto porcentaje de hispano hablantes: *Nueva York; Los Ángeles; Miami; Houston; San Diego; Washington, D.C.; Phoenix; Chicago; Dallas; San Antonio; El Paso; Boston; otras*

Tamaño: *9.4 millones de kilómetros cuadrados*

Población de hispanos: *Aproximadamente 40 millones*

Producto Interno Bruto: *500 billones de dólares estadounidenses*

Exportaciones: *Maquinaria, computadoras, software, maquinaria industrial, instrumentos científicos, equipo telefónico, equipo de transporte, medicinas, plástico, productos elaborados, maquinaria agrícola, frutas, otras*

Importaciones: *petróleo crudo, automóviles, textiles, zapatos, radios, estereos, televisores, electodomésticos, equipo fotográfico, ropa, papel, café, mariscos, otras*

Gramática: The Spanish Subjunctive

Many students of Spanish head for *las montañas* when the topic turns to the subjunctive. But the good news is that with careful explanation, it really isn't that bad. Meet my "kinder, gentler subjunctive."

So What the #@$%&! Is the Subjunctive?

The subjunctive is not a tense. It's more of a "mood." The subjunctive is the "alter ego" of the indicative. It is a second form of the verb that serves an entirely different grammatical function.

The subjunctive removes the subject a few steps away from the certainty of the action or state of the verb: "I did it" (indicative), compared with "It is possible that I might have done it, but nobody is really sure at this moment in time" (subjunctive). While the indicative mood is certain, quantifiable, and solid, the subjunctive is possible, doubtful, indirect, emotional, pliable, opinionated, and (sometimes) contrary to fact.

There are both present and past forms of the subjunctive. There's also a future sub-junctive, but it's only used in legal writings. We'll focus on the present subjunctive in this chapter.

Acuérdate _____

Verbs that end in *–cer*, such as *conocer*, *establecer* (to establish), *parecer* (to seem/ to appear), and *crecer* (to grow) change to *conozco*, *parezco*, *establezco*, and *crezco* in the first person *yo* form. When forming the subjunctive of such verbs, you must maintain this ending throughout: *conozca*, *establezcas*, *parezcan*, *conozcamos*, and so on.

Forming the Present Subjunctive

Making the present subjunctive is sort of like putting the wrong ending on the verb. With his shoes on backwards, you can imagine how the poor verb feels: unsure, vul-nerable, and plagued by self-doubt. In the subjunctive, *–ar* verbs take the endings that you worked so hard to learn for the *–er* and *–ir* verbs, and the *–er* and *–ir* verbs take the endings used by *–ar* verbs. The only real deviation from this paradigm is that the first-person singular *yo* form is now the same as the third-person (*él, ella, usted*). If you need to review the subjunctive endings, consult your beginning text or Appendix A.

The key to forming the present subjunctive is to start with the *yo* form of the verb in the indicative and then build your subjunctive from there. I'll show you why in a minute. In most cases, the whole thing is pretty straightforward.

For example, let's say we're dealing with our regular old friend *hablar*. Here are the steps you'll need to follow to form the present subjunctive:

1. Recall the endings for *–er* verbs (remembering the change in the *yo* form).

2. Form the *yo* form of the verb in the indicative (*hablo*).

3. Remove the *–o*, and put the subjunctive ending in its place: *hable*.

The steps you'll need to follow for *–er* and *–ir* verbs are the same. Only the endings have changed:

1. Recall the endings for your –ar verbs (remembering the change in the yo form).

2. Form the yo form of the verb (comer = como; vivir = vivo).

3. Remove the –o, and put the subjunctive ending in its place: coma, viva.

The only hard part to remember is that you must start with the indicative yo form (until you have memorized the subjunctive forms, when they will come naturally to you) and use it as your template for the subjunctive. Any changes in the stem that occur there will be reflected in the present subjunctive form.

The Subjunctive and Those Spelling Rules

Adding this "wrong" ending can necessitate some spelling changes. Take for example the verb *pagar*. If we follow the steps for forming the present subjunctive, we start with *pago*. Now, because this is an –ar verb, we remove the –o and add –e, which gives us *page*. But this would be pronounced as "*pah hay*" because the g goes soft before e and i. Therefore, we must add u after the g to protect it from the softening effects of the –e. So the present subjunctive of *pagar* is *pague*. The u remains a silent partner.

Right and Wrong Spelling with the Subjunctive

Verb	First Person Indicative	Wrong!	Right!
sacar	*saco*	"*sace*"	*saque*
arrancar	*arranco*	"*arrance*"	*arranque*
jugar	*juego*	"*juege*"	*juegue*

When to Use the Subjunctive

Forming the subjunctive is relatively straightforward. The real confusion tends to come when trying to figure out how to use it. I hope the following section clears up any remaining questions that you might have.

Usted Commands

Directly telling someone to do or not to do something is known as a command or imperative. When you're addressing someone in the *usted* form (or *ustedes*, for more than one person), you must use the subjunctive form of the verb for all commands.

Hable con el cocinero, por favor.
Please speak to the cook.

Paguen la cuenta en la caja, señores.
Pay the bill at the cashier, gentlemen.

Dígame por favor si Adela está lista o no.
Please tell me if Adela is ready or not.

No vayan al restaurante que está detrás del hotel.
Don't go to the restaurant behind the hotel.

Hágame el favor de decirme la hora.
Please give me (do me the favor of telling me) the time.

Tráigame un nuevo tenedor.
Bring me a new fork.

Ten Cuidado

Even though the *usted* command forms are more polite than the direct *tú* commands, you should still add courteous phrases such as *por favor* when using them. The *por favor* doesn't have to come next to the command: *Hágame el favor de decirme la hora, por favor* means "Please tell me what time it is." Nobody likes being told what to do, and *por favor* should be used as much as possible.

Indirect Commands

When someone's will is directed at or imposed upon something or someone else, the subjunctive form of the verb must be used. If I say "I want Jorge to jump in a lake," I'm expressing my will that Jorge do something. It doesn't matter whether Jorge and I use *tú* with each other. I am placing my will and desire on something other than myself. And if Jorge replies that he's not a fool and wants me to jump off a bridge, the subjunctive must also be used when he places his will on me:

No quiero que Juan coma todo el pan.
I don't want Juan to eat all the bread.

El jefe quiere que Julio venga temprano al trabajo.
The boss wants Julio to come to work early.

Deseamos que los ciudadanos sean felices.
We wish the citizens to be happy.

María no permite que su esposo tome cerveza.
Maria doesn't allow her husband to drink beer.

Paco desea que el mesero vuelva en unos minutos.
Paco wishes the waiter to return in a few minutes.

Nosotros insistimos en que tú nos pagues el dinero ahora.
We insist that you pay us the money now.

Mis padres quieren que yo haga los quehaceres.
My parents want me to do my chores.

Su novia quiere que yo conozca a su hermana.
His girlfriend wants me to meet her sister.

Acuérdate _____

Some people like to use "NEEDS PAWS" as a device to remember under what conditions the subjunctive is used. These letters stand for: Necessity, Emotion, Exaggeration, Demanding, Seeming, Possibility, Asking, Wishing, Supposing. If this sort of thing helps you, learn NEEDS PAWS.

Acuérdate _____

When one noun places its will on a different noun, the subjunctive is required: *Quiero que tú vayas* means "I want you to go." But when the noun places its will on itself, there is no need for the subjunctive, and an infinitive is all you'll need: *Quiero ir* would mean "I want 'myself' to go."

Impersonal Expressions

It doesn't always have to be a person doing the wanting. The subjunctive must also be used in "impersonal" expressions showing opinion or emotion such as "It's wonderful that …" or "It's too bad that …."

Es fantástico que Antonio haya conseguido empleo.
It's great that Antonio has found work.

Es una lástima que María no conozca mejor a su esposo.
It's a shame that Maria doesn't know her husband better.

¡Qué lástima que no puedas venir a la fiesta!
What a shame you can't come to the party!

Negative Tú Commands

When you tell a child, friend, or family member not to do something, the *tú* form of the subjunctive is required:

No me digas que vas a vender tu casa.
Don't tell me you're going to sell your house.

Jaimito, no toques el libro de Juan.
Jaimito, don't touch Juan's book.

Juanito, no juegues con tu comida.
Juanito, don't play with your food.

No me dejes solo, mi amor.
Don't leave me alone, my love.

Impersonal Wishes, Hopes, and Letting Someone Else Do It

You'll see what I mean by the examples. These are usually preceded by *que*. In sentences expressing hope, the verb *esperar* ("to wait"; "to hope") or *ojalá* ("it is hoped") are optional:

> *Que la pague mi cuñado.*
> Let my brother-in-law pay it. (*la cuenta*)

Que lo repare el gobierno.
Let the government fix it.

(Espero) Que sirvan la comida ahora mismo.
I hope they serve the food right now.

(Ojalá) Que gane mi equipo.
I hope my team wins.

¡Que coman pastel!
Let 'em eat cake!

Que descanse en paz.
May he rest in peace

¡Viva el Rey! (the *que* is understood)
Long live the King!

Unspecified Future Time

Use the subjunctive when the exact time a future event will (or may) occur is uncertain or unimportant. These sentences often translate as "whenever" in English:

Pagaremos la deuda cuando llegue el cheque.
We'll pay the debt whenever the check gets here.

Te llamo cuando pueda.
I'll call you whenever I can.

Nadie sabe cuando vaya a acabar el mundo.
Nobody knows when the world will end.

Felipe dice que lo hará cuando termine la cena.
Felipe says that he'll do it whenever he finishes dinner.

María, cuando crezcas serás presidente. (crecer)
Maria, when you grow up you'll be president.

After Certain Stock Phrases

By their very nature, some phrases take the subjunctive. Most end in *que*. Here are just a few examples:

aunque   although

es posible que   it's possible that

hasta que   until

después de que   after

es importante que   it's important that

puede ser que   it may be that

tan pronto como   as soon as

en cuanto   as soon as

a pesar de que   in spite of the fact that

Ten Cuidado

Avoid stand-alone subjunctives such as: *Yo haga*, *Él no sepa*, and *Ellos vayan*. You'll need to start these with phrases such as *Es posible que* or *Es importante que* to make them work. You can, however, say *Lo que sea*, which means, "Whatever (it may be)."

Here are some additional subjunctive situations. The examples will serve as explanation:

◆ **Something unlikely or uncertain:** *Es posible que mi equipo gane mañana.* It's possible that my team may win tomorrow. (Who knows if they will ….)

◆ **After expressions of doubt:** *No creo que mi hermano vaya a poder cruzar la frontera solo.* I don't think that my brother will be able to cross the border alone. (He's not too bright.)

◆ **Statement colored by emotion:** *Estoy tan triste (de) que tú me hayas abandonado.* I'm so sad that you have abandoned me.

◆ **Statement doubtful or not true:** *Es poco probable que María tenga el dinero para pagarlo.* It's unlikely that María has the money to pay it.

Sometimes both the indicative and the subjunctive are possible in a particular sentence. The decision to use the one or the other depends on how certain, opinionated, or emotional the speaker feels. For example:

Aunque Julio es inteligente, no puede solucionar el problema.
Although Julio is intelligent, he can't solve the problem. (There is no doubt that Julio is an intelligent man.)

Aunque Julio sea inteligente, no puede solucionar el problema.
Although Julio may be intelligent, he can't solve the problem. (Here the speaker is casting some doubt as to Julio's intelligence.)

No es cierto que existe Papá Noel. (existir)
Santa Claus does not exist. (We now have scientific proof.)

No es cierto que exista Papá Noel.
There is no Santa Claus. (But some people still believe in him, and I can't prove that he doesn't exist.)

> **Acuérdate**
>
> Use the subjunctive whenever there is doubt and the subject of the second verb is different from the subject of the first verb: *Yo dudo que Juan pueda hacerlo.* ("I doubt that Juan can do it.") You can say *Yo dudo que puedo hacerlo* without a subjunctive because the subject of the two verbs is the same.

Unknown but Potential Existence

¿Hay alguien aquí que hable el inglés?
Is there anyone here who speaks English?

The reason that *hablar* is in the subjunctive (*hable*) here is that we're not sure whether such a person exists. Even if there is an English-speaker around, we can't know (and don't particularly care) who he or she might be. Another translation of this sentence might be: "Is there anyone here who might be able to speak English?" If we replace *hable* with the indicative *habla*, the sentence might mean "So, there's someone here who speaks English? Well, good! I look forward to meeting this person."

El Web

A great source of information on Hispanics living in the United States is www.hispaniconline.com. The site is mostly in English, but it contains links to Spanish-language sites as well.

Also, search for Spanish subjunctive tutorials online or visit www.studyspanish.com/lessons/subj1.htm.

Risa del Día

I'm not sure why, but there seems to be no shortage of jokes in Spanish about ducks. Most of these ducks talk. Here is an example:

Entra un pato a un bar y dice:

Un sandwich de pollo y un refresco, por favor.

El barman se queda estupefacto y con la voz temblorosa le dice:

¿Cómo puede ser que un pato hable?

¿Y qué? ¿Usted no habla acaso?

Sí, bueno …. ¿Y cómo descidió honrarme entrando a mi bar?

Es que trabajo de albañil en la obra de aquí a la vuelta y vine a comprar la comida. ¿Qué tiene de raro?

El pato paga y se va. El barman se va corriendo al circo y le cuenta lo sucedido al dueño. Juntos se van a la obra a buscar al pato y lo encuentran construyendo una pared. El dueño del circo le dice:

Por favor señor pato, véngase conmigo a trabajar en el circo.

El pato contesta: ¿Y para qué necesitan a un albañil en el circo?

Vocabulario Útil:

refresco	soft drink; soda	*albañil*	mason; bricklayer
quedarse	to become; to remain	*a la vuelta*	around the corner; nearby
estupefacto	astonished	*tener de raro*	be strange
voz	voice	*obra*	work; project; construction site
tembloroso	shaky	*circo*	circus
acaso (no)	by chance; "I suppose you don't"	*dueño*	owner
honrar	to honor	*lo sucedido*	what had happened

The Least You Need to Know

◆ Spanish-speakers have a long history in the United States.

◆ Forming the subjunctive is a bit like putting the wrong ending on the verb.

◆ Build the subjunctive by using the first-person singular indicative as your template: *salgo*, *salgas*, and so on.

◆ The subjunctive must be used when someone tries to impose their will on someone or something else.

◆ The subjunctive must also be used when there is doubt or emotion and there is a change of subject of the second verb.

Part 3

La Vida Cotidiana (Everyday Life)

The *lecturas* in the following chapters are about friends, family, food, religious customs, and *fiestas*. After all, why bother learning Spanish in the first place if you can't have fun, meet new people, and deepen your knowledge of the culture? The grammar sections will be slightly shorter than those in Part 2. This time I'll go into greater detail about *haber*, *tan*, and *tanto*, the present progressive, prepositions, *por* versus *para*, *usted* versus *tú*, and a few other sundries about grammar and usage.

Chapter **12**

La Familia Latina

In This Chapter

- *Lectura:* la unidad familiar

- *Gramática:* por versus para

- *Palabras para ti:* terms of kinship

- *Diálogo:* Juanita y Mario

The family unit is one of the most important social institutions in the Spanish-speaking world. The *familia hispana* often extends beyond the nuclear family, and it is not uncommon for one's grandparents, uncles, aunts, cousins, and other family members to be living under the same roof—or at least nearby. It is also quite acceptable for children to continue to live at home with their parents until they marry.

Many families in Spain and Latin America still follow the traditional family model with respect to gender roles, although a growing number of women have found it necessary to find work outside the home for economic reasons. It is not uncommon for mothers in middle-class families to remain at home, while the father brings home the *tocino*. Wealthier families often employ a live-in maid or nanny, who will eventually be considered as "a member of the family." It is important to remember, however, that every Hispanic family is unique in its own way, and may not follow the traditional models.

Lectura: La Unidad Familiar Hispana

Here is a short reading about the Latin family. It is challenging, so you may want to read it a few times:

La familia es una de las instituciones sociales más importantes para el individuo hispano. De ella procede en gran medida su identidad y bienestar personales y su sentido de seguridad y estabilidad. La familia latina representa un apoyo para el individuo a la vez que reafirma su dignidad y posición en la sociedad. Une a todos los miembros, incluso a los parientes, y les hace sentir como parte de una unidad íntima y fuerte, en la que pueden tener confianza. Por eso, en muchos casos, un joven hispano puede permanecer en la casa de sus padres hasta que se case.

La unidad familiar hispana incluye el concepto de la familia extendida. No es raro que, por razones económicas, sociales o personales, los parientes de cierta familia (abuelos, tíos, primos) vivan una temporada o permanentemente con ésta en su casa. Es una costumbre común y aceptada y demuestra la solidaridad e intimidad de la familia hispánica.

Cultura Latina

Godparents are very important to the Latin family structure. The institution of godparenthood is known as *el compadrazgo*. The godparents, or *padrinos*, are usually friends or relatives of the family who do all they can to treat their godchildren as if they were their own. This can include gifts for holidays and special events, and the promise to be helpful throughout the lives of their godchildren.

Vocabulario Útil:

institución	institution	*apoyo*	support
proceder	proceed; to come from	*reafirmar*	to reaffirm
identidad	identity	*dignidad*	dignity
bienestar	well-being	*posición*	position
temporada	season, a period of time	*sociedad*	society
sentido	sense; feeling	*unir*	to unite; to tie
seguridad	security	*permanecer*	to remain
estabilidad	stability	*miembro*	member

costumbre   custom; way of doing something

común   common

aceptado   accepted

demostrar (o → ue)   to demonstrate; to show

solidaridad   solidarity

intimidad   intimacy

pariente   relative (not "parent")

unidad íntima   intimate unit

fuerte   strong

confianza   trust; confidence

Análisis del Texto

Now let's take a closer look:

La familia es una de   Did you notice that *una* is feminine? This ties it to *familia*: "The family is one of the …."

el individuo hispano   Here is an example of how you sometimes need to expand your thinking about cognates. The word *individuo* is indeed a cognate with the English word "individual." But in English, using the word individual to mean "a person" sounds like it's from a police report. In Spanish, *individuo* doesn't sound quite as stilted as individual might in English. It just means "person."

De ella procede en gran medida   Here, *ella* means "it" and refers to *familia* (linked by gender). The subject pronouns can also stand in for inanimate and abstract nouns. The phrase *en gran medida* literally means "in great measure." A better translation would be: "for the most part."

identidad y bienestar personales   The adjective *personales* is pluralized by the *s* to show that it modifies both *identidad* and *bienestar*. If it had been left in the singular, it would have modified only *bienestar*, which would have made sense but wouldn't have been what the author wanted to say.

a la vez que reafirma   The phrase *a la vez que* literally means "at the time that." A better translation is "while."

Acuérdate

Just a reminder that *y* changes to *e* before words that begin with an "ee" sound (*i, hi,* and occasionally *y* when followed by a consonant and sounding as "ee," as in *Ybarra*). It still means "and." We see this in the text in *solidaridad e intimidad.*

incluso a los parientes   The word *incluso* means "even," as in "Even I can understand this." It is used adverbially and thus doesn't change to *inclusa*.

en la que pueden tener confianza Note that *en la que pueden* literally means "in that [feminine thing] in which they can ...." The *la* is linked to *unidad* by its gender. A better translation is "in which."

hasta que se case The verb *casar* is subjunctive here. *Hasta que* always takes a subjunctive: "Until whenever they may marry."

no es raro que ... vivan Another subjunctive here is *vivan* (from *vivir*). *No es raro que* takes a subjunctive. *Raro* borders on being a false cognate and usually means "strange," not "rare." All together the phrase means "It isn't unusual that ...." The idea to follow is doubtful and uncertain, and the statement is in the negative. So the whole thing just feels subjunctive: "It isn't unusual that the relatives might ...."

con ésta en su casa Where the heck did this *ésta* come from? Good question. Well, it must be linked to something feminine, so we'll have to look back in the sentence. This *ésta* is linked to *cierta familia* and is acting as a pronoun (note the *tilde*). Translated, it just means "it."

Gramática: Para vs. Por

Of the many Spanish prepositions, *para* and *por* seem to cause more grief and confusion than all the others. Why? Both are often translated as "for" in English, so it's no surprise that many people have difficulty knowing when to use one and not the other.

Para

Para definitely translates as "for" in most cases. It may also translate as "to" or "in order to." It indicates where things are going and what things are used for. Study the following examples closely to learn how to use para correctly:

Algo Nuevo

The expression *para nada* does indeed mean "for nothing," as in *No sirve para nada*, which means, "It isn't good for anything." It can also mean "not at all" and can serve to intensify a negative: *¿Te gusta la salsa picante?* ("Do you like spicy salsa?") *No, para nada.* ("No, not at all.")

◆ **Destination:** *Mañana saldré para Bogotá.*
I leave for Bogota tomorrow.

◆ **Use:** *Necesito comprar mucha ropa para niños.*
I need to buy a lot of children's clothes ("clothes for children").

◆ **Purpose:** *Habrá una reunión para festejar tu cumpleaños.*
There will be a party (in order) to celebrate your birthday.

◆ **Comparisons:** *Para un inglés, usted baila muy bien.*
You dance pretty well for an Englishman.

◆ **Future time:** *La fiesta está programada para el próximo lunes.*
The party is scheduled for next Tuesday.

◆ **Tell it like it is:** *Para mí, esto es un evento maravilloso.*
In my opinion (As for me), this is a marvelous event.

Por

Por is used more in the sense of "by," "by means of," "through," and "on behalf of." Study the following examples to see what I mean:

◆ **Motive:** *Lo hacen por necesidad.* They do it out of need (for necessity's sake).

◆ **Favor:** *Voté por el otro candidate.* I voted for the other candidate (in favor of).

◆ **Reason:** *¿Por qué no vas al baile?* Why aren't you going to the dance?

◆ **Behalf:** *Lo hice por mi esposa.* I did it for my wife. (If this had been *para* instead of *por*, it would have meant "I made it [some thing] for my wife.")

◆ **Exchange:** *Me dieron diez pesos por un dólar.* They gave me 10 pesos for 1 dollar.

◆ **Time (duration):** *Voy a estar en este pueblo por una semana.* I'll be in this town for a week.

Por is also used to express the passive "by" and "by means of." It is used where we would say "per," as in "per year." Observe:

La canción fue compuesta por mi cuñado.
The song was composed by my brother-in-law.

Te enviaré el archivo por correo electrónico.
I'll send you the file by e-mail.

Me cobran diez pesos por hora.
They charge me 10 pesos per hour.

Acuérdate

To help you with *por*, think of "MFRBET": Must Fix the Roof for Bernardo, use Esteban's Tools. These stand for: Motive, Favor, Behalf, Reason, Exchange, and Time duration.

(This one is even dumber, but at least this time I can say that I made it up all by myself.)

You know that *¿por qué?* means "why?" You probably also know that *porque*, written together, means "because." The word *porqué*, with the *tilde*, is a noun and can mean "reason" or "motive," as in *No me dijo el porqué de su comportamiento*, which translates as "He didn't tell me the reason for his behavior."

Palabras Para Ti

Here's a complete list of the ways that someone can be your *pariente*.

You know they're in your *familia* when they're your …

abuelo/a grandfather/mother

ahijado/a godson/daughter

bisabuelo/a great-grandfather/mother

bisnieto/a great-grandson/daughter

comadre "like a sister"

compadre "like a brother"

concuñado spouse's sister's husband

concuñada spouse's brother's wife

cuñado/a brother/sister-in-law

esposo/a spouse

hermano/a brother/sister

hijo/a son/daughter

madrastra stepmother

madre mother

madrina godmother

marido husband

medio/a hermano/a half-brother/sister

nieto/a grandson/daughter

nuera daughter-in-law

padrastro stepfather

padre father

padrino godfather

primo/a cousin

sobrino/a nephew/niece

sobrino/a político/a spouse's nephew/niece

suegro/a father/mother-in-law

tatarabuelo great-great-grandfather/mother

tatarnieto great-great-grandson/daughter

tío/a uncle/aunt

tío/a político/a uncle/aunt-in-law

yerno son-in-law

Diálogo: Mario y Juanita

Here is your first *diálogo*. Mario and Juanita are friends at a high school in Santiago, Chile. They are just getting to know each other. Let's listen in:

Mario: *Hola, Juanita. ¿Cómo estás?*

Juanita: *Muy bien, Mario. Gracias. ¿Y tú?*

Mario: *Bien, pero estoy muy ocupado hoy día. Oye, te quería hacer una preguntita, ¿tienes hermanos?*

Juanita: *Sí, dos. Un hermano y una hermana. Aquí tengo una foto de mi familia (ella saca una foto de su bolsa). Mira, él es mi padre, y ella es mi madre. La que está a la derecha es mi hermana, Adelita, y el que está a la izquierda es mi hermano, Roberto. Atrás están los primos, los tíos, los abuelos y los padrinos. Soy yo ahí, sentada en el piso.*

Mario: *Parece que tu familia es grande. La mía también es grande. Tengo cinco hermanos y muchos parientes. Mañana te enseño una foto.*

Juanita: *Está bien. Nos vemos entonces. Chau.*

Mario: *Chau, Juanita. Hasta mañana.*

Now, here's a translation of the *diálogo*. See how well you did:

Mario: Hi, Juanita. How are you?

Juanita: Very well, Mario. Thanks. And you?

Mario: Fine, but I'm very busy these days. Hey, I wanted to ask you a question. Do you have (any) brothers and sisters? (siblings)

Juanita: Yes, two, a brother and a sister. Here, I have a picture of my family (she takes a photo out of her bag). Look, he is my father, and she is my mother. The (person) on the right is my sister, Adelita, and the one who is on the left is my brother, Roberto. Behind are (my) cousins, aunts and uncles, grandparents, and godparents. That's me there, sitting on the floor.

Mario: It seems that your family is big. Mine is also big. I have five brothers (and sisters?) and a lot of relatives. I'll show you a picture tomorrow.

Juanita: Okay. We'll see each other then. Bye.

Mario: Bye, Juanita. See you tomorrow.

El Web

If you need more info on *por* and *para*, visit www.studyspanish.com/lessons/porpara.htm or http://spanish.about.com/cs/grammar/a/porpara.htm.

Risa del Día

All its strengths aside, the Latin family also seems to be a great source of humor. There are many jokes about relationships, marriage, in-laws, and related topics. Many of these jokes are definitely not tasteful and thus are unsuitable for publication in this book. Here are two fairly harmless examples:

1. *Se encuentran dos amigas y una llorando le dice a la otra:*

   Mi médico me dio una semana de vida.

   La otra le contesta:

   Bueno, te dejo a mi marido por esta semana.

   ¿Pero para qué lo quiero a tu marido?

   Porque con él en tu casa la semana te va a parecer una eternidad.

2. *Conversaban dos hombres en un bar cuando uno pregunta:*

   Disculpa la pregunta, ¿pero a ti te cae bien tu suegra?

   No, para nada.

   Entonces ¿por qué llevas una foto de ella en el paquete de cigarros?

   Ah! Es que quiero dejar de fumar.

Vocabulario Útil:

se encuentran are found	*parecer una eternidad* seem like an eternity
llorar to cry	
médico doctor	*caerle bien* to like (a person)
una semana de vida "a week to live"	*para nada* not at all; "no way"
	dejar de fumar to quit smoking

The Least You Need to Know

◆ Family life is very important in Spanish and Latin American cultures.

◆ *La familia* usually extends beyond the nuclear family.

◆ *Para* and *por* both mean "for" but have different uses.

13

Nuevos Amigos

In This Chapter

◆ *Lectura:* Un joven español en busca de amigos

◆ *Gramática:* usted versus tú

◆ *Diálogo:* María, Alejandro, y Tom

Close friendships seem to play an even greater role in the lives of Spanish-speakers than they often do in the world of Anglophones (that's us). Statistics show that in the United States, many adults can name only a handful of close friends whom they have had continuous contact with all their lives. But because it is far more common for Latinos to grow up and live in the city of their birth, they usually can list far more lifelong friends than we can. This attitude toward friendship usually carries over to their long-distance friends as well. Once you've made a good Latin friend, there's a good chance that you will know this person a long time—if you give as much as you receive, of course (ah, the lessons of life).

Lectura: Un Joven Español Busca Amigos

This is an example of a letter you might see posted on an Internet bulletin board. Here we have a young man from Spain who is looking for new friends to exchange e-mail with. This text is a good example of how someone might write about his or her life in the hopes of making new friends.

This guy is fictitious, so don't send him any e-mail. If you're interested, you can find thousands of nonfictitious Spanish-speakers on the web. Just search for "*amigos*" or "*chat español*," and surf around until you find something (or someone) interesting.

Me llamo Juan Antonio Garza Muñoz, aunque profesionalmente se me conoce como Juan Garza. Tengo 23 años, y soy escorpión.

Nací en un pequeño pueblo del suroeste de España, El Rocío (ubicado a 50 klm. de Sevilla), en una casita en la ladera de una colina. Nací a las 10 de la noche, el 13 de noviembre de 1976. Todo fue a la antigua, podemos decir, ya que a mi madre le asistió al parto solamente una partera. Nací en una pequeña cama y mi madre lo pasó mal (supongo que no tan mal, porque le quedaron ganas de tener tres hijos más).

A los cinco años, vinimos a Madrid a vivir, a intentar salir adelante. Éramos una familia modesta (por no decir pobre). Mi padre, Felipe, era conductor de taxi y de camiones. Mi madre se dedicaba a cuidar de la casa y de la família. Mi infancia fue feliz, supongo. Los niños son felices jugando con sus cosas y con sus amigos.

Mi adolescencia no fue tan feliz, ya que estuvo marcada por dos cosas, muy importantes para mí. La primera es que desde que tenía nueve años mis padres empezaron a trabajar el turno de noche, y dormían de día. Yo los veía solamente una hora al día y, al no tener hermanos de mi edad (son menores todos), la lectura y la música me acompañaban. Menos mal que tenía a mi abuelita, que nos cuidaba durante el día. La otra cosa que marcó mi adolescencia fue la muerte de mi hermanita María cuando yo tenía 15 años. Es algo que me ha costado muchos años para superar (si es que lo he superado).

A los 19 años me fuí de la casa para trabajar de taxista en Valencia. Invertía la mayor parte del dinero que ganaba en la Bolsa de Valores. Fue probablemente la mejor decisión que pude tomar en aquella época. Gané mucho dinero, conocí a gente superdivertida, y ayudé a gente a conseguir trabajo. ¿Qué más podía pedir?

A grandes rasgos así soy yo. Siempre me interesa mantener correspondencia con nuevos amigos. Si os interesa escribirme, tengo correo electrónico: jgarza@lux.intercomws.es (éste es el de mi casa), o si no, jgarza.@datbasepnd.dingo.com.es (éste es el del trabajo).

Cultura Latina

Spaniards and Latin Americans tend to stand quite close to one another when they talk. You might find yourself feeling a bit boxed in by your new Latin friends. But from their perspective, standing close to you is an indication of their concern and politeness (and a good way to let you know what they had at their last meal). If you keep backing off, they might get the message that you are cold and aloof. Of course, over e-mail all of this is a moot point.

Vocabulario Útil:

escorpión   Scorpio (zodiac sign)

nacer   to be born

ubicarse   to be located

casita   little house (*casa* + *ita*)

ladera   side; bank

colina   hill

a la antigua   old-fashioned way; the old way

asistir a   to attend (false cognate)

parto   birth

partera   midwife

suponer   to suppose

modesto   modest; not rich

salir adelante   to get ahead (economically)

adolescencia   adolescence

turno   shift (here, "night shift")

acompañar   to keep one company; to go with

menos mal   it was good that …; I'm glad that …

superar   to get over; to come through

Bolsa de Valores   the stock market

tomar una decisión   to make a decision

aquella época   that time (of my life)

conseguir   to get; to acquire

pedir   to ask for

a grandes rasgos   the big picture; "in a nutshell"

correo electrónico   e-mail

Algo Nuevo

You already know that *pero* means "but." Now learn *sino*, which means "but rather." *No soy inglés, sino canadiense* means "I'm not English, but (rather) Canadian"; *Mis padres no hablaban el italiano, sino el portugués* means "My parents didn't speak Italian, but (rather) Portuguese." Use *sino* when the first part of your sentence is negative and you wish to make a correction to something stated or assumed. *Sino* as a noun means "fate."

Análisis del Texto

Okay, now let's take a closer look:

se me conoce como Juan Garza   The *se* makes the statement passive, and the *me* is the direct object pronoun. So, this means, "I am known as Juan Garza."

a la antigua   The *a la* + feminine adjective means "in the style of X." You can say, *a la española* ("in a Spanish style") and *a la mexicana* ("in a Mexican style").

ya que a mi madre le asistió al parto solamente una partera You may need to take this apart to understand what's going on. Literally, we have "*to my mother to her attended to the birth only a midwife.*" This, of course, doesn't make sense. The *le* is the INDOP, the *al parto* is the direct object, and the *a mi madre* just clarifies who the *le* refers to. *Ya que* means "since," so a better translation of this would be: "… since only a midwife attended my mother's delivery."

lo pasó mal The neuter pronoun *lo* here refers to the experience of giving birth in general, which has no gender assigned to it in this sentence, so *lo* is used. Translation: "She had a hard time."

le quedaron ganas de tener más hijos The verb *quedar* means "to remain." A literal translation might be "to her there remained desires to have." A better translation would be: "She still wanted (had desire left) to have more children."

A los cinco años The preposition *a* can be used in numerous time expressions: *a las cinco de la tarde* means "at five o'clock in the afternoon." Here, this phrase translates as "When I was five years old." He could also have written *Cuando yo tenía cinco años*.

modesta (por no decir pobre) The use of *por* here is interesting. Juan calls his family *modesta*, almost as a euphemism for *pobre*. So this might translate as "My family was modest (rather than calling it poor)." There is a bit of tongue-in-cheek attitude here.

Menos mal que tenía a mi abuelita *Menos mal* is a rather odd but useful phrase for saying "at least" or "It's a good thing that …" By itself it often means "It could have been worse."

me ha costado muchos años When someone says *me cuesta* or *me ha costado*, it may not have anything to do with money. *Costar* can also be used in the sense of "to be difficult" or "to cause difficulty," or even "to take a lot out of someone (physically, emotionally, or in some other way)." Here, this sentence might translate as "It has taken me many years (of my life)."

Ten Cuidado

The *usted* versus *tú* debate is rarely as clear-cut as some textbooks would have you believe. Entire Ph.D. theses have been written on this topic. As your exposure to the language and culture grows, you'll eventually figure out how *usted* and *tú* are being used by the people around you. Until you do, be careful and stick to the general rules about *usted* and *tú*.

Gramática: Usted vs. Tú

As you already learned in your beginning course, you have a choice between two pronouns and verb forms when addressing people: *tú* and *usted*.

In very general terms, *usted* is used with strangers, superiors, and people for whom you wish to show respect. You also may use *usted* when you wish to keep a certain distance and professionalism between yourself and someone. *Tú* is used for friends, family members, young children, and one's peers. While *tú* is not in itself disrespectful, it must be used appropriately.

> *¿Cómo está usted?*
> How are you? (polite)

> *¿Cómo está tú?*
> How are you? (familiar)

While *usted* is almost always appropriate when meeting someone for the first time, it also may be used with people whom you have known for years. For example, my dentist lives in Mexico, and I've been hopping across the border to seek his excellent care for nearly 20 years. He calls me Esteban, and I call him Raúl. Nonetheless, we always use *usted* with each other. Why? Because even though our interaction is quite friendly and relaxed (he even teases me about my old metal fillings), ours is still a professional relationship. I am his client, and he is my health-care provider. He respects me as his patient by using *usted*, and I respect him as a professional by using *usted* back. If we were to start using *tú*, there would be a palpable change in the nature of our relationship from that of a professional one to one of equal friends. If one day Raúl is no longer my dentist, then we might feel comfortable using *tú*. But perhaps not.

Tú is usually used in these instances:

♦ When speaking to a child

♦ When you are a child and are talking to friends

♦ When speaking to a family member (most of the time)

♦ When praying (supreme beings are addressed as *tú*)

♦ When speaking to a fellow student or someone your age

♦ When you and the other person have agreed to use *tú*

♦ When someone insists that you use *tú* with them

Except when addressing children, your peers, and fellow students (if you happen to be a student yourself), it would be best to begin your conversations with *usted* and the third-person singular verb form that goes with *usted*. Unless you have a clear reason for not addressing someone as *usted* (see the previous list), you risk unintentionally insulting people by using *tú*. If you inadvertently start off with *usted* when the situation would have allowed for *tú*, you'll be kindly instructed to use *tú* (children will usually laugh about it). As a non-native speaker, it's unlikely that any offense will be taken. However, it's a lot harder to backpedal once you have started using *tú* with someone to whom you should have said *usted* from the very beginning.

There's actually a verb that means "to use *tú* with someone." The verb is *tutear*. If someone says "*Me puedes tutear*," it means that you can call him or her *tú* if you wish. No, there's no verb "*ustedear*," except, perhaps, as a joke.

What They Didn't Tell You About Tú and Usted

Now that I've covered the "textbook" uses of *usted* and *tú*, I must tell you that the ways in which *usted* and *tú* are used in practice can vary considerably from place to place. In parts of Central America, you may hear people using *tú* (or *vos*) and *usted* in the same sentence with the very same person (*usted* can sometimes be used simply to emphasize a point). You will hear Colombians using *usted* with their close friends and even their pets, and Chileans using *usted* verb forms with their young children. On the other hand, in the Caribbean, *usted* is rarely used at all. Cubans and Puerto Ricans can be heard using *tú* with just about everybody, all the time, from the very beginning. Using *usted* in a situation that would clearly have called for *tú*, or with people you have used *tú* with for years, can convey anger or dismay.

Algo Nuevo

In parts of Latin America, there's another word for *tú*. In Argentina, Uruguay, much of Central America, highland Ecuador, and a few other places, people say *vos*. *Vos* is an old form for "you" that disappeared from most Spanish, just as *thou* faded away in English. The *vos* form of the verb is a bit different from the *tú* form. To form the *vos* form in the present indicative (the only tense that matters), remove the final *r* from the infinitive, replace it with *s*, and accent the final syllable: *vos hablás, venís, tenés,* and so on. Commands are formed by removing the same final *r* and accenting the remaining *a, e,* or *i*: *Hablá vos*. If you're in a country where people say *vos*, you'll pick it up quickly. Just use *tú* until you do, and you'll be fine.

Nevertheless, in spite of the many subtleties involved, it's still best to follow the general rules I've outlined above until you are comfortable with the way the locals do it. With adults, use *usted* until you're 100 percent sure that *tú* is appropriate.

Diálogo: Nuevos Amigos

Here is another *diálogo*. This one is much longer than the last one. The scene takes place in Peru, in the colonial city of Cuzco, not far from Machu Picchu. Tom is an American backpacker. He has read *The Complete Idiot's Guide to Intermediate Spanish, Second Edition*, so his Spanish is tip-top. While sitting at a table in a café, he is approached by two Peruvians, Alejandro and María. Here's their conversation:

María: *Hola. ¿Qué tal? ¿De dónde eres?*

Tom: *Hola. Soy de los Estados Unidos.*

Alejandro: *¿Ah, sí? ¿De cuál estado?*

Tom: *De Ohio. Soy de Cleveland. Me llamo Tom.*

María: *Me llamo María, y mi amigo se llama Alejandro. ¿Podemos tomar asiento aquí contigo?*

Tom: *Sí, cómo no. Ustedes son de aquí, ¿verdad?*

Alejandro: *Pues, sí, somos de acá. Pero no de aquí de Cuzco. Yo soy de Lima y María es de Arequipa. De hecho, somos turistas aquí también. ¿Qué te parece el Perú?*

Tom: *Me encanta. Llegué apenas anteayer. No me he acostumbrado todavía a la altura. Anoche no pude dormir bien y me dio un dolor de cabeza horrible. Ahora, parece que ya me ha pasado todo. Y ustedes, ¿qué están haciendo en Cuzco?*

María: *Pues, tú sabes, estamos haciendo el Camino Inca. No es solamente para los turistas extranjeros, ¿verdad?*

Tom: *Claro que no. Es una maravilla.*

Alejandro: *Dime una cosa. ¿Cuánto gana un trabajador por día en los Estados Unidos? Tú sabes, acá la cosa es muy difícil. Uno trabaja muy duro, pero los sueldos son muy bajos. O sea, creo que ustedes están ganando mucho más que nosotros.*

Tom: *Bueno, eso depende de la clase de trabajo que uno haga. Yo, siendo estudiante, vivo en parte de una beca y de lo poco que me están pagando de mi trabajo temporal en la cafetería universitaria.*

Alejandro: *Pero, por hora, ¿cuanto te pagan?*

Tom: *Pues, se trata del sueldo mínimo permitido por ley. Son unos seis dólares por hora, más o menos.*

Alejandro: *¡Caray! En comparación con lo que se gana aquí, es mucho dinero.*

Tom: *Tal vez. Pero hay que tener en cuenta que allá todo cuesta mucho más. Aunque parezca mucho dinero, en realidad no lo es.*

María: *Oye, Alejandro. Basta con las preguntas acerca del dinero. ¿No ves que le estás molestando a Tom?*

Tom: *No te preocupes, María. Todo el mundo me hace las mismas preguntas.*

María: *Mira, vamos a ir a una peña esta noche a las 9:00. ¿Quieres ir con nosotros? Sería más divertido si podríamos ir contigo.*

Tom: *¿Conmigo? Bueno, sí, por supuesto. A mí me gustaría ir con ustedes.*

María: *Muy bien. Entonces, vete a la plaza central a las ocho y media. Podemos encontrarnos frente a la catedral y de ahí, podemos ir juntos a la peña.*

Tom: *Perfecto. Nos vemos entonces a las 8:30.*

Alejandro: *¡Sensacional!*

Tom: *Bueno, hasta entonces. Oye, Alejandro, antes de que te vayas, hazme un favor. ¿Me puedes sacar una foto? Aquí tienes mi máquina de fotos. Es muy fácil de usar. Oprimiendo este botón, se saca la foto.*

Alejandro: *¿Listo? (Saca la foto.) Bueno, ya la saqué.*

Tom: *Gracias. Ah, una última pregunta. ¿Qué es una peña exactamente?*

María: *Es una fiesta andina con musica tradicional.*

Tom: *¡Qué bueno! Nos vemos entonces.*

Alejandro: *Muy bien. Hasta luego.*

Cultura Latina

In some Spanish-speaking countries, it's expected that a man should kiss a woman on one cheek the first time they are being introduced (if the two are about the same age and social standing). Interestingly, in Brazil it's two kisses; in Argentina and Uruguay, it's one. In Mexico, it's not a good idea until you've known the person for a long time. Men may hug if they are good friends. Do be careful with all this, however. Spend some time observing what the people around you are doing before you start running around hugging and kissing people.

Now here's the text of the *diálogo* translated:

Maria: Hi. How are you? Where are you from?

Tom: Hi. I'm from the United States.

Alejandro: Really? From which state?

Tom: From Ohio. I'm from Cleveland. My name is Tom.

Maria: My name is Maria, and my friend's name is Alejandro. Can we take a seat here with you?

Tom: Yes, of course. You're from here, right?

Alejandro: Well, yes we're from here. But not from here in Cuzco. I'm from Lima, and Maria is from Arequipa. In fact, we're tourists here, too. What do you think of Peru?

Tom: It's great. I just arrived the day before yesterday. I haven't gotten used to the altitude yet. Last night I couldn't sleep well, and I got a horrible headache. Now it seems that it has all passed. And you? What are you doing in Cuzco?

Maria: Well, you know, we're doing the Inca trail. It's not just for the foreign tourists, you know ….

Tom: Of course not. It's wonderful (a wonder).

Alejandro: Tell me something. How much does a worker earn each day in the United States? You know, things are pretty tough here (the thing is …). You work very hard (one works), but the wages are very low. I mean, I think (believe) that you all are making a lot more that we are.

Tom: Well, that depends on the kind of work you do (one does). Being a student, I live partly from a scholarship and partly from the little (I earn) from my part-time job at the school cafeteria.

Alejandro: But, per hour, how much do they pay you?

Tom: Well, it's the minimum wage allowed by law. It's about six dollars per hour, more or less.

Alejandro: Wow! In comparison with what (that which) people earn (is earned) here, that's a lot of money.

Tom: Perhaps. But you have to keep in mind that everything costs a lot more there. Although it might seem like a lot of money, in reality it isn't.

Maria: Hey, Alejandro. Enough with the questions about money. Can't you see that you're bothering Tom?

Tom: Don't worry, Maria. Everybody asks me the same questions.

Alejandro: Look, we're going to go to a *peña* tonight at 9:00. Do you want to come with us? It would be more fun if we could go with you.

Tom: With me? Well, yes, of course. I'd love to go with you.

Maria: Great. So, go to the central plaza at 8:30. We can meet in front of the cathedral and then we can go together to the *peña*.

Tom: Perfect. We'll see each other then at 8:30.

Alejandro: Cool!

Tom: Well, see you then. Hey, Alejandro, before you go, do me a favor. Can you take a picture of me? Here's my camera. It's really easy to use. Just push this button to take the picture.

Alejandro: Ready? (Takes picture.) Okay, I took it.

Tom: Thanks. Uhhh, one last question. What exactly is a *peña?*

Maria: It's an Andean party with traditional music.

Tom: That's great! We'll see each other later then.

Alejandro: Okay. See you later (until later).

Algo Nuevo

You've probably heard the word *gringo* before as an insult meaning Anglo-Saxon. In Mexico, it almost always means someone from the United States regardless of one's ethnic background. But don't automatically assume that you are being insulted if someone calls you a *gringo,* especially if it is done in humorous tone of voice. I was once called a *gringo* on Mexican television, and no insult was ever intended. In some countries, it simply refers to an English-speaker, although in Argentina, a *gringo* could mean someone from Italy. The term is not used much in Spain. The word *yanqui* is universally understood for American, even if you're from the South.

El Web

You can hook up with new friends at many websites on the Internet. Yahoo, AOL, and MSN all have Spanish forums. Just search for "Spanish Chat" and you'll find something. The verb *chatear* has been coined in Spanish. You can guess what it means.

Also, find out more about the *vos* pronoun at http://leonardo.sfasu.edu/ccuadra/ 32vos.htm. If this site goes under, just search for *Spanish Voseo*.

Risa del Día

This, I suppose, is a dumb joke. Why? Because I made it up myself. You can see why I didn't go into comedy professionally. I've added a little extra verbiage here and there for you to practice your reading skills. The text is presented to you as it might appear in a Spanish language book. Notice the dashes to indicate dialogue and breaks in the conversation:

Un amigo a otro:

Juan, ¿sabes qué?—dijo Miguel.

No—dijo Juan, molesto, girando la cabeza hacia su compañero.

Que ya va para tres años que nos conocemas y hasta la fecha nunca hemos podido pasar una semana entera sin pelearnos.

Miguel se quita el sombrero y lo pone sobre una mesa—. Estoy pensando que quizá sea mejor que no sigamos siendo amigos. Me cuesta discutir tanto, y a decirte la verdad, ya no me gusta pasar tiempo contigo. ¿Tú qué opinas?

Bueno,—le dijo Juan a Miguel—. ¿Pero si tú eres mi mejor amigo?

Cómo puedo yo ser tu mejor amigo si cada semana nos peleamos?

Pues claro, si con mis otros amigos me peleo cada día ….

Vocabulario Útil:

molesto   bothered; perturbed

girar la cabeza   to turn one's head

va para tres años   it's going on three years

hasta la fecha   until today; so far

entero   entire; whole

pelearse   to get into a fight

discutir   to argue

a decirte la verdad   to tell you the truth

opinar   to think; to have an opinion

pues claro   Well, sure …

cada día   every day

The Least You Need to Know

♦ Latin friends often make friends for life.

♦ The Internet is a good place to meet *e-amigos*.

♦ Many subtleties are involved in deciding whether to use *tú* or *usted*.

♦ Follow the general rules about *tú* and *usted* until you learn otherwise.

La Gastronomía y el Buen Comer

In This Chapter

- ◆ *Lectura:* Receta para tamalitos
- ◆ *Gramática:* las preposiciones
- ◆ *Diálogo:* La Fonda

You don't need anyone to remind you that both Latin America and Spain boast some of the best foods on the planet! We've all heard of burritos, tacos, and tostadas. But that's just a tiny fraction of the many delectable dishes that await you from *la buena cocina.*

The Complete Idiot's Guide to Intermediate Spanish, Second Edition, is not a cookbook. This is unfortunate, but there are so many different dishes prepared in Latin America and Spain that it would be impossible to discuss them all here and still have room for grammar. If you're getting hungry for some authentic Latin American or Spanish food, see if there are any ethnic restaurants in your area. You can usually find something if you're in a large city, but if you're in a more isolated or rural area, you may have to cook the food yourself. I'll suggest a few websites at the end of the chapter where you can find some great recipes if you're interested in more information about Spanish and Latin American cuisine.

Lectura: Receta para Tamalitos Mexicanos

Rather than tease you with a *lectura* about how good all the food is and how much Spanish speakers like to eat it with their friends and family (you knew this already), I decided to use a real recipe as the reading for this chapter. I liked this text because of the interesting style in which it is written and because studying it might help you with other recipes written in Spanish.

The main meal in Latin countries usually comes at midday. Eating with family and friends also tends to take longer than you may be used to because lengthy conversations are always expected once the food is consumed. These activities are called *la sobremesa*.

Tamalitos Mexicanos

Para 6 personas

Ingredientes:

Para la masa:

> 7 elotes desgranados
>
> 120 gramos (4 onzas) de mantequilla
>
> 2 cucharadas de azúcar
>
> 2 cucharaditas de sal
>
> hojas de elote

Para la salsa:

> 4 chiles poblanos asados, pelados, despepitados y rebanados en rajitas finas
>
> ½ kilo (un poco más de una libra) de tomate asado y pelado
>
> ½ cebolla mediana
>
> 1 cucharada de mantequilla
>
> sal al gusto
>
> 350 gramos (12 onzas) de queso cortado en tiras

Preparación

Las hojas de elote se ponen a remojar en agua fría, se escurren y se secan. En el procesador de alimentos se muelen los granos de maíz. La mantequilla se bate con el azúcar y la sal hasta que esté cremosa y se le añaden los elotes molidos. Se hacen los tamalitos untando una cucharada de pasta en una hoja de elote; se doblan como tamales y se van colocando parados en una tamalera o en una olla con tapa a la que se le habrá añadido un poco de agua y se ponen a cocer durante 45 minutos, aproximadamente. Se sirven acompañados por la salsa y, si lo desea, por un poco de crema ácida.

Nota: También se pueden hacer en la olla express, en cuyo caso tardarán aproximadamente 15 minutos.

Salsa: El tomate se muele con la cebolla, se cuela y se sofríe en la mantequilla; se le añade sal al gusto y se sazona durante aproximadamente 10 minutos; si queda muy espesa se le puede añadir un poquito de agua. A los 10 minutos se le agregan las rajas y el queso y se sirve.

Acuérdate

The word for "bean" varies widely throughout the Spanish-speaking world. In Mexico and most of Central America, it's *frijol*. In Venezuela, it's *caraota*; in Colombia, it's *fríjol* (accent on the *í*); and in Ecuador, it's *fréjol*. *Argentinos* and *Uruguayos* call them *porotos*.

Presentación

Se colocan paraditos sin desenvolver en una cazuela; en una salsera aparte se sirve la salsa y, si lo desea, en otra salsera crema ácida. También se pueden servir en un platón ovalado, desenvueltos y bañados con su salsa.

Ten Cuidado

Be careful when asking for butter. *Mantequilla* is the usual word, but in some countries (such as Argentina and Uruguay) the word is *manteca*, which elsewhere means "pork lard." Also, be careful when talking about corn. Most people say *maíz* for corn, but words such as *jojoto*, *elote*, *mazorca*, and *cholco* are also possible.

Vocabulario Útil:

masa dough; filling

elote corn on the cob (Mexico and Central America)

desgranar to remove kernels/grains

gramo gram

libra pound

onza   ounce

mantequilla   butter

mediano   medium-sized

cucharada   tablespoonful

cucharaditas   teaspoonful

hoja   leaf; husk

asar   to roast; to grill

pelar   to peel

despepitar   to remove seeds

rebanar   to slice

raja, rajita, tira   strip

sal al gusto   salt "to taste"

remojar   soak

escurrir   to drip

procesador de alimentos   food processor

tapa   lid

batir   to beat; to mix

moler   to grind

untar   to spread

doblar   to bend; to turn

colocar   to place; to put

parar   to stand up

tamalera   a tamale holder

cocer   to cook; to boil

si lo desea   if you wish

crema ácida   sour cream

olla express   pressure cooker

tardar   to take (time)

colar   to drain; to strain

sofreír   to sauté

sazonar   to season

espeso   thick

desenvolver   to unwrap

cazuela   casserole

salsera   a salsa dish

platón   a big plate

Cultura Latina

A tip is *una propina*. In most Spanish and Latin American restaurants, the wait staff does not depend on tips for income as in the United States, and doesn't necessarily expect you to leave a tip. Of course, a small tip will always be appreciated if you wish to reward your waiter for good service. Larger tips may be expected in upscale restaurants that cater to tourists. But as a general rule, you don't need to tip the waiters at smaller eateries.

Análisis del Texto

Getting hungry? So am I. Let's take a quick look at what this recipe has to teach us:

cucharadas … cucharaditas   These words mean "tablespoonful" and "teaspoonful." As you know, *cuchara* means "spoon." The suffix *–ada* means "an amount of" or "–ful." We'll talk a bit more about suffixes in a later chapter.

se ponen a remojar   Did you notice that there are several *se* passives throughout this text? Here, p*oner* is followed by *a* + infinitive to mean "to put to" or "to make X," as in "to put it to soaking": *El jefe me puso a trabajar* means "The boss put me (made me) to work." A better translation usually leaves the word "put" out of it all together.

hasta que esté cremosa   *Hasta que* is always followed by a subjunctive.

se hacen los tamalitos untando   *Untar* means "to spread onto something (like butter)" Here, the present participle *untando* means "by spreading."

se van colocando parados   This is a compound tense with *ir* + present participle, and translates as "going along doing something." Here we have, "are being placed standing up."

en una olla con tapa a la que se le habrá añadido   I love this construction! Confused? Let's break it up. The first part is easy enough: "in a pot with lid." Then we have *a*, which means "to." Next is the *la que*. The *la* must stand in for something feminine: *olla*. After that is the *se* (passive), the *le* (to it), the future of *haber*, and the past participle of *añadir* ("to add to"), which is *añadido*. Literally this works out as "in a pot with lid to which (feminine) will have been added." A better translation: "In a lidded pot to which has been added …."

la olla express, en cuyo caso   Now and then you may see the words *cuyo*, *cuya*, and their plural forms. These mean "of which," "in which," "of whom," and "whose," and mostly are used in the written language: *Un hombre cuyo caballo es veloz* means "A man whose horse is fast." You needn't worry about *cuyo* in the spoken language because there are always ways around it: *un hombre que tiene un caballo veloz* means "a man who has a fast horse." Here we have "a pressure cooker, in which case …."

se colocan paraditos   You have seen the *–ito* suffix before: *Casa* changes to *casita*. This ending can also be added to adjectives. Because the *tamalitos* are already smaller than regular old *tamales*, the writer decided to also use the *–ito* suffix on the adjective. This makes them sound more dainty, I suppose.

platón   The suffix *–ón* is an enlarger. *Plato* (plate) is made bigger by calling it a *platón*. If you think this book is big, you could call it a *librón*. We'll talk more about suffixes in a later chapter.

Algo Nuevo

You know that *desayuno* is breakfast, *almuerzo* is lunch, and *cena* is dinner. But there's a lot of variation from country to country. In Cuba and Peru, dinner is *la comida*. In Mexico, *la comida* is definitely lunch, and *un almuerzo* is a light snack eaten around 10:00 in the morning. This would be called *las mediasnueves* or *la mediamañana* in Colombia. In Ecuador, dinner is *la merienda*, which in most other countries would mean "a snack." In Mexico, a "snack" is called *una botana*. A *botana* can be any little thing: a small bag of potato chips, nuts, or sometimes even what we would call an appetizer. In other countries, words such as *merienda, refrigerio, pasaboca,* and *bocado* are used instead. In Spain, a *merienda* is a light afternoon meal, which in Colombia might be called *las onces*.

Gramática: Las Preposiciones

Just a quick bite of grammar this time—about those little morsels we call prepositions.

A preposition is defined as an "invariable particle that unites two words or phrases establishing a dependent relationship between them." Huh? Okay, okay. In plain English, a preposition is a short word or phrase that tells you where something belongs, where something is positioned, or how something is related to something else.

You already know many Spanish prepositions. Here's a list to help you fill in the gaps. Some can take infinitives, as in *antes de comer*, which means "before eating." You should be able to translate these examples on your own.

Using Prepositions

Preposition	Definition	Example
a	to	*al doctor*
alrededor (de)	around	*alrededor de mí*
ante	before	*ante el juez*
antes (de)	before	*antes de comer*
a través de	across; through	*a través del parque*
bajo	under	*bajo la ley*
cerca (de)	near	*cerca de mi casa*
con	with	*con las manos*
contra	against	*contra la pared*
de	of, from	*de mi familia*
desde	from	*desde la montaña*

Preposition	Definition	Example
debajo (de)	under	*debajo de la cama*
delante (de)	in front of	*delante de mí*
después (de)	after	*después de comer*
detrás (de)	behind	*detrás de él*
en	in	*en mi casa*
encima (de)	on top of	*encima de la mesa*
entre	between; among	*entre nosotros*
frente a	in front of	*frente a la casa*
hacia	toward	*hacia las montañas*
lejos (de)	far (from)	*lejos de aquí*
según	according to	*según el texto*
sin	without	*sin saber; sin tí*
so	under (legal)	*so pena de muerte*
sobre	over; about; on	*sobre la tierra*
tras	after	*día tras día*

Cultura Latina

The word for "waiter" changes from place to place: *mesero* (most of Latin America), *mesonero* (Venezuela), *garzón* or *mozo* (Argentina), *camarero* (Spain, the Caribbean). You may need to ask the locals, "*¿Cómo se dice 'mesero/camarero' aquí?*" to find out what word people use where you are.

Diálogo en el Restaurante "La Fonda"

Let's see what happens to Jose and Maria when they stop for lunch at a small restaurant:

El mesero: *Bienvenidos a La Fonda.*

María: *Gracias, joven. Una mesa para dos personas, por favor.*

El mesero: *Cómo no, señora. Síganme por favor. Su mesa está cerca de la ventana.*

José: *¿Ah, sí? Excelente. Tenemos mucha hambre. (Toman asiento.)*

El mesero: *Muy bien. Díganme, ¿qué desean tomar?*

María: *Para mí, una limonada. Ya sé que mi esposo va a querer un jugo de naranja.*

José: *No, querida, no quiero nada de eso. Joven, tráigame una cerveza bien fría.*

María: *Pero, mi amor, no te olvides de tu salud, y del problema que tienes con el hígado y todo, tú sabes ....*

José: *Pues, tienes razón. Entonces, déme un vaso de leche, por favor. (Sale el mesero ... vuelve con las bebidas.)*

El mesero: *Aquí tienen las bebidas. Ahora, ¿qué van a querer?* (also: *pedir, ordenar, comer*)

José: *Es que no estamos listos todavía, joven. Dénos la oportunidad para estudiar (leer) el menú, y vuelva en dos minutos, si no sería gran molestia.*

El mesero: *Está bien. (Sale el mesero. Regresa 15 minutos después). Bueno, ¿ya están listos?*

María: *Sí, joven, ya. Yo voy a probar el filete de pescado.*

José: *Y yo el caldo de res, y el pollo asado. Pero dígame una cosa, joven. ¿Es picante el caldo?*

El mesero: *No, señor. No tiene nada de picante.*

José: *Está bien, entonces. Usted sabe ... por lo del estómago ... hay que tener cuidado.*

El mesero: *Sí. El pollo va acompañado de frijoles y arroz.*

José: *Eso está muy bien. Ahora, lleve los vasos vacíos a la cocina y dígale al cocinero que prepare la comida de una vez. Es que tenemos mucha prisa.*

El mesero: *Sí, señor. Como usted quiera.*

José: *Espere, tengo una pregunta más. ¿Qué pasa con los cubiertos?*

El mesero: *Enseguida se los traigo. (Va a la cocina y le grita al cocinero) ¡Oye, Juan! Hay un tipo en la cinco que quiere que hagas la comida de una vez.*

El cocinero: *¿Ah, sí? ¡Qué lástima! Es que estoy muy cansado. Ya no quiero cocinar. Que espere hasta que yo tenga ganas.*

Acuérdate

When referring to something abstract, we need *lo*, the neuter pronoun. In the dialogue, Jose says, "*lo del estómago.*" This translates literally as "the thing about the stomach" and more freely as "my stomach problems." As other examples, *lo de Juan* means "the issue (problem, idea) with Juan"; *lo único que no sé hacer* means "the only thing I don't know how to do"; and *lo que me dices* means "the thing (subject, issue) you are telling me."

Translation

El mesero: Welcome to La Fonda.

Maria: Thanks. You're very kind. A table for two, please.

El mesero: Very good. Please follow me. Your table is near the window.

Jose: Is that right? Excellent. We're very hungry.

El mesero: Great. What would you like to drink?

Maria: For me, a lemonade. I already know that my husband is going to want orange juice.

Acuérdate

The word for a drinking straw also changes from place to place. In Mexico, it's a *popote*. Most other places call it a *pitillo* or *pajilla*, but *pajita*, *sorbete*, and *carrizo* are also possible. In Argentina, Uruguay, and Paraguay, a *bombilla* is a metal straw for drinking *mate*, a green tea that is popular there. Elsewhere, a *bombilla* is usually a light bulb. Go figure.

Jose: No, dear, I don't want anything like that. Young man, bring me a very cold beer, please.

Maria: But honey, don't forget about your health, and the problem with your liver, you know ….

Jose: Well, you're right. In that case, I'm going to order a glass of milk. (waiter leaves; returns)

Ten Cuidado

Use *hay* (not *tener*) when asking about eggs and milk. Yes, eggs are *huevos*. But that word can also mean "the male generative organs." If you ask someone "*¿Tiene huevos?*" you aren't asking if there are eggs available, but if he (or she!) has testicles. Also avoid "*¿Tiene leche?*", which translates as "Are you lactating?" Say "*¿Hay huevos?*" and "*¿Hay leche?*" instead.

El mesero: Here are your drinks. Now, what are you going to order?

Jose: Well, we're not ready yet. Give us a chance to study the menu, and come back in two minutes, if it wouldn't be too much trouble.

El mesero: All right. (exit waiter; returns 15 minutes later). So, are you ready now?

Maria: Yes, young man, we are. I'm going to try the fish fillet.

Jose: And I'm going to try the beef stew and the rotisserie chicken. But tell me something, young man. Is the stew spicy?

El mesero: No, sir. There's nothing spicy in it.

Jose: Well, that's fine then. You know … my stomach problems … you have to be careful.

El mesero: Right. The chicken comes with beans and rice.

Jose: That's fine. Now, take these empty glasses to the kitchen and tell the cook to prepare the food at once. We're in a hurry. ("We have a lot of hurry.")

El mesero: Yes, sir. As you wish.

Jose: Wait, one more thing. What about the silverware?

El mesero: I'll bring it to you right away. (goes to kitchen; yells to the cook) Hey, Juan! There's a guy (*tipo* means "type") at table five (*la* refers to *mesa*) who wants you to make his food right away.

El cocinero: Oh yeah? What a shame! You see, I'm very tired. I don't want to cook anymore. Let him wait until I feel up to it.

Algo Nuevo

Literally, *Es que* means "It's that …." But a better translation might be "You see …," "What's happening is that …," "The thing is that …," and so on. By starting with *Es que*, the cook is explaining his actions or situation. In the right context, the statement *Es que Elias no tiene dinero* could mean, "You see, the problem is that Elias doesn't have any money … (so that's why he can't buy/do the thing we're talking about)."

El Web

Visit these websites for recipes and information about Spanish and Latin American food, or use your favorite search engine to find more:

www.afuegolento.com

www.top-tour-of-spain.com/authentic-spanish-food-recipes.html

www.ma.iup.edu/Pueblo/latino_cultures/recipes.html

Risa del Día

I suppose that these are old jokes. Food is held in such high regard that there aren't too many jokes about food. So here are a couple of short ones:

1. *Jaimito, ¿vos rezás antes de comer?* (*Vos* verb form indicates that this joke is probably from Argentina)

   No, maestra. Mi mamá no cocina muy bien, pero no es para tanto!

2. *Camarero, ¡el pollo está crudo!*

   ¿Como lo sabe, si no lo ha probado?

   Es que se está comiendo mi ensalada.

Vocabulario Útil:

rezar   to pray

cocinar   to cook

para tanto   that bad; "that extreme"

crudo   raw; uncooked

se está comiendo mi ensalada   he's eating my salad

The Least You Need to Know

◆ The main meals in Spanish-speaking countries tend to come at midday.

◆ The words for many foods change from country to country.

◆ The words for the main meal of the day change from country to country.

◆ Prepositions show relationship and position; some can take an infinitive.

La Iglesia y la Religión

In This Chapter

- ◆ *Lectura:* La Virgen de Guadalupe
- ◆ *Gramática:* the present progressive tense
- ◆ Palabras para ti

Historians of both Spain and Latin America have long identified the Roman Catholic Church as one of the most important forces in culture, society, and politics. In 1492, the Spanish *reconquista* finally came to an end when the last of the Moors were ousted from Granada and the entire Iberian Peninsula came under the religious control of the church. That same year, Catholicism was introduced to the New World (or maybe it was the other way around).

Catholicism and Latin American Culture

The Catholic Church brought profound changes to *las Américas.* It introduced a new moral code, the holy sacraments, the notion of heaven and hell, the Virgin, the saints, monogamy, and, of course, the crucified Christ. The human sacrifices and cannibalism practiced by some native peoples were replaced by the consumption of the host and wine (body and blood of Christ). Cathedrals were built on the sites of the old native worshipping grounds, and Christian saints replaced native deities.

Today, the Roman Catholic Church is still an integral part of the cultural and religious life of most Spaniards and Latin Americans. It is important to note, however, that not all Spanish-speakers are Roman Catholics. Protestant denominations (including several evangelical groups), Judaism, Mormonism, Native American religions, and atheism (just to mention a few) are also represented throughout the region. Nonetheless, statistics show that 99 percent of Spaniards and 87 percent of all Latin Americans are at least nominally Roman Catholic, and that nearly 40 percent of the world's Catholics speak Spanish as their first language. Thus, even if you have different religious beliefs, or none at all, you should have at least a passing understanding of the role the Church plays in Ibero-American history and society.

If you plan to travel to Spain or Latin America, there's a good chance that at some point you'll find yourself in a church or cathedral during a religious service, as Masses are held every day of the week. I have included the Spanish versions of the *Ave María* and the *Padre Nuestro* as sidebars in this chapter just so you might have a clue as to what's going on during the service.

Algo Nuevo

To give you an idea of the kind of language you'll find in a religious text, here's "In the beginning ..." from the *Book of Genesis*:

En el principio creó Dios los cielos y la tierra. Y la tierra estaba desordenada y vacía, y las tinieblas (darkness) estaban sobre la faz del abismo, y el Espíritu de Dios se movía sobre la faz de las aguas. Y dijo Dios: Sea la luz; fue la luz. Y vio Dios que la luz era buena; y separó Dios la luz de las tinieblas. Y llamó Dios a la luz Día, y a las tinieblas llamó Noche.

Lectura: La Virgen de Guadalupe

Our Lady of Guadalupe, also known as *la guadalupana*, is Mexico's patron saint. Her image can be seen in cathedrals, churches, chapels, and just about anywhere else you could possibly imagine: kitchen walls, key chains, napkins, candle holders, posters, hats, T-shirts, automobiles, you name it. Faith in the apparition of *la guadalupana* runs deep in the Mexican religious psyche, and her image is a constant reminder of the miracles she still performs (testimonials appear daily in newspapers) and of Mexican national pride.

According to legend, *la Virgen* appeared to Juan Diego, a Mexican Indian, in 1531 on a hill outside Mexico City called *Tepeyac*. The *Virgen* appeared several times to Juan Diego over the course of several days. She told him that she had a special love for the native Mexican people, and that a shrine should be built on the hill in her honor.

Cultura Latina

Most Latin American countries have a patron saint, and many cities and towns also have their own patron or patroness. Nearly every day of the year is associated with a particular saint (in the United States, we only seem to know St. Patrick's Day and St. Valentine's Day). When your town's saint's day comes up, it's time for a *fiesta*, known as a *fiesta patronal*.

Whether you believe the story or not, this event gave the Catholic Church a much stronger message to deliver to the indigenous population—that *la Virgen* appeared directly to one of their own people and that she cared about the welfare of the native Mexicans.

Today, the Basilica of the Virgin of Guadalupe is still on *Tepeyac* hill and is visited by 10 million pilgrims each year. The original cloth on which her image miraculously appeared is on display, and pilgrims are shuttled past on a series of people-movers to view it. Here's the story:

Cultura Latina

The Festival of Our Lady of Guadalupe falls on December 12 and is celebrated throughout Mexico. The main event is held at *Tepeyac*, in the great atrium of the *Basilica de Guadalupe*. Many groups specializing in different native dances arrive from all over the country to perform during the festival. The most famous native dance is called *los matachines*.

La Virgen de Guadalupe se apareció al indio Juan Diego el sábado 9 de diciembre de 1531 en las faldas del cerro del Tepeyac, situado en las afueras de la ciudad de México, para anunciarle que deseaba que en ese lugar se construyera un templo en su honor, para en él mostrar su amor, su compasión, su auxilio y su defensa a los hombres, y le pidió que hiciera llegar su mensaje al obispo de México, Juan de Zumárraga. Juan Diego cumplió con el encargo de la Virgen, pero el obispo no le creyó.

Aquella misma tarde Juan Diego volvió a pasar por el Tepeyac, le contó a la Virgen lo sucedido y le pidió que enviara a otro mensajero, pero ella insistió en que Juan Diego lo intentara de nuevo al día siguiente.

Siguiendo las instrucciones de la Virgen, Juan Diego volvió a presentarse ante el obispo, quien entonces le pidió alguna señal que demostrara que lo que decía era verdad.

Ese mismo día por la tarde, Juan Diego tuvo su tercer encuentro con la Virgen. Al hacerle saber la petición del obispo, la Virgen le pidió que volviera a encontrarla al día siguiente, y que entonces le daría la señal que pedía el obispo.

Pero al día siguiente—lunes 11—el tío de Juan Diego, Juan Bernardino, se enfermó gravemente a causa de la peste, y esto impidió a Juan Diego presentarse ante la Virgen. Esa misma noche empeoró el estado de Juan Bernardino, por lo que Juan Diego tuvo que ir a la ciudad de México en busca de un sacerdote.

Transcurrían las primeras horas del 12 de diciembre cuando, en su camino a la ciudad, Juan Diego pasó a la altura del Tepeyac. Avergonzado por no haber cumplido la promesa que le había hecho a la Virgen, decidió rodear el cerro para evitar un nuevo encuentro. Sin embargo, la Virgen se apareció a Juan Diego en el llano que se extiende junto al cerro. Le dijo a Juan Diego que no debía temer más por la salud de su tío y le pidió que subiera a la cumbre del Tepeyac, en donde encontraría unas rosas de Castilla—que no florecían en el cerro—las que serían la señal que debía entregar al obispo.

Ten Cuidado

Hacia means "toward." So in the text we have "toward noon on that twelfth of December." When written as *hacía* with the *tilde*, it's the past imperfect of *hacer*. The two are pronounced differently ("HAH seeyah" and "hah SEE ah") but look almost the same.

Mientras Juan Diego se dirigía a casa del obispo, la Virgen se apareció ante el moribundo Juan Bernardino y lo sanó. Le explicó el encargo que había dado a Juan Diego, y le pidió que hablara al obispo de su enfermedad y la forma como había sido curado por ella.

Hacia el mediodía de aquel 12 de diciembre Juan Diego le dijo al obispo que le había traído la señal que le había pedido. Entonces desenvolvió su ayate y las rosas de Castilla cayeron al suelo, y en la manta apareció la imagen de la Virgen de Guadalupe.

Vocabulario Útil:

aparecer   to appear

falda   side (of a hill or mountain); skirt

cerro   hill

auxilio   help

mensaje   message

obispo   bishop

cumplir   to keep; uphold; make good on

encargo   mission; assignment; task

lo sucedido   what had happened

mensajero   messenger

siguiente   following

volver a + infinitive   to repeat X; to do it again

de nuevo   again; another time

presentarse   to come before; to present oneself

señal sign

encuentro meeting; encounter

petición request

enfermarse to get sick

gravemente gravely; seriously

a causa de because of; due to

peste plague; epidemic

impedir to stop; to impede

estado condition; state

empeorar to worsen; to get worse

por lo que and so; for this reason

sacerdote cleric; priest

transcurrir to transpire; to happen

avergonzado ashamed

rodear to go around

llano low, flat land

temer to fear

cumbre top; summit

florecer to grow; to flower; to bloom

dirigirse to head toward; to go toward

moribundo deathly ill

sanar to heal; to cure

enfermedad sickness

manta rug; carpet; cloth on the floor

Análisis del Texto

Now let's look at our text more closely:

deseaba que en ese lugar se construyera un templo This is a simple past tense with a past subjunctive. You knew that already, right? *Construir* needs that *y* to form the past subjunctive because its stem ends in a vowel. The literal translation is, "She wanted that in that place be built a temple." A better translation would move the "in that place" to the end: "She wanted them to build a temple in that place."

para en él mostrar su amor The *él* stands in for *templo*.

y le pidió que hiciera llegar su mensaje *Hiciera* is past subjunctive of *hacer*. *Hacer* can be used with another infinitive as a helping verb: "She asked him to get the message to him" (to make it arrive).

pero el obispo no le creyó Believing is done with the indirect object pronouns (INDOPs) in Spanish: *No te creo* means "I don't believe (to) you." In this example, we know that the Bishop didn't believe Juan Diego personally. If the text had read *"pero el obispo no lo creyó,"* this would have meant that he didn't believe what Juan Diego said ("didn't believe it") rather than not believing that Juan was an honest person. The INDOP, as you know, is invariable for gender: *No le creo a María* means "I don't believe Maria." You may sometimes see *No se lo creo*, which means "I don't believe him/her/*usted*, and I don't believe what he/she/*usted* said, either."

Aquella misma tarde   This phrase means, "that very same afternoon." The use of *aquella* helps to distance the reader from the event. This did happen in 1531, after all ….

al día siguiente   This should be understood as "on the following day," not "to the following day."

le pidió alguna señal que demostrara   Here we have the past subjunctive in *demostara*. The *obispo* is unsure of what sign might be given: "asked him for a sign that might show …." Because it is unknown what kind of sign *la Virgen* might give, the subjunctive is required.

por lo que Juan Diego tuvo que ir   The *lo* refers to the whole situation of the illness of Juan Diego's uncle, and offers a cause-and-effect link between the two statements: "Juan Bernardino's condition worsened, and so (for this reason) Juan Diego had to go …."

Transcurrían … cuando … Juan Diego pasó   This is a fine example of how a preterit tense (*pasó*) can interrupt the events being described in the imperfect (*transcurrían*).

Gramática: The Present Progressive Tense

When something or someone is involved in an activity in a particular moment (often, but not always, the present moment), Spanish uses what is known as the present progressive tense. This tense corresponds to the *–ing* tenses we use all the time in English.

You have seen several verbs in the present progressive in previous *lecturas* and examples. Now let's look at the tense in greater detail:

Forming the Present Progressive Tense

Verb	Ending	Present Participle	Definition
hablar	*–ando*	*hablando*	"talking"
cantar	*–ando*	*cantando*	"singing"
comer	*–iendo*	*comiendo*	"eating"
vivir	*–iendo*	*viviendo*	"living"
oír	*–yendo*	*oyendo*	"hearing"

Ten Cuidado

The participle is always invariable. No matter who you are or what you're doing, the *o* at the end never becomes *a*. It also is never pluralized with an *s*.

The present progressive in Spanish is basically the same as the English construction "someone or something *is* doing:" *estar* (to be) + present participle. Most verbs form regular present participles. But, of course, a few common *–er* and *–ir* verbs have slightly irregular forms. Stem-changing *–ir* verbs such as *pedir* (pido) and *dormir* (duermo) change the *e* to *i* and the *o* to *u* in the present participle:

> *venir* changes to *viniendo*
>
> *decir* changes to *diciendo*
>
> *sentir* changes to *sintiendo*
>
> *pedir* changes to *pidiendo*
>
> *dormir* changes to *durmiendo*
>
> *morir* changes to *muriendo*
>
> *poder* changes to *pudiendo*

Acuérdate

The present participle of *ser* is *siendo* It isn't used often, but it's handy for saying "Being X …," as in: *Siendo hombre, no pudo entender los dolores de parto de su esposa.* ("Being a man, he couldn't understand his wife's labor pains.")

If the verb stem ends in a vowel (*creer, caer, oír, leer*), then the *i* in *–iendo* becomes *y*: *creyendo, cayendo, oyendo, leyendo.* Verbs ending in *–eír*, such as *reír* ("to laugh") and *sonreír* ("to smile"), lose both the *e* and the *tilde: riendo, sonriendo.*

Here are some basic sentences using the present progressive tense:

> *Estoy escribiendo una carta a mi viejo amigo.*
> I'm writing a letter to my old friend.
>
> *Antonio está viajando por España.*
> Antonio is traveling through Spain.
>
> *Están recibiendo comunión.*
> They are receiving communion.
>
> *Estamos construyendo una nueva iglesia.*
> We are building a new church.

Cultura Latina

Here is the Spanish text for the Lord's Prayer:

Padre Nuestro que estás en el Cielo, santificado sea tu nombre; venga a nosotros tu reino y hágase tu voluntad en la tierra como en el cielo; danos hoy nuestro pan de cada día y perdona nuestras ofensas, como también perdonamos a los que nos ofenden, no nos dejes caer en la tentación, y líbranos del mal. Amén.

The present participle can also be used after verbs such as *seguir* and *continuar* (both mean "to continue") and the verb *ir* ("to go"):

Siguen charlando.
They're still talking.

Voy entendiendo un poco mejor del español.
I'm getting to understand Spanish a bit better.

Continuarán reparando la capilla durante toda la semana.
They will be continuing to repair the chapel during the entire week.

Algo Nuevo

The verb *ir* works well with the present participle: *Voy caminando por la calle* means, "I am walking along the street (and making progress)." Its use implies motion. I could also say *Estoy caminando por la calle*, but with *estar* the focus is more on *what* I am doing rather than on the fact that I am getting somewhere. Sometimes the sense of motion is figurative: *Voy entendiendo* means, "I'm moving toward understanding" (I understand more and more each time).

The present participle also has some uses by itself. Use it to say "By doing X ...," as in the following examples:

Trabajando se gana la vida.
You live by working (one lives ...).

Leyendo un poco cada día, tu español mejorará.
By reading a little every day, your Spanish will improve.

Note that the tense of *estar* can vary. With helping verbs, you can use it in the imperfect, conditional, future, or even the subjunctive:

Juan estaba hablando con el cura cuando sonó el teléfono.
Juan was talking to the priest when the phone rang.

Había estado mirando la televisión durante una hora cuando se me cortó la luz.
I had been watching television for an hour when the power went out on me.

Es posible que esté leyendo.
It's possible that he may be reading.

Estaré viajando durante el próximo mes.
I will be traveling during the coming month.

Palabras Para Ti

Here are some more words related to religion and religious life:

orar; rezar   to pray

misa   Mass

misal   missal; book used for Mass

crusifijo   crucifix

ídolo   idol

biblia   Bible

pecado   sin

cura (masculine)   priest

culto   form of Christianity other than Catholicism (not necessarily a "cult" in the English sense)

protestante   Protestant

judío   Jewish

musulmán   Muslim

hindú   Hindu

templo   temple

mezquita   mosque

comunión   communion

inclinarse la cabeza   to bow your head

confesar   to give confession

bendecir   to bless

ángel   angel

espíritu santo   Holy Spirit

Cultura Latina

Here is the Spanish version of the *Ave María:*

Dios te salve María, llena eres de Gracia, el Señor esté contigo; bendita eres entre todas las mujeres y bendito el fruto de tu vientre Jesús. Santa María, Madre de Dios, ruega por nosotros los pecadores ahora y en la hora de nuestra muerte. Amén.

El Web

If you need more information or vocabulary for Roman Catholicism, go right to the source and visit the Vatican's official website at www.vatican.va. Several languages are available, including Spanish.

Risa del Día

Jokes of a religious nature abound in Spanish. Many are *chistes verdes*. The following joke was among the tamest I could find. I think it's actually pretty funny:

Un misionero va caminando por la jungla cuando de repente se topa con un tigre de aspecto feroz y muerto de hambre. Ante la desesperación se arrodilla y reza:

¡Oh, Padre, infunde sentimientos cristianos a esta fiera!

El tigre, sorprendido, mira a su alrededor y a continuación se arrodilla y dice:

¡Oh, Padre, bendice este alimento que voy a recibir!

Vocabulario Útil:

misionero missionary

de repente all of a sudden

toparse to run into; to come upon

muerto de hambre dying of hunger; famished

ante "faced with"

desesperación despair

arrodillarse to kneel down

infundir to fill with

fiera wild beast

a continuación next; and then

bendecir bless

alimento food

recibir to receive

The Least You Need to Know

◆ Roman Catholicism is the predominant religion in Spain and Latin America.

◆ The Virgin of Guadalupe is Mexico's patroness.

◆ The present progressive is the *–ing* form of the verb.

◆ You can change the tense of the helping verb (*estar, continuar, ir,* and so on) to create more complex tenses.

Chapter 16

Las Fiestas

In This Chapter

- ◆ *Lectura:* Las Fiestas de Madrid
- ◆ More about *haber*
- ◆ *Tan y tanto*
- ◆ Here, there, everywhere
- ◆ *Los días festivos*

How would you like to tie a red bandana around your neck and run for dear life within a few feet of several angry bulls with hundreds of people yelling at you and no way to escape? Sounds crazy, right? And yet each July people from all over the world travel to Pamplona to participate in the Running of the Bulls and the Festival of San Fermín, one of the most internationally celebrated festivities in Spain.

What If I Don't Like Bulls?

Okay, so if running away from vicious *toros* is not your style, then maybe you should consider the Tomatina, a much more "civilized" festival where everyone gets together and throws tomatoes at each other. Can't believe it? Well, as columnist Dave Barry would say, "I swear I'm not making this up." Since 1944, each year on the last Wednesday of August in the little town of Buñol (30 miles west of Valencia), people flock to fight a war with over-ripe tomatoes. *¿Por qué?* Well, *¿por qué no?*

Both Spaniards and Latin Americans find reasons to celebrate many events throughout the year. Some of the celebrations are religious holidays, even though the tone of the *fiestas* themselves may not seem overly religious. Other fiestas date back to pre-Christian pagan festivals, or, in the case of Latin America, to pre-Columbian times (that's before old Chris Columbus got there).

Yes, *fiesta* does mean "party," but fiestas are usually on a much grander scale than a mere get-together at a friend's house. *Un día de fiesta* may be a national or religious holiday. For a smaller party with friends, say *una reunión* (although *fiesta* would still be understood).

Lectura: Las Fiestas de Madrid

The following *lectura* discusses Madrid and the various fiestas held in the city throughout the year. It's a challenging text because its tone is a bit more literary than most of your previous readings. Feel free to read it several times if you need to. Have your dictionary on hand for any new words, and take your time:

Madrid es una ciudad muy alegre. Ofrece todo tipo de espectáculos propios de una gran capital. También tiene el encanto de conservar aún el sabor tradicional de "la villa." Y es cierto que en algún sentido y en lo profundo de su alma Madrid sigue siendo esa villa, esa ciudad de barrio que aún ofrece toda la autenticidad de un pequeño pueblo. Encantadora y versátil se presentará al visitante, si tiene la oportunidad de saborear algunas de estas fiestas que acontecen desde los primeros segundos en que comienza el año: El Año Nuevo comienza con el gran espectáculo. Casi 40 millones de españoles estarán pendientes cada año a la media noche del gran reloj de la Puerta del Sol, que emitirá las tradicionales 12 campanadas para las que una gran muchedumbre, allí congregada (y el resto de los españoles que lo siguen por televisión), tomen las 12 uvas a su son, durante los 12 últimos segundos del año. Este momento marcará el inicio de la fiesta que se despliega por toda la ciudad.

El 5 de Enero tiene lugar la tradicional y vistosa Cabalgata de los Reyes Magos, que desfila por la zona de Hortaleza. Parece carnaval y representa la entrada de los Magos en la ciudad. Es también una tradición que se repetirá por numerosas ciudades españolas.

El 15 de Mayo, se celebran las Fiestas de San Isidro, patrón de la ciudad, con numerosos festejos típicos como verbenas, romerías y las mejores corridas de toros del año. También se celebran conciertos de rock y jazz, teatro y ferias de artesanía.

Durante los meses de Julio y Agosto se celebran los Veranos de la Villa, campaña de teatro, cine, y espectáculos musicales organizados por el ayuntamiento. Del 6 al 15 de Agosto se celebra la Verbena de la Paloma, una de las fiestas más castizas de la ciudad, caracterizada por su colorido y el gran optimismo que se respira por la calle. En ella se resucitarán los típicos trajes del chulo madrileño, bailes, y los bellos mantones de manila, y lo mejor del folklore madrileño.

Septiembre, es la gran temporada de estreno en teatros, cines y espectáculos en general. Durante este més se celebran los Festivales de Otoño y la Fiesta de la Melonera en Arganzuela, cuyos origenes se remontan al siglo XVIII. Del 8 al 12 de Octubre, se celebra la Fiesta del Pilar. En Noviembre tienen lugar las tan diversas celebraciones de la tradicional Almudena, en contraposición con la Fiesta Internacional de Jazz.

Diciembre cierra el año con la exposición y venta de nacimientos y árboles de Navidad en puestos tradicionales situados en la Plaza Mayor, todo un espectáculo de luz y colorido con todo el encanto y romanticismo que acompaña a tan tradicionales fiestas.

> ### Cultura Latina
>
> In Madrid, a *verbena* is an open-air celebration on the eve of a saint's day. In the south of Spain and elsewhere, this would be called a *feria*. A *romería* is a "pilgrimage," especially popular in the South of Spain. Both *verbenas* and *romerías* are extremely festive occasions with all sorts of activities going on throughout the day and night.

Vocabulario Útil:

encanto   enchantment; charm

aún   still; yet

espectáculo   event; show

villa   village; town

sentido   sense; feeling

alma   soul

barrio   neighborhood

encantador   enchanting; charming

visitante   visitor

saborear   to experience; to taste

acontecer   to occur

estar pendiente   to be watchful; be waiting for

campanada   sounding of a bell; chiming

muchedumbre (feminine)   crowd

son   sound

inicio   beginning

desplegarse   to unfold; to spread out

tener lugar   to take place

vistoso   bright and colorful

cabalgata   ride (on horses)

desfilar   to parade

ayuntamiento   city government

castizo   traditional; pure

colorido   colorful atmosphere

estreno debut

cuyos whose

remontarse to date back to

nacimientos nativity scenes

puestos stand; stall; kiosk

Cultura Latina

The *chulo madrileño* is a typical working-class figure from certain areas of Madrid. The word *melonera* comes from *melón*. So *La Fiesta de la Melonera* celebrates the late-summer melon harvest. *La Virgen de la Almudena* is the patroness of Madrid, and the *almudenas* are *verbenas* held in her honor.

Análisis del Texto

Okay, you survived. Wonderful. Let's look at a few phrases from the text—nothing too difficult:

todo tipo de espectáculos Note that the plural of *espectáculos* doesn't require that *tipo* (type; kind) be pluralized. In fact, Spanish often presents us with a singular collective when a plural is understood: *El Cubano habla muy rápidamente* means "Cubans speak very fast." Here, *todo tipo* would be translated in English as "all kinds," even though it's singular in Spanish.

en lo profundo de su alma *Lo profundo* means "the deep part." So this means "in the bottom of its soul …."

Encantadora y versátil se presentará al visitante Here is a great example of how you can't always find the subject of the sentence in the sentence itself. In fact, we have to go way back to the beginning of the previous sentence to see that *encantadora y versátil* and the verb *se presentará* are all referring back to *la villa de Madrid*. To translate this effectively into English, we almost need to bring the subject back into the sentence. And the charming and versatile part actually would come later in an English sentence: "The village of Madrid will appear charming and versatile to the visitor who …."

estarán pendientes … del gran reloj *Estar pendiente* is a great way to say that someone is waiting for something, or is expecting something, or is being watchful with great expectation.

12 campanadas para las que … tomen las 12 uvas a su son This construction can be a little tricky if you aren't careful. The *las* refers back to *campanadas* (chimes of the bell). So at each chime of the big bell, Spaniards eat a grape until the New Year arrives.

el gran optimismo que se respira por la calle   You have to use your imagination here—there is no shortage of flowery language in Spanish: "The great optimism that is breathed on the street." A better translation might substitute something like "can be felt" for "breathed."

cuyos orígenes se remontan al siglo XVIII   Here is *cuyo* again. It means "whose" and is mostly used only in writing. The gender is not affected by the subject, but rather by the thing possessed—in this case, *orígenes*. Centuries ago, *cuyo* was actually a more common possessive: *¿Cuyo es aquél caballo?* meant "Whose horse is that?" But that was in the days of Don Quixote.

Gramática: More About Haber

We have already discussed the helping verb *haber* as part of the *Yo he hablado* ("I have spoken") construction. *Hay* and *hubo* also come from *haber*. But *haber* can do a lot more for you because it can legitimately take any tense. It also takes a subjunctive mood in *haya* (present) and *hubiera/hubiese* (past). You can use *haber* with past participles to form the more complex "compound tenses."

Usually your instincts will guide you as to what these mean, because we use similar constructions in English. Take a quick look at the following examples:

> *La fiesta habrá terminado a esa hora.*
> The fiesta will have finished at that time.

> *Si yo hubiera ido a la reunión, te habría podido dar este regalo.*
> If I had gone to the party (but I didn't), I would have been able to give you this present.

> *Habiendo terminado su bebida, lanzó la copa al piso.*
> Having finished his drink, he threw the glass to the floor.

> *María lo habría hecho, pero no hubo tiempo.*
> Maria would have done it, but there wasn't time.

> *Es posible que no haya pan manána.*
> It is possible that there won't be any bread tomorrow.

Here, There, Everywhere

Most of these you have already seen. This is just a quick review with added explanation. You'll need these to express where and directions.

aquí	here	*atrás*	behind
acá	here, over here (see below)	*a la derecha*	on the right
ahí	there (in general)	*a la izquierda*	on the left
allá	there (in general)	*a un lado*	to one side
allí	there (more specific)	*derecho, recto*	straight ahead
más allá	beyond	*en frente*	in front; across from; facing
allende	beyond (literary)		

Both *aquí* and *acá* mean "here." In parts of South America (Argentina, Uruguay, and Chile), *acá* is more common than *aquí*. Purists will tell you that *aquí*, however, is the preferred word. *Acá* can be correctly used when the "here" you're talking about is rather general: *Acá en los Estados Unidos se fuma mucho, pero no aquí en me casa* means, "Here in the United States people smoke a lot, but not in my house." Use *acá* with verbs of motion: *Vente para acá* (often "sinalefized" as *vente paracá* or even *vente pacá*)—"Come over here."

Tan y Tanto: So, So Much

The adverbs *tan* and *tanto* are used to say "so much" and "how much." *Tanto* also can be used as an adjective, placed before a noun or nouns, and must match gender and number. When used adverbially (*Te quiero tanto* means "I love you so much"), it remains in what looks like a masculine singular form.

> *La fiesta fue tan divertida.*
> The fiesta was so much fun.

> *Tantos libros, tan poco tiempo para leerlos.*
> So many books, so little time to read them.

> *Tanta fue su emoción que comenzó a llorar. Y lloró tanto.*
> He felt so much emotion that he started to cry. And he cried so much.

Acuérdate _____

In Mexico, *tanto* can mean "an amount," and *tantito* is "a little bit." So you'll hear people say *¿Me das tantito?* for "Can you give me a little bit (of something)?" This usage is most popular in Mexico and may not be understood elsewhere.

The Holidays

Here's a list of the major holidays celebrated throughout Latin America and Spain. Of course, there are hundreds more regional holidays, but these are the big ones. Most are religious:

Miércoles de Ceniza   Ash Wednesday

Domingo de Ramos   Palm Sunday

Viernes Santo   Good Friday

Día de Pascua   Easter

Día de Todos los Santos   All Saints Day

Nochebuena   Christmas Eve

La Navidad   Christmas Day

Noche Vieja   New Year's Eve

El Año Nuevo   New Year's Day

Acuérdate

You already know that *feliz* means happy. Thus, *Feliz Navidad* means "Merry Christmas"; *Felices Pascuas* means "Happy Easter"; and *Feliz cumpleaños* means "Happy birthday." For a more general "Happy holidays," you can say *Felices fiestas*.

Cultura Latina

El Día de los Reyes Magos ("Day of the Wise Men") falls on January 6 (the Epiphany). It is on this day, rather than on Christmas, that most gift-giving takes place. On a different note, the equivalent of Friday the Thirteenth in Latin countries is Tuesday the Thirteenth. Don't ask me why.

Los puertorriqueños celebrate two special days: November 19, the day Christopher Columbus discovered the island or *Borinquen;* and July 25, the day the Puerto Rican constitution was signed. Some Puerto Ricans also celebrate the Fourth of July.

Fiestas Patrias: Independence Days

Of course, every Spanish-speaking country other than Spain was once a colony of Spain and thus ruled by the Spanish crown. Over the course of the nineteenth century, each gained its independence. Sounds like a good reason to throw a party to me. Here's a list of the Independence Day holidays for Spain's former colonies:

Argentina   el 9 de julio

Bolivia   el 6 de agosto

Chile   el 18 de septiembre

Colombia   el 20 de julio

Costa Rica   el 15 de septiembre

Cuba   el 20 de mayo

La República Dominicana   el 22 de febrero

El Ecuador   el 3 de octubre

Las Filipinas (Philippines)   el 12 de junio

El Salvador   el 15 de septiembre

Guinea Ecuatorial   el 12 de octubre (1968)

Guatemala   el 15 de septiembre

Honduras   el 15 de septiembre

México   el 16 de septiembre

Nicaragua   el 15 de septiembre

El Panamá   el 28 de noviembre (from Spain), el 3 de noviembre (from Colombia)

El Paraguay   el 14 de mayo

El Perú   el 28 de julio

Uruguay   el 25 de agosto

Venezuela   el 5 de julio

El Web

A list of links about various Latin fiestas can be found at www.lasculturas.com/lib/libHolidays.htm.

Risa del Día

Here are two short jokes to brighten your *día*:

1. *Mamá, mamá ....*

   ¿Puedo ir a una fiesta de 15 años?

   No, nena, es demasiado larga.

2. *Un ladrón a otro:*

   Rápido, que viene la policía. ¡Salta por la ventana!

   Pero si estamos en el piso 13 ....

   ¡Éste no es el momento para ser supersticioso!

Vocabulario Útil:

nene/nena   child

demasiado   too

saltar   to jump

piso   floor

supersticioso   superstitious

Cultura Latina

An important day in the life of most Mexican girls is her fifteenth birthday party, known as *la quinceañera*. Traditionally, a girl can marry at the age of 15 (although this is highly unusual outside of the most rural areas). The family prepares a large celebration and, if they can afford it, rents a hall for dancing and other festivities. *La festejada* (the girl being celebrated) wears a very beautiful dress.

The Least You Need to Know

◆ In both Spain and Latin America, *fiestas* are common and lots of fun.

◆ The helping verb *haber* takes many tenses and can be used with the past participle to express complex ideas.

◆ *Tan* is an adverb that means "so" and sometimes "such."

◆ *Tanto* means "so much" and is both an adjective and an adverb. When used as an adjective, it must agree in gender and number.

◆ There are several words for "here" and "there," such as *aquí, acá, allí,* and *allá*.

Part 4

Arts and Leisure

¡Olé! It's time to enjoy some of the finer things in life.

In this part, your *lecturas* will discuss literature, sports, art, music, and handicrafts. There's also a chapter devoted to travel-related dialogues. Our grammar sections will cover the past subjunctive, numbers, fractions, percentages, and interrogatives. You'll also learn the magic of Spanish prefixes and suffixes. Amaze your *amigos* by being able to accurately guess what a word means, even if you've never seen it before!

You're doing great. *¡Manos a la obra!* (Let's get to it!)

Chapter 17

Don Quixote de la Mancha

In This Chapter

- ◆ *Lectura: El Ingenioso Hidalgo Don Quixote de la Mancha*
- ◆ *Gramática:* the past subjunctive
- ◆ *Diálogo:* Quixote, Sancho Panza, y los molinos de viento

Miguel de Cervantes Saavedra (1547–1616) is considered by many to be one of the greatest Spanish authors who ever lived. Some call him the "Spanish Shakespeare"; others call Shakespeare the "English Cervantes." At any rate, *El Ingenioso Hidalgo Don Quixote de la Mancha*, first published in 1605 (a second part was published in 1615) is most certainly one of the masterpieces of world literature. The book has had a tremendous influence on the development of prose fiction and the modern novel, and has been translated into all modern languages.

The Man from La Mancha

The tale of Don Quixote describes the adventures of an idealistic Spanish *hidalgo* (nobleman) named Alonso Quijano who, after reading far too many books about knights, dragons, and chivalry, goes a bit *loco* and comes to believe that he himself is a knight who must battle against the injustices of the world. Together with his loyal *escudero* (squire), Sancho Panza, Quixote travels through the arid landscape of La Mancha in search of adventure, dedicating his noble deeds to a Dulcinea (known by the locals, in every sense, as Aldonza), whom he sees as his lady and eternal love. Quixote's imagination often runs away with him. He sees windmills as giants, flocks of sheep as enemy armies, and country inns as castles. His romantic view of the world, however, is balanced by Sancho Panza's down-to-earth perspectives on life.

Acuérdate

Remember that the letter *j* replaced the letter *x* several centuries ago for the *h* sound. Thus, you will see both *Don Quixote* and *Don Quijote*. Both spellings are correct, although *Quijote* is more common in Spain.

The tale of Don Quixote paints a rich picture of Spanish life as it presents the reader with countless philosophical insights. Quixote's idealism seems like madness in a world that often views heroism and love as forms of insanity. This has led many readers to consider *Don Quixote* a tragedy despite its humorous style and many satirical episodes. But others have found the story to be uplifting, as evidenced by the 1965 Broadway hit musical *Man of La Mancha* (music by Mitch Leigh), renewed by the message that "life should not be lived as it is, but rather as it should be."

Lectura: Don Quixote: Capítulo Uno

This *lectura* is a condensed and simplified version of the opening chapter of *Don Quixote*. Reading it in the original sixteenth-century Spanish is extremely tedious. (Imagine reading Shakespeare if you're not a native English-speaker.) Pay close attention to the first sentence: *En un lugar de la Mancha* …. This line is as famous in Spanish as "To be or not to be" is in English. Don't worry if you don't understand some of the words in the text; even this version is difficult and old-fashioned.

En un lugar de la Mancha, de cuyo nombre no quiero acordarme, vivía no hace mucho tiempo un hidalgo de los del antiguo estilo. Con él vivían un ama que no pasaba de los cuarenta y una sobrina que no llegaba a los veinte, además de un hábil mozo de campo y plaza.

La edad de nuestro hidalgo rondaba los cincuenta años; era de complexión recia, seco de carnes, enjuto de rostro, gran madrugador y amigo de la caza. Alonso Quijano era su nombre. Este hidalgo, los ratos que estaba ocioso (que eran los más del año), se daba a leer libros de caballería. Tanta era su afición a dichos libros que llegó a olvidarse de la caza y a descuidar la adminstración de su hacienda. Incluso vendió una parte de sus tierras para adquirir todos los libros de caballeróas que pudo.

Leía en aquellos libros cosas como ésta: "La razón de la sinrazón que a mi razón se hace, de tal manera mi razón se enflaquece, que con razón me quejo de vuestra hermosura".

Con estas razones perdía el pobre el juicio. Enfrascado en sus lecturas, se le pasaban las noches y los días, viendo cada vez más turbio lo claro y menos claro lo turbio. Y así, del poco dormir y del mucho leer se le secó el cerebro.

Su fantasía se llenó de todo lo que leía en los libros: de encantamientos y pendencias, de batallas y desafíos, de heridas y amores, de tormentos y disparates imposibles. Y todos estos disparates se convirtieron para él en la historia más cercana del mundo.

Rematado ya su juicio, en la cabeza se le metío el loco pensamiento de hacerse caballero andante. Le pareció que debía irse con sus armas y caballo a buscar aventuras que le dieran eterno nombre y fama.

Y lo primero que hizo fue limpiar unas armas que habían sido de sus bisabuelos, que desde hacia siglos estaban olvidadas en un rincón. Fue luego a ver a su rocín, y aunque era éste flaco y desgarbado, le pareció que le pareció que ningún otro caballo le igualaba. En su imaginación buscó un nombre que le fuese bien y, tras larga reflexión, vino a llamarlo Rocinante.

Después, y durante ocho días, buscó otro nombre para sí. Al cabo de su deliberación se dio el de Don Quijote. Pero, acordándose que el valeroso Amadís no se había contentado con llamarse Amadís a secas, sino que añadió el nombre de su reino y patria, para hacerla famosa, y se llamó Amadís de Gaula, así quiso, como buen caballero, añadir al suyo el nombre de la suya y llamarse Don Quijote de la Mancha.

Algo Nuevo

The name of Don Quixote's horse is actually a play on words. *Rocín* means "an old nag." The *ante* part comes from *antes,* which means "before." So *Rocinante* means "used to be an old nag." This makes sense, because the horse now belongs to a famous knight errant. Sancho Panza is also a humorous name. The word *panza* means "belly" or "stomach." If you remove the *s* from Sancho, you get *ancho,* which means "wide" or "stretched out." Need I say more?

Vocabulario Útil:

un ama (feminine)	mistress	*rostro*	face; countenance
hábil	capable; skillful	*madrugador*	gets up early
rondar	to round out to; to be about	*caza*	hunting
recio	robust; sturdy	*ocioso*	idle; leisurely
enjuto	lean; gaunt	*darse a*	to be given to

caballería   chivalry

afición   love of

dichos   said; aforementioned

descuidar   to neglect; opposite of *cuidar*

hacienda   estate

adquirir   to acquire

razón   reason

sinrazón   injustice; wrong

enflaquecer   to become thin

enfrascado   immersed; bottled up

turbio   unclear; murky

cerebro   brain; mind

encantamiento   spell; enchantment

pendencia   fight; scuffle

batalla   battle

desafío   challenge

herida   wound

tormento   torment

disparate   nonsense; a foolish thing

cercano   close; nearby

rematado   finished off; "gone"

pensamiento   thought

caballero   knight

andante   errant; going from place to place

aventura   adventure

limpiar   to clean

armas   arms

rincón   corner

flaco   skinny; weak

desgarbado   ungainly; unsteady on foot

igualar   to equal; to be as good as

sí   here, "himself"

al cabo de   after; at the end of

deliberación   deliberation; thinking

contentarse   to be happy with; to content

a secas   alone; by itself

patria   homeland

Análisis del Texto

I know this was rough. Please don't jump off a *puente*. Let's take a look at what we got out of this *lectura*:

de cuyo nombre   This means "of whose name …."

un hidalgo de los del antiguo estilo   An *hidalgo* was the lowest rank of nobility in Spain during Don Quixote's day. It comes from *hijo de algo* which means "son of something." *Del antiguo estilo* means "of the old style." Today, Hidalgo is a common *apellido* (surname).

que no pasaba de los cuarenta y una sobrina que no llegaba a los veinte   Understanding this sentence requires a little extra thinking. You know that the articles can stand in for nouns, using gender and number as a link between them. But until now, the noun being referenced has always been around somewhere. Here, *los* refers to a masculine plural noun. But where is the noun? You won't find it anywhere in the passage.

The noun, in this case, is implied by the context: *no pasaba de los cuarenta* means that the subject "wasn't over forty." So, *los* refers to *años*.

> ### Cultura Latina
>
> Don Quixote and Sancho Panza have been the subjects of many works of art. Quixote has also been the inspiration for two operas, a symphonic poem by German composer Richard Strauss, several motion pictures, ballets by Petipa and Balanchine, and, of course, the 1965 musical *Man of La Mancha*.

un hábil mozo de campo y plaza   This is an old-fashioned expression meaning that the young man (*mozo*) is as capable at physical labor (*el campo*) as he is at taking care of the duties of the house.

que llegó a olvidarse   Here *llegar a* is acting as a helping verb. It translates as "to come to" or "to happen to," as in "I came to realize that my wallet had been stolen." So here, our hidalgo "came to forget" or even "came to the point of forgetting."

"La razón de la sinrazón que a mi razón se hace, de tal manera mi razón se enflaquece, que con razón me quejo de vuestra hermosura".   Forget this! It doesn't make sense. And it isn't really supposed to: "The reason of the unreason with which my reason is afflicted so weakens my reason that with reason I complain of your beauty."

The idea is so confusing that it pushes Quijano over the edge. Don't try to understand it, or you'll soon find yourself doing battle with windmills.

Acuérdate

The *se le* (*se me*, *se te*, and so on) configuration is used frequently in Spanish to express what I call the "don't look at me, it wasn't my fault" concept: *Se me olvidó tu nombre* literally means "Your name forgot itself on me." This is how many Spanish-speakers would say, "I forgot your name"; *Se te cayeron las llaves* means "The keys dropped themselves from you," which you would actually translate as "You dropped your keys."

cada vez más turbio lo claro y menos claro lo turbio   I like this. *Cada vez más* means "more and more." *Cada vez menos* means "less and less," even though the *cada vez* is only stated once. So, this means that he saw "more and more clearly what was unclear, and more and more unclearly what was clear."

Cultura Latina

The word *flaco* is also a popular nickname for anyone who is skinny: *Oye Flaco, ¿cómo te va?* means "Hey, Skinny, how's it going?" They used to call me "el flaco" 20 years ago, but alas, no longer.

en la cabeza se le metío el loco pensamiento   This means, "The crazy idea got into his head."

aunque era éste flaco   Note that *éste* stands in for his *rocín* (old nag). When *éste* or *ésta* is used as a pronoun, it is often translated as "the latter." To say "the former," one would use *aquél* or *aquélla*.

durante ocho días   Why eight days? Good question. The answer is that in Spanish, *ocho días* is synonymous with "one week" because it counts the present day.

buscó otro nombre para sí   You know that *sí* means "yes." *Sí* also has an interesting secondary usage as a third-person pronoun meaning "self." It can be singular or plural: *entre sí* (among themselves).

It can be modified by *mismo/a/os/as* for clarity: *Compró un juguete para sí misma* means "She bought a toy for herself." Check your dictionary under *sí* for additional examples.

Acuérdate

La Mancha is a region of Spain southeast of Madrid on the *meseta* between Albacete, Ciudad Real, Toledo, Valdepeñas, and Cuenca. Interestingly, the word also means "stain," as in *Mi camisa tiene una mancha.* ("My shirt has a stain on it.")

se dio el de Don Quijote   *Dar* has many secondary uses in addition to "to give." Here, *se dio* means, "it gave itself," meaning "it presented itself," or, actively, Don Quijote "came up with it." The *el* refers back to *nombre.*

Amadís de Gaula   Amadis of Gaul is the title of a series of medieval romances of chivalry, written in prose and relating the adventures of a legendary hero of the same name. The story was first published in 1508. In many ways, Don Quixote is a satire of the tales of *Amadís de Gaula* and other such works.

añadir al suyo el nombre de la suya   You have learned *suyo* as the third-person possessive adjective "his," "hers," and so on. With the article, *suyo* and its permutations can serve as a noun: "to add to his (name) the name of his (homeland)."

Gramática: The Past Subjunctive

Most basic texts don't cover the past subjunctive tense, but I personally think it's fun, and very necessary. So, let's take a look:

Forming the Past Subjunctive

For regular verbs, adding the following endings to the verb stem makes the past subjunctives:

Forming the Past Subjunctive –*ar* Verbs

Ending	Verb	Example
–*ara*	*hablar*	*hablara*
–*aras*	*pagar*	*pagaras*
–*ara*	*contar*	*contara*
–*áramos*	*cantamos*	*cantáramos*
–*arais*	*mandar*	*mandarais* (Spain)
–*aran*	*pensar*	*pensaran*

And for –*er* and –*ir* verbs, we have these:

Forming the Past Subjunctive with –*er* and –*ir* Verbs

Ending	Verb	Example
–*iera*	*comer*	*comiera*
–*ieras*	*vivir*	*vivieras*
–*iera*	*salir*	*saliera*
–*iéramos*	*entender*	*entendiéramos*
–*ierais*	*meter*	*metierais* (Spain)
–*ieran*	*ocurrir*	*ocurrieran*

Verbs that form irregular preterits will form irregular past subjunctives. Start with the *yo* form of the preterit verb, remove the ending, and add the past subjunctive –*er* and –*ir* endings, even for –*ar* verbs:

Forming the Irregular Past Subjunctives

Verb	Stem	Subjunctive
hacer	*hice*	*hiciera*
saber	*supe*	*supiera*
poder	*pude*	*pudiera*
andar	*anduve*	*anduviera*
estar	*estuve*	*estuviera*

There is an alternate form for the past subjunctive that uses the following endings:

For *–ar:*   *–ase, –ases, –ase, –ásemos, –aseis, –asen*

For *–er* and *–ir:*   *–iese, –ieses, –iese, –iésemos, –ieseis, –iesen*

This form is slightly less popular than the *–ara/–iera* forms. You may hear it in parts of South America or read it from time to time in a text. This secondary form (which is actually older than the *–ase/–iese* form) is becoming less common, and many people never use it at all. You should know about it, but you don't have to use it if you don't want to. The other form will be understood everywhere.

The verbs *ir* and *ser* have the same form in the past subjunctive: *fuera, fueras, fuera, fuéramos, fueran.* The context of the sentence will always indicate which verb it is.

Using the Past Subjunctive

The past subjunctive works like the present subjunctive, only in the past. What I mean is, if you want someone to do something in the present, you use the present subjunctive: *Quiero que Juan lo haga* means "I want Juan to do it." But if you wanted someone to do something in the past, you need to use the past subjunctive form: *Quería* (imperfect past) *que Juan lo hiciera* means "I wanted Juan to do it." All the rules that you learned previously about how and when to use the subjunctive apply to the past subjunctive—only now, the time or action of the sentence must have occurred in the past.

Acuérdate

You'll notice that the first-person and third-person singular forms for the past subjunctive are the same. Usually the context makes it clear who the subject of the sentence is. But whenever there is a risk of confusion, simply add the subject pronoun *yo, él, ella,* or *usted.*

The *–ir* verbs with stem changes in the present indicative change to *i* in the past subjunctive tense: *pedir* is *pidiera, sentir* is *sintiera.*

One of the most common uses you'll have for the past subjunctive is in "contrary to fact" sentences. When you say "if something were possible (but it's not)" or "if this were true (but it isn't)," you will use the past subjunctive, even if the situation is going on currently. Often, it is used with the conditional tense. Observe:

Si yo pudiera hablar el francés, ganaría mucho dinero.
If I could speak French (but I can't), I could make a lot of money.

Si estuviéramos en la Argentina, podríamos ir a Tierra del Fuego.
If we were in Argentina (but we're not), we could go to Tierra del Fuego.

Si yo fuera Don Quixote, compraría un nuevo caballo.
If I were Don Quixote (but I'm not), I would buy a new horse.

Diálogo: Los Molinos

I suppose that this isn't a true-to-life dialogue. But here we have Don Quixote and Sancho Panza in their conversation during Quixote's famous "battle" with the windmills/giants. Note the use of the dashes to open and close the dialogue:

La ventura va guiando nuestras cosas; porque ves allí, amigo Sancho Panza, donde se descubren treinta o pocos más, desaforados gigantes, con quienes pienso hacer batalla y quitarles a todos las vidas.

¿Qué gigantes? —dijo Sancho Panza.

Aquellos que allí ves —respondió su amo— de los brazos largos.

Mire vuestra merced —respondió Sancho— que aquellos que allí se parecen no son gigantes, sino molinos de viento, y lo que en ellos parecen brazos son las aspas.

Ellos son gigantes; —respondió Don Quijote— y si tienes miedo, quítate de ahí, y ponte a rezar que yo voy a entrar con ellos en fiera y desigual batalla.

Y con esto, dio de espuelas a su caballo Rocinante, sin atender a las voces de su escudero Sancho. Iba diciendo a grandes voces— ¡No huyáis, cobardes y viles criaturas; que un solo caballero es el que os acomete!

> ### Algo Nuevo
>
> *Vuestra merced* ("Your mercy" or "Your grace") was a common form of address from inferior to superior in the sixteenth and seventeenth centuries. The modern formal *usted* is a contraction of *vuestra* and *merced*.

Se levantó en esto un poco de viento, y las grandes aspas comenzaron a moverse; lo cual visto por Don Quijote dijo— ¡Pues aunque mováis más brazos que los del gigante Briareo, me lo habéis de pagar!

Y encomendándose de todo corazón a su señora Dulcinea, con la lanza en ristre, arremetió a todo el galope de Rocinante, y embistió con el primer molino, dándole una lanzada en el aspa. El viento volvió el aspa con tanta furia que hizo la lanza pedazos, llevándose tras sí al caballo y al caballero, que fue rodeando muy maltrecho por el campo. Acudió Sancho Panza a socorrerle, a todo el correr de su asno, y cuando llegó le halló que no se podía menear.

¡Válgame Dios! —dijo Sancho—. ¿No le dije yo a vuestra merced que mirase bien lo que hacía, que no eran sino molinos de viento?

Calla, amigo Sancho —respondió don Quijote—; que las cosas de la guerra; que aquel sabio Frestón ha vuelto estos gigantes en molinos por quitarme la gloria de su vencimiento: tal es la enemistad que me tiene.

Vocabulario Útil:

ventura   fortune

se descubren   "are revealed"

desaforado   terrible; monstrous

vuestra merced   your mercy

amo   master

molinos de viento   windmill

aspa   blade/wing of a windmill

fiera (adjective)   fearsome

desigual   unequaled

espuelas   spurs

a grandes voces   shouting

huir   to flee; to run away

cobarde   coward

acometer   to attack

encomendarse   to entrust oneself

lanza   lance

pedazos   pieces

en ristre   at the ready

arremeter   to charge (in battle)

embestir   to charge (same as *arremeter*)

furia   rage

tras sí   behind itself; after itself

maltrecho   in bad shape; exhausted

socorrerle   to help him

menear   to move one's body

¡Válgame Dios!   "Lord, give me strength!"

enemistad   enmity (opposite of *amistad*)

Análisis del Texto

Normally, I'd probably just provide you with a translation of a dialogue, but since we're dealing with literature, I think some analysis is required:

con quienes pienso hacer batalla   This would mean "with whom I plan ("am thinking") to do battle."

quítate de ahí y ponte a rezar   Literally, this means "remove yourself from there and start praying." *Quitarse de* does indeed mean to "get out of somewhere."

Briareo   This is a mythological giant with 100 arms and 50 heads.

haber de pagar   The verb *haber* with *de* means about the same thing as *tener que*. It is an older form to express obligation, but is still used today by many speakers (*Has de hacerlo* is the same as *tienes que hacerlo*). This could also be translated as a future expression: "You'll pay for this!"

El Web

If you travel to Spain, you can follow the steps of Don Quixote himself along the *Ruta de El Quijote*. Check out the map and text (many links are also available to other Quixote stuff) at http://es.wikipedia.org/wiki/Ruta_de_Don_Quijote.

Risa del Día

The word for tongue-twister in Spanish is *trabalenguas.* Here's one that would have made Quixote proud. The word *dicho* as a noun means "an old saying." It is also the past participle of "to say." So, this starts out with "They tell me that I have said a saying …."

"Me han dicho que he dicho un dicho, … pero ese dicho no lo he dicho yo, … porque si ese dicho … que han dicho que he dicho yo lo hubiera dicho yo, … estaría bien dicho … por haberlo dicho yo."

The Least You Need to Know

- Don Quixote (Quijote) is one of the masterpieces of world literature.

- The past subjunctive follows the same rules for usage as the present subjunctive, only for past actions or events.

- The past subjunctive can be used for "contrary to fact" statements such as "If I were king (but I'm not) …."

Chapter **18**

El Museo del Prado

In This Chapter

- ◆ *Lectura:* Ficha Práctica del Museo del Prado
- ◆ *Gramática:* more about numbers
- ◆ Fractions
- ◆ Percentages
- ◆ Addition and subtraction

Many exceptional art museums are located throughout the Spanish-speaking world. Yet Madrid's *Museo del Prado* continues to welcome more visitors than any other art museum in Spain or Latin America. The Prado houses more than 3,000 works of the finest paintings, sculptures, drawings, furniture, and decorative art, and is one of Spain's most popular attractions.

El Prado

Construction of the Prado began in 1810 during the reign of King Fernando VII and his wife, Doña Isabel de Braganza. The original building has had numerous extensions added to it since then. Today the collection is divided between the original Villanueva building, which houses paintings from the Middle Ages to the nineteenth century, and the *Casón del Buen Retiro*, which houses nineteenth-century works formerly displayed in the Modern Art Museum.

The museum's collection consists principally of works donated to the Spanish royal collection between the sixteenth and nineteenth centuries. Of particular interest are the paintings by Titian, commissioned by Charles V and Philip II in the sixteenth century, and a series painted by Rubens for Philip IV in the early seventeenth century. The Prado also houses an exceptional collection of paintings from the Spanish school, including works by El Greco, Velázquez, and Goya.

Lectura: Ficha Práctica del Museo del Prado

Here's a reading I'm sure you'll find somewhat more useful than Don Quixote. This time we have the visitor information guide from the Prado Museum itself. It contains all the facts about touring the museum that you'll ever need to know. Even if you won't be traveling to Spain soon, the vocabulary in the text will be helpful at any museum you might visit during your travels.

Direcciones:

Edificio Villanueva Paseo del Prado, s/n. 28014 Madrid. Tel. (91) 330 28 00. Fax: (91) 330 28 56

Casón del Buen Retiro c/ Alfonso XII, 28. 28014 Madrid. Tel. (91) 420 05 68 - (91) 429 29 30

Sede Administrativa:

c/ Ruiz de Alarcón, 23. 28014 Madrid Tfnos. (91) 330 28 00. 330 29 00. fax (91) 330 28 56. Correo electrónico: museo.nacional@prado.mcu.es

Con motivo de las obras de remodelación y ampliación del edificio del Casón del Buen Retiro (c/ Alfonso XII, 28), las Salas de Exposiciones de dicho edificio permanecerán cerradas al público a partir del 2 de Agosto de 1997.

Teléfono de Información:

(91) 330 29 00.

Teléfono de Información del Ministerio de Educación y Cultura (24h): 906 32 22 22.

Horario:

Martes a Sábado: 9,00–19,00

Domingos, festivos, 24 y 31 de diciembre: 9,00–14,00

Lunes: Cerrado

Primer día de enero, Viernes Santo, 1 mayo y 25 diciembre: Cerrado

Transportes:

Metro: Estaciones de Banco de España y Atocha

Autobuses: 9, 10, 14, 19, 27, 34, 37, y 45

Ferrocarril: Estación de Atocha

Precio de entrada:

6 €: Tarifa general

3 €: Titulares Carnet Joven, estudiantes o sus equivalentes internacionales; grupos culturales y educativos (previa solicitud).

> ### Cultura Latina
>
> Spain has produced some of the world's most famous painters: Salvador Dalí, Pablo Picasso, El Greco, Goya, Velázquez, and others. You can find lots of information on each of these artists and see examples of their *obras* (works) at any library and on the Internet. Just seek, and you shall find.

Gratis: Mayores de 65 años o jubilados; menores de 18 años.

Miembros de la Fundación Amigos del Museo; voluntarios culturales y educativos; desempleados.

Gratis a todos: Sábados de 14,30 a 19,00 y Domingos de 9,00 a 14,00

Planos del Museo:

Disponibles en las taquillas del Museo.

Gratis los siguientes Días:

18 de Mayo. Día Internacional de los Museos 12 de Octubre. Fiesta Nacional de España 6 de Diciembre. Día de la Constitución.

Abonos: Paseo del Arte:

Tarifa general 36 €

Incluye una visita al Museo del Prado, Fundación Thyssen Bornemisza y Museo Nacional Centro de Arte Reina Sofía.

Tarifa reducida 18 €

Con este abono se puede acceder al Museo de Prado durante un año.

Tarifa general: 36.06 €

Con este abono se puede acceder, durante un año, a todos los Museos de Titularidad Estatal. Todas estas tarjetas se pueden adquirir en las taquillas de Museo.

> ### Acuérdate
>
> *Durante* does mean "during," but with a specified time it also can mean "for X amount of time." So, *durante un año* would translate as "for a year," not "during a year."

Condiciones de entrada para grupos escolares:

Los grupos escolares (máximo de 25 alumnos por profesor) deberán de ir provistos de su correspondiente (y obligatoria) autorización del Museo. Los profesores deben solicitarla con anticipación—al menos dos semanas—a la Oficina de Visitas de Grupos del Museo de Prado.

Cafetería:

El horario de la cafetería es de 9,30 a 18,00

Autoservicio:

Martes a Sábados 11,30–16,00

Librería y Tienda:

Martes a Sábado 9,00–18,30

Domingo y festivos 9,00–13,30

Otros servicios:

Accesos especiales para minusválidos

Salón de actos

Vocabulario Útil:

ficha   file; card; "guide"

práctico   practical; useful

dirección   address

s/n   sin número (no number)

c/   calle (street)

sede   seat; office; headquarters

administrativo   administrative

con motivo de   due to; "with the reason of"

a partir de   as of, after

horario   schedule; timetable

festivo   holiday (*día festivo*)

ferrocarril   rail; train

tarifa   fee; price

titular   holder of; named owner of

carnet   ID card

educativo   educational

previa   having obtained previously

solicitud   request; application

gratis   free; no cost

mayores de   older than

jubilado   retired person

menores de   younger than

voluntario   volunteer

desempleado   unemployed; out of a job

plano   map; plan

disponible   available

taquilla   ticket window

siguiente   following

abono   season ticket; payment

escolar   school (adjective)

provisto   to carry; to be equipped with

correspondiente   corresponding

obligatorio   obligatory; mandatory

autorización   permission

deber   to be obligated to

solicitar   to apply

con anticipación   in advance

al menos   at least

autoservicio   self-service

librería   bookstore

minusválido   disabled; handicapped

salón de actos   event hall; conference hall

Análisis del Texto

This text isn't too difficult; just a few minor points here and there:

28014 Madrid   Notice that the *código postal* (ZIP code or postal code) comes before the name of the city, not after it. Most Spanish-speaking countries follow this order, although Puerto Rico and Mexico do not. Some smaller countries do not have postal codes.

Ten Cuidado

You must write a *tilde* over the letter *o* when it comes between numbers: *345 ó 592* means "345 or 592." This is to distinguish the letter *o* from the number zero.

Con motivo de las obras de remodelación y ampliación   *Motivo* is indeed related to the English word "motive," but while "motive" seems a bit formal, the Spanish word *motivo* can be used in everyday conversation. It simply means "reason," as in *¿Cuál es el motivo de su llamada?* ("What is the reason for your call?").

9,00–19,00   The use of the 24-hour clock in Spanish-speaking countries is more common than in the United States. Note also that the comma is used here instead of the colon. Both the colon and the comma can be used for times (9,00 or 9:00) in Spanish.

previa solicitud   The word *previo* does mean "previous." However, when placed before the noun, it can also convey the idea of "having fulfilled the requirement of ...." For example, *consulta previa petición de hora* means "consultation by appointment only"; and *sus pertenencias se entregarán previo pago de la suma mencionada* means "Your belongings will be handed over upon receipt of the aforementioned amount." So here, *previa solicitud* means "upon having filed an application." This construction is usually found in formal writing only.

36 € Most prices in Spain are now given in euros, the currency of the European Union.

Gramática: More About Numbers

Yes, I know that you've learned the numbers already. But there may be a few things about them that you didn't get to when you were a beginning student. So, let's take a closer look.

The Ordinals: First, Second, Third, and So On

The ordinal numbers are all adjectives, and thus must match the gender and number of the noun or nouns they modify. They are usually, but not always, placed before the noun:

primero (primer)	first
segundo	second
tercero (tercer)	third
cuarto	fourth
quinto	fifth
sexto	sixth
séptimo	seventh
octavo	eighth
noveno	ninth
décimo	tenth
undécimo/decimoprimero	eleventh
duodécimo/decimosegundo	twelfth
decimotercero	thirteenth
decimocuarto	fourteenth
decimoquinto	fifteenth

Ten Cuidado _____

Ordinal numbers are usually placed before the noun they modify, but they must be placed after the noun if it is part of a title: *Juan Carlos Segundo* means "Juan Carlos the Second." Make sure that you don't translate these as "the second Juan Carlos."

decimosexto sixteenth

decimoséptimo seventeenth

decimoctavo eighteenth

decimonoveno nineteenth

vigésimo twentieth

vigesimoprimero twenty-first

vigesimosegundo twenty-second

vigesimotercero twenty-third

trigésimo thirtieth

cuadragésimo fortieth

quincuagésimo fiftieth

sexagésimo sixtieth

septuagésimo seventieth

octogésimo eightieth

nonagésimo ninetieth

centésimo hundredth

Algo Nuevo

The ordinal numbers beyond *décimo* (tenth) are rarely used in conversation and may be replaced by the cardinal number: *el cuarenta aniversaro* or *el cuadragésimo aniversario* both mean "the fortieth anniversary." Cardinal numbers are also used in titles when the number is above 10: *Luis XII* translates as *Luis doce*; *Juan Carlos XX* means *Juan Carlos veinte*.

Here are a few examples:

El primer pintor español de la etapa.
The first Spanish painter of the period.

La tercera exhibición del año.
The third exhibition of the year.

Juan Pablo Segundo.
Pope John Paul the Second.

Es el segundo Juan Pablo que he visto hoy.
He's the second guy named John Paul I've seen today.

Fractions

You may not have learned these as a beginner, so here are the fractions that you are most likely to use in daily conversation.

½	*un medio*		⅕	*un quinto*
⅓	*un tercio*		⅔	*dos tercios*
¼	*un cuarto*		²⁄₄	*dos cuartos*

When a fraction is not used in a strictly scientific or mathematical sense, it may be expressed in the following ways. Notice that gender may come into play:

un kilo y medio   one and a half kilos

media naranja or *la mitad de una naranja*   half an orange

cuatro de cada cinco médicos   four out of five doctors

la quinta parte del dinero   one fifth of the money

Addition and Subtraction

A few good examples should suffice here:

$2 + 3 = 5$ *dos más tres son cinco*

$7 - 3 = 4$ *siete menos tres son cuatro*

$2 \times 9 = 18$ *dos por nueve son dieciocho*

$20 \div 5 = 4$ *veinte dividido por cinco son cuatro*

Acuérdate

You know that the words *mayor* and *menor* mean "older" and "younger," respectively. But with numbers, *mayor* means "greater than," and *menor* means "less than."

Algo Nuevo

Longer numbers such as telephone numbers or ID numbers are usually read in groupings of two, unlike in the United States, where we tend to read each number individually. Odd numbers that can't be paired up may be read alone. So if my phone number is 921-547-3601, I would read it as *nueve veintiuno, cinco cuarenta y siete, treinta y seis cero uno.* Of course, people will understand you if you read the numbers one by one, but it sounds more natural in Spanish the other way.

Percentages

When giving the percent (%) of a number, you must use an article. The indefinite article translates as "by." Here's what I mean:

el quince por ciento de la población
15 percent of the population

Mis ingresos han subido un 10 por ciento.
My income has increased by 10 percent.

El Web

If you can't travel to Madrid anytime soon, you can visit the Prado online at the museum's official website: http://museoprado.mcu.es/home.html.

Risa del Día

Here we have a joke about modern art:

Un tipo en un museo de arte moderno está explicando un pintura a un amigo:

Pues esto es un amanecer, como indican sus colores cálidos que rompen la imagen clásica del cubismo y arte abstracto para plasmarse más allá de la realidad que involucra el sueño que uno tiene por la mañana ....

En esto que se acerca otro tipo y dice:

¡Huy! ¡Pero si eso es un atardecer!

¿Cómo que un atardecer? ¡Esto es un amanecer!

¡Pero cómo puede usted asegurar que es un amanecer!

Mire, yo he estudiado en Cambridge y Harvard, he hecho tres masters en arte moderno, así que estoy seguro que es un amanecer.

Pues mire, yo conozco al pintor y ése jamás se levanta temprano, así que estoy seguro que es un atardecer.

Vocabulario Útil:

tipo	guy; person	atardecer	sunset
pintura	painting	asegurar	to assure
amanecer	sunrise	jamás	never ever
plasmarse	to be expressed	levantarse	get up
involucrar	to involve	temprano	early
uno	one; a person; "you"		

The Least You Need to Know

♦ The Prado is Spain's most important art museum.

♦ Ordinal numbers are adjectives and are usually placed before the noun.

♦ Percentages require an article.

♦ Fractions can be expressed in several ways.

♦ *Más, menos, por,* and *dividido por* mean "plus," "minus," "times," and "divided by," respectively.

Chapter **19**

La Música Latina

In This Chapter

- *Lectura:* salsa y cumbia
- *Gramática:* prefixes
- *Cielito Lindo*

Both Spain and Latin America present a rich variety of musical heritages—from Andalucian flamenco music, to the classical guitar concertos of Joaquín Rodrigo; from the haunting sounds of the Andean pan flute, to the many rhythms of Latin jazz and popular song: *rumba, mambo, cumbia, cha-cha-chá, canto, bolero, guaguancó, plena, timba, toque, bamba, merengue, bachata, son, guajira* … just to name a few.

The Sound of Many Cultures

The popular music of the Spanish-speaking world has always been an expression of the meeting of diverse peoples. The Moors and Gypsies shaped the tonality and harmonic structure of flamenco. New World musicians incorporated European instruments into their music, including the accordion, harp, guitar, trumpet, and woodwinds. West Africans and Native Americans contributed new instruments such as the marimba and the conical drum, as well as their native dances and rhythms, to create what we know collectively as Latin American music. The influence of Latin music has reached far beyond its borders. American jazz has also been greatly influenced by Latin styles.

Today, numerous crossover stars have made significant inroads into American pop culture with hits such as the *Macarena, La Vida Loca,* and *Mambo No. 5.* And, of course, who could ever forget the first crossover rocker, Richie Valens, and his hit *La Bamba.*

> **Cultura Latina**
>
> The *bolero* originated in Cuba in the late 1800s, but it had also become extremely popular in Mexico by the 1940s and 1950s. Boleros are essentially ballads of love or love lost. Interestingly, a *bolero* in Mexico is also "a shoe-shiner." So if you call out for someone to play you a *bolero,* you may find someone coming to shine your shoes instead.

Lectura: Salsa y Cumbia

It wasn't easy to pick a *lectura* for this chapter; the various styles of Latin music are practically endless, and it seemed a shame to skip over so many different genres of Latin music. Still, both salsa and cumbia have become quite popular outside of their countries of origin, so I thought that the following text might be appropriate.

Salsa is associated primarily with Puerto Rico, and the size and vibrancy of the *boricua* communities in the United States has done much to popularize this art form. Cumbia, although originally an Afro-Colombian beat, has become so popular in Mexico that it can be heard on Spanish-language radio stations along the border as well as in any large U.S. city with a sizeable Mexican population.

Salsa es un estilo de música latinoamericana que surgió en Nueva York como resultado del choque de la música afrocaribeña traída por puertorriqueños, cubanos, colombianos, venezolanos, panameños y dominicanos, con el Jazz y el Rock de los norteamericanos. Desde ese entonces, vive deambulando de isla en isla, de país a país, incrementando de tal manera, su riqueza de elementos.

La salsa no es una moda pasajera, sino una corriente musical establecida, de alto valor artístico y gran significado sociocultural: en ella no existen barreras de clase ni de edad.

La cumbia, en cambio, es el aire musical más representativo de Colombia. Es producto del aporte de tres culturas: negra africana, indígena y blanca. La cultura negra aportó la estructura rítmica y la percusión (tambores); la indígena aportó las flautas (caña de millo y las gaitas) y parte de la línea melódica; la blanca, por su parte, las variaciones melódicas y coreográficas, y la vestimenta de los danzantes. La cumbia expresa claramente el mestizaje de la cultura colombiana. El ritmo se ha popularizado mucho en México.

Definitivamente, pues, la música es parte de nuestra raíz, nos identifica con un determinado momento y lugar. Y, en gran medida, nos identifica como raza. La musica es, para nosotros los latinos, un vehículo de cultura, la esencia misma de lo que nos hace ser quienes somos.

Vocabulario Útil:

surgir	to arise	*clase*	here, social class
resultado	result	*en cambio*	"in comparison"
choque	collision	*aire*	aspect; "air"
afrocaribeño	Afro-Caribbean	*representativo*	representative
entonces	time; period	*aporte*	contribution
deambular	to roam	*indígena*	indigenous; native
incrementar	to increase	*rítmica*	rhythmic
tal manera	such a way	*vestimenta*	clothing; costumes
riqueza	richness	*definitivamente*	undoubtedly
moda	fashion; style	*pues*	then
pasajero	fleeting (adjective)	*raíz*	root
sino	but rather	*determinado*	certain; determined
corriente	current; style	*raza*	race (ethnicity)
significado	meaning	*vehículo*	vehicle
barrera	barrier		

Cultura Latina

The *corrido* is a story/song form similar to the American country music ballads. *Corridos* became popular in Mexico during the revolution as a means of retelling historic events or passing along folklore, or as a narrative of battles and revolutionary heroes. Today, any person or event can be the subject of a *corrido;* the lyrics may be satirical, political, or tragic.

Análisis del Texto

¡Fantástico! Now, let's look a little closer:

desde ese entonces   You probably know the word *entonces* as "then" or "so," as in *Entonces, ¿quién me va a llevar al concierto?* ("So, who's going to take me to the concert?"). But *entonces* has a secondary meaning as "time" or "period" in phrases such as this one: *En aquel entonces todavía era soltero.* ("At that (distant) time I was still a bachelor.")

vive deambulando   I'll bet you weren't expecting to see the present participle being used with *vivir* as a helping verb. It isn't common, but because the verb *vivir* here implies action or motion, it's a natural fit with the present participle: *Vivo durmiendo* means "I'm walking through my life asleep."

en ella no existen barreras de clase ni de edad   Just a quick reminder that you'll need to look all the way back to the beginning of the previous sentence to find the noun that is linked to *ella*. Notice here also the use of *ni* for "nor," and that the *de* is repeated.

la negra africana, la indígena y la blanca   Notice how much work the writer is getting out of *la*. It is standing in for *cultura*, linked by gender, three times. We could add in the word *cultura* if we wanted to (*la cultura negra africana, la cultura indígena,* and so on), but *la* (or *el,* if it had been a masculine noun) can do the job all by itself once the subject has been stated.

por su parte   This is just a way of setting the third element (*la cultura blanca*) a little farther from the first two elements. *Por su parte* means "for its part" but can often be left out of a translation because it usually doesn't add to the meaning of the text. It's a literary device that makes the writer sound smarter.

definitivamente, pues, la música es parte   The little word *pues* usually means "well." *Pues, lamento haberme olvidado de los boletos del concierto* means "Well, I'm sorry I forgot the concert tickets." However, at other times *pues* means "then," as it does here: "Without a doubt, then, music is part …."

la esencia misma   You know that *mismo* means "same," but it also can be translated under certain circumstances as "very": *Aquí mismo* means "this very place"; *Eso mismo me dijo* means "He said that very thing to me." In *la esencia misma,* the best translation would be "the very essence," not "the same essence."

Gramática: Prefixes

Let's face it. There are tens of thousands of Spanish words out there, and it would be all but impossible to learn them all. In fact, nobody knows them all. I certainly don't.

But I'm going to share a few tricks with you that can help you expand your vocabulary without having to memorize long lists of words.

Spanish, like English, utilizes many prefixes and suffixes to create new words or to alter the meaning of existing ones. With this in mind, one of the most efficient ways to expand your Spanish vocabulary is to learn the meanings of the various prefixes and suffixes. In this chapter, we'll examine the prefixes; in the next two chapters, we'll tackle the suffixes.

Using Prefixes

You probably already know that a prefix is a letter, particle, or mini-word that can be affixed to the beginning of another word. We use many of them in English: *pre–*, *sub–*, *anti–*, *ex–*, *ob–*, *in–*, and so on. Many of these English prefixes are the same (or darn close) in Spanish. This is because most English and Spanish prefixes come from Latin or Greek (we talked about the similarities between the two languages back in Chapter 1). So in most cases, you'll already know what a prefix means in Spanish because it will sound and look a lot like the corresponding English prefix.

Here's a list of some of the more common prefixes. The meaning of the Spanish examples should be obvious to you.

Common Prefixes

Prefix	Meaning	Example
ante–	before	*antemano*
anti–	against	*antibiótico*
auto–	self	*autoservicio*
bi–, bis–, biz-	two	*bilateral*
cent–	hundred/hundredth	*centavo*
contra–	against	*contrario*
com–, con–	with	*communidad*
de–, des–	take apart; "un"	*desempleado*
entre–	among, between	*entrevista*
ex–	out	*extraer; éxodo*
homo–	same	*homogenizado*
in–, im–,	opposite of	*increíble; imposible*
inter–	between, among	*intercambio*
mal–, mala–	bad	*malévolo*

continues

Common Prefixes (continued)

Prefix	Meaning	Example
meta–	beyond	*metafísico*
mono–	one	*monolingüe*
para–	together, with	*paramédico*
poli–	many	*polifónico*
pre–	before	*precertificado*
pro–	in favor of	*proponer* (to propose)
re–	with intensity	*revisión; refreír*
re–	again	*repasar* (review)
semi–	medium; half	*semiautomático*
seudo–	false	*seudónimo*
sobre–, super–	above; superior	*superficial*
sub–	under	*subterráneo*
tele–	at a distance	*telescopio*
uni–	one; singular	*unidimencional*

Cielito Lindo

I'm not sure why, but of all the lovely songs sung in Spanish, *Cielito Lindo* ("Beautiful Heaven") seems to be the most recognizable to Americans. The song was popularized in the 1940s by Hollywood star Deanna Durbin. But maybe that antacid commercial from the 1980s is to blame? Who knows ….

Either way, it's not that great of a song, folks. In fact, if it weren't for the "Ay Ay Ay Ay" part, this tune would have died a quiet death at the end of the Mexican Revolution.

Cultura Latina

Considered the most romantic music in the Latin world, the style known as *el trio* plays simple but beautiful music that usually combines vocal harmonies with romantic guitars. Most of the songs performed are *boleros*.

But just get a few *gringos* together in a cantina, add a couple rounds of tequila, and sooner or later someone starts bellowing, "Ay Ay Ay Ay." And that's the only part that anyone knows!

Well, here are the real lyrics (some of them, anyway). If you plan on singing this little ditty anytime soon, why not impress your friends by performing the whole thing? You'll be forever remembered as the only one in the room who could get past the "Ay Ay Ay Ay" part.

De la Sierra Morena, cielito lindo, vienen bajando un par de ojitos negros, cielito lindo, de contrabando.

Ay, ay, ay, ay, canta y no llores, porque cantando se alegran, cielito lindo, los corazones.

Pájaro que abandona, cielito lindo, su primer nido, si lo encuentra ocupado, cielito lindo, bien merecido.

Ese lunar que tienes, cielito lindo, junto a la boca, no se lo des a nadie, cielito lindo que a mi me toca.

Ay, ay, ay, ay, canta y no llores, porque cantando se alegran, cielito lindo, los corazones.

Vocabulario Útil:

ay oh	*nido* nest
venir bajando coming down	*merecido* deserved
par pair	*lunar* mole (on the skin)
contrabando contraband	*a mí me toca* it's my turn (for a kiss?)
alegrarse to cheer up	

Risa del Día

This joke almost appeared back in the chapter about religion. There are hundreds of *San Pedro* (Saint Peter) jokes in Spanish, usually of the "Three guys die and go to heaven and meet Saint Peter at the pearly gates" variety. The last of the three usually receives some undeserved injustice. As always, *chistes verdes* abound. But this one had a musical punch line, so I've included it here. No offense meant to any fellow musicians out there ….

Cultura Latina

Considered the national music of Mexico, *mariachi* originated in the late nineteenth century as a traditional folk music form. The music evolved into a symphonic ensemble that included harp, trumpet, violin, *guitarrón* (big guitar to play the bass line), and *vihuela* (small guitar). The outfits—typically tight pants, short jackets, and big sombreros—were derived from the first Mexican *charros*, or cowboys.

San Pedro está recibiendo a los recién llegados a las puertas del cielo, y el primero viene de Texas. "¿Dime, que hacías en vida?" pregunta San Pedro.

El tejano responde, "Bueno, yo extraía petróleo, me hice rico, pero no me senté en los laureles—Repartí todo mi dinero entre toda mi familia, de forma tal que están aseguradas las próximas tres generaciones".

San Pedro responde, "Eso está muy bién. ¡Que pase el siguiente!"

El segundo de la fila había escuchado la conversación y dijo, "Yo gané mucho dinero en la bolsa, pero no quise beneficiarme de ello yo sólo, como hizo el tejano. Así que doné cinco millones a la caridad".

"Maravilloso" dice San Pedro. "Adelante. ¿Quién sigue?"

El tercero también había oído todo, así que dijo tímidamente, "Bueno, yo sólo gané quinientos dólares en toda mi vida".

"¡Cielos!" dice San Pedro. "¿Y qué instrumento tocabas?"

> ### Cultura Latina
>
> Perhaps the most well-known form of Spanish music is *el flamenco*. Once considered a low art form, *flamenco* was all but banned during Franco's 40-year reign. But today *flamenco* music and dance have become world-famous, due in part to *flamenco* supergroups such as the Gypsy Kings.

Vocabulario Útil:

recién llegados   new arrivals

tejano   Texan

extraer   to extract

sentarse en los laureles   to rest on one's laurels

repartir   to distribute

el siguiente   the next guy

fila   line

beneficiarme   to benefit

caridad   charity

maravilloso   marvelous

quién sigue   who's next?

tímidamente   timidly; with shyness

¡Cielos!   Heavens!

instrumento   instrument

tocar   to play an instrument

El Web

Check out www.lamusica.com for all the latest news about popular Latin music. If you're interested in more information about Mariachi music, visit www.elmariachi.com.

The Least You Need to Know

◆ There are many different styles of music in Spain and Latin America: *cumbia*, *bolero*, *salsa*, and *merengue*, just to name a few.

◆ Prefixes build Spanish words and can help you increase your vocabulary more easily than memorizing long lists of words.

◆ *Cielito Lindo* has more words than just the "Ay Ay Ay Ay" part.

Chapter 20

El Fútbol

In This Chapter

- ◆ Un Juego Nacional
- ◆ *Lectura:* La Copa de Oro
- ◆ *Gramática:* suffixes, part one

In terms of mass appeal and overall participation, sports in Spain and Latin America basically comes down to one thing: *fútbol* (a.k.a. soccer). Sure, *beisbol* is also a serious sport in the Caribbean and parts of Central America. And, yes, here and there, other sports such as rugby, jai alai, horse racing, and basketball are also popular. But no other sport—not even bull fighting—can evoke such passion as soccer, in spite of the fact that the game was originally introduced to the Spanish-speaking world by the English.

El Juego Nacional

Children seem to start kicking the soccer ball around practically from the day they learn to walk. Everyone is proud of their national teams and the skill of their players. Universities and cities compete in national championships, and national teams are formed to compete internationally. An important victory can provoke mass hysteria and spontaneous celebrations across the country.

Unfortunately, sometimes *el fútbol* can be taken a bit too seriously, as was evidenced during the 1994 World Cup when a Colombian player was assassinated after accidentally kicking the ball into his own goal during a game against the United States. The loss of an important tournament can have serious repercussions and can even impact a country's economy, suicide rate, and national elections. The bottom line seems to be that it's not how you play the game that counts, but whether you win.

Lectura: La Copa de Oro

Several international tournaments are played in professional soccer. The following text discusses Mexico's disappointing performance against Canada during the Gold Cup playoffs:

La Selección de México tuvo un sorpresivo y triste adiós de la Copa de Oro, al caer 2–1 ante Canadá, un rival chico que hizo ver muy mal a los verdes.

México, tres veces campeón de este certamen, tuvo que hacer las maletas en forma prematura, pues casi nadie esperaba que no llegara ni siquiera a la Semifinal del torneo en la que estuvo rodeado de rivales con una calidad supuestamente inferior a la suya.

Antes de los dos minutos del primer tiempo extra el canadiense Richard Hastings anotó el gol de oro con un tiro de zurda por arriba de scar "Conejo" Pérez, con lo que culminó un fugaz contragolpe luego de que el equipo de la hoja de maple comenzó mal contra el equipo méxicano, que había cobrado un tiro de esquina.

Los más de 18 mil espectadores que estaban reunidos en el estadio, casi todos ellos mexicanos, reaccionaron con estupefacción ante la anotación.

Mientras que "El Conejo" permanecía congelado en su área y sus demás compañeros salían cabizbajos, en cuestión de segundos, los elementos canadienses se trepaban unos a otros en el suelo en señal de festejo, y Hasting permanecía con los brazos en alto.

México llevó en su pecado una gran penitencia, ya que tuvo el balón durante casi todo el partido, pero casi nunca se atrevió a tirar al arco, si acaso se acercó con un envío en la primera parte que el arquero Forrest le sacó con apuros a Francisco Palencia.

Hasta este lamentable partido el futuro pareció prometedor para un Tricolor que no veía en Canadá a un rival suficientemente peligroso. Pero en lo que ha sido un torneo de sorpresas, el fantasma de lo insospechado parecía rondar en el ambiente y eso se hizo realidad cuando al minuto 83 Martin Nash dio un centro desde la derecha que ni Claudio Suárez ni Rafael Márquez pudieron evitar que fuera rematado por Carlo Corazzin, cuyo cabezazo produjo el 2–1.

Vocabulario Útil:

selección   select team

sorpresivo   surprising

Copa de Oro   Gold Cup

campeón   champion

certamen   competition; contest

hacer las maletas   to pack (their) bags

prematuro   premature

torneo   tournament

rodear   to surround

supuestamente   supposedly

tiempo extra   overtime

anotar   to note; to rack up a goal

zurda   left; from the left foot

"Conejo"   a nickname, "the Rabbit"

culminar   to culminate; to end

fugaz   very fast

contragolpe   counterattack

cobrado   here, "made a goal successfully"

tiro   shot

esquina   corner

espectador   spectator

reunir   to come together; to meet

estadio   stadium

reaccionar   to react

estupefacción   astonishment; stupefaction

anotación   racking up of goals, score

permancer   to remain

congelado   frozen

cabizbajo   heads bowed

en cuestión de   in a matter of

elementos   here, team members

treparse   to climb up

suelo   ground

señal   signal

festejo   celebration

en alto   up in the air

pecado   sin

penitencia   penitence

balón   ball

atreverse   to dare

tirar   here, "to kick; to shoot"

arco   net; goal

acaso   here, "just barely"

acercarse   to get close to

envío   here, "a pass"

arquero goalie, goalkeeper	*fantasma* ghost, specter
le sacó took it out	*insospechar* to not expect
con apuros hurriedly	*rondar* here, "to permeate"
lamentable unfortunately	*ambiente* environment; atmosphere
partido game; match	*un centro* pass to the center
suficientemente sufficiently	*rematado* finished off; completed
peligroso dangerous	*cabezazo* hit with the head
de sorpresas "of surprises"	

Acuérdate

In soccer, each team has 11 players on the field. Usually there are four forwards (*delanteros*), two players in midfield (*mediocampistas*), and four defensive players in the back (*defensas*). Of course, the goalie guards the net (*portería, arco*) and is the only person who can touch the ball with his or her hands. The soccer field itself is delineated by sidelines, which are called *líneas de banda* in Spanish.

Análisis del Texto

It is time now for some analysis:

al caer 2–1 ante Canadá   Here the contraction *al* before an infinitive means "upon doing X," as in *Al concluir el partido, nos fuimos del estadio* ("When the game ended [upon ending], we left the stadium").

hizo ver muy mal a los verdes   *Los verdes* is just an elegant variation for the Mexican soccer team (they wear green uniforms). Notice the use of *hacer ver*: "… made the 'Greens' look very bad."

Algo Nuevo

Notice the construction *en forma prematura* from the *lectura*. This is an adverbial phrase and means "prematurely." Such constructions (*en forma X, de manera X*) are common in Spanish and usually are translated with a regular adverb in English. So *Maradona envió el balón de manera muy rápida* should not be translated as "Maradona passed the ball in a very quick manner," but simply as "Maradona passed the ball very quickly." In the previous example, *en forma prematura* could have been written as *prematuramente*, but often the *–mente* adverbs are avoided because they can get a bit too long.

que había cobrado un tiro de esquina   You'll find the verb *cobrar* used most often with money to mean "to take money" or "to charge": *Me cobraron tres pesos por los boletos* means "They charged me three pesos for the tickets." Here, *cobrar* means "to register *against the other team*," or "*to rack up a point*." *Un* tiro de esquina is "a corner shot."

reaccionaron con estupefacción ante la anotación   Note the use of the "Night-Before-Christmas" construction: "They reacted with disbelief."

los elementos canadienses se trepaban unos a otros en el suelo en señal de festejo   This literally means "The Canadians climbed on top of each other on the ground in celebration."

si acaso se acercó   *Acaso* is one of those words with several lives. Sometimes the word *acaso* simply adds doubt or reinforces the uncertainty of a question: *¿No sabes acaso si el equipo brasileño ya llegó?* would be translated as "Do you happen to know if the Brazilian team already arrived?" The phrase *por si acaso* means "just in case." In this example, *acaso*, together with *si*, would be translated as "if they ever got near the goal at all." Look up *acaso* in your dictionary for additional examples.

un Tricolor que no veía en Canadá a un rival suficientemente peligroso   *Un Tricolor* (there are three colors in the Mexican flag) refers to the Mexican team. It's just more elegant variation. Translated, this means: "A Mexican team who didn't think (see) that Canada was a sufficiently dangerous rival."

el fantasma de lo insospechado parecía rondar en el ambiente   Here we have a Spanish metaphor—literally, "the ghost of the unsuspected seemed to permeate the atmosphere." Remember that you may have to look beyond the usual meanings of words to understand what is being talked about, and that metaphors and flowery language are common in Spanish.

> ### Ten Cuidado
>
> Elegant variation is very common in sportswriting. Don't get thrown off by phrases such as *el equipo de la hoja de maple*. You could translate this as "the Maple Leaf team" if you wanted to, but in most situations, simply saying "the Canadians" would sound more natural in English.

no pudieron evitar que fuera rematado por Carlo Corazzin, cuyo cabezazo produjo el 2–1
Take a quick look at that past subjunctive (*fuera*): "They couldn't avoid that it (the center kick from the left) was finished off by Carlo Carazzin, whose hit with the head produced the 2–1." *Evitar* has the effect of placing an impersonal desire (that an event should not happen) on something else, so we need the subjunctive after it: *El medio campista no pudo evitar que se le quitara el balón* means "The mid-field player couldn't avoid having the ball taken from him."

Gramática: Suffixes, Part One

Suffixes are exactly like prefixes, with one major difference … they always show up late at parties. You already know many suffixes, though you may not realize it. Each suffix has a particular role to play and can alter or expand the meaning of a word.

Ten Cuidado

Remember that although a suffix may look exactly the same in English and Spanish, the two are not pronounced the same: For example, *-ble* is "bull" in English and "blay" in Spanish.

Unfortunately, the use of suffixes is not an exact science, and it isn't always possible to know what a word means simply by knowing the root word and the suffix. Still, a suffix usually can point you in the right direction and can be a wonderful tool in understanding and creating new words.

We'll be looking at suffixes in both this chapter and the next. Let's begin with a list of suffixes that are cognates of English. The examples are all pretty faithful cognates:

Some Suffix Examples

Suffix	English	Examples
–aje	–age	*garaje*
–algia	–algia	*nostalgia*
–ancia	–ance/ancy	*discrepancia*
–arquía	–archy	*anarquía*
–ario	–ary	*sumario*
–ático	–atic	*fanático*
–bio	–b/–ian	*microbio; anfibio*
–ble	–ble	*razonable*
–cida	–cide	*insecticida*
–cidio	–cide	*suicidio*
–ción	–tion	*infección*
–culo	–cle	*obstáculo*
–cultura	–culture	*agricultura*
–cracia	–cracy	*democracia*
–crecía	–cracy	*hipocresía*
–crata	–crat	*demócrata*
–dad/–tad	–ity	*libertad*
–dor	–tor	*pintor*

Suffix	English	Examples
–endo	–endous	estupendo
–esa	–ess	princesa
–ectomía	–ectomy	apendectomía
–endo	–end	dividendo
–fico/a	–fic	magnífico
–filo/ia	–phile	bibliófilo
–fobia	–phobia	agorafobia
–fóbico/a	–phobic	claustrofóbico
–fono	–phone	gramófono
–génico	–genic	fotogénico
–iatra	–ician	pediatra
–icio/a	–ice	justicia; servicio
–ico	–ic/ical	rústico; práctico
–íficar	–ify	identificar
–ismo	–ism	comunismo
–ista	–ist	artista
–ita	–ite	israelita
–itis	–itis	artritis
–itud	–tude	actitud
–iz	–ess	actriz
–izo	–ish	rojizo
–logo	–logist	antropólogo
–ograma	–ogram	cardiograma
–ónimo	–onym/–mous	sinónimo
–nomo	–omer	astrónomo
–or/a	–er/or	doctor
–oso/a	–ous	escandaloso
–tivo	–tive	representativo
–tomía	–tomy	anatomía
–torio	–tory	laboratorio
–voro	–vorous	omnívoro

El Web

The International Soccer Federation, known as FIFA (for its French title *Fédération Internationale de Football Association*), maintains its own website. You can review the rules of the game and hundreds of important statistics in both English and Spanish at www.fifa.com.

Acuérdate _____

The word for referee in Spanish is *árbitro*. In soccer, *el árbitro* keeps time on his own watch, not on an official time clock as in most other games.

You might also want to visit www.diegomaradona.com, a website "dedicated to the greatest soccer player of all time and to all those who grew with the magic of Maradona in their eyes." Although he isn't as popular as he once was, Maradona, who grew up in a poor district of Buenos Aires, is still considered by many to be one of the best soccer players who ever lived.

Risa del Día

Soccer is especially popular in Argentina. The following joke seems slightly more humorous because it's told in the *vos* form of address, which is common in Argentina. Notice that *escuchame* ("es cu CHA me") and *querés* are the forms when using *vos*. Normally, these would be *escúchame* and *quieres*. *Jugás* is the *vos* present indicative, which in most places would be *juegas*:

Dos amigos:

Ché Ernesto, escuchame … ¿en el cielo habrá cancha de fútbol?

Yo creo que sí, Jorge, porque si allá todo es perfecto, tiene que haber cancha de fútbol.

Bueno, hagamos una cosa. El primero que muera que se lo diga al otro, ¿eh?

Listo, quedamos así.

Al cabo de unos años, Jorge muere. Al día siguiente, Ernesto escucha una voz de ultratumba:

¡Joooorge, Jooorge, Joooorge! ¡soy Ernesto!

¿Qué querés?

Te tengo dos noticias, una buena y otra mala ….

¿La buena?

Que yo tenía razón, en el cielo hay una cancha espectacular, con plateas, un pasto perfecto y unas instalaciones alucinantes.

¿Y la noticia mala?

Que vos jugás mañana a las 11:00.

Vocabulario Útil:

ché   "hey" (in Argentina)

cancha   field (for sport)

listo   here, "all right"

al cabo   at the end

ultratumba   beyond the grave

plateas   benches; bleachers

pasto   grass; turf

instalaciones   buildings; equipment

alucinante   amazing; incredible

The Least You Need to Know

◆ *Fútbol* is generally the most popular team sport in the Spanish-speaking world.

◆ As with prefixes, many suffixes that come from Greek or Latin are English cognates.

◆ Suffixes build Spanish words and can help you increase your vocabulary more easily than memorizing long vocabulary lists.

Chapter 21

Artesanías Mexicanas

In This Chapter

- ◆ Mexican handicrafts
- ◆ *Lectura:* Cómo hacer una piñata
- ◆ *Gramática:* suffixes, part two

Mexico produces a broad and most beautiful collection of handcrafted objects. Handicrafts are known collectively as *artesanías*, and someone who makes them is an *artesano* or *artesana*. Of course, other countries also produce *artesanías*, but for this chapter, we'll focus on those of Mexico specifically.

Las Artesanías Mexicanas

Each region of Mexico specializes in a particular craft. For example, many ceramic items are made in the state of Jalisco, most notably in the town of Tonalá, which has long been considered an important center for handicrafts. In the state of Chihuahua, near Casas Grandes, local potters have revived the ancient art of pottery making, known as *alfarería*, in the style of the ancient Paquimé and Mimbreño peoples. In the 1960s, the Seri Indians of Isla Tiburón (located between coastal Sonora and Baja California) began carving figurines in ironwood, depicting natural motifs such as fish, dolphins, whales, turtles, and bears. These figurines have become very popular in recent years, and although their supply of ironwood has dwindled, a few hundred Seri Indians still carve the wooden figurines.

The state of Oaxaca is famous for its brightly colored animal figurines, known as *alebrijes*, and for its *tapetes*, or "woven rugs." The Zapotec Indians are one of the few remaining Native American cultures in Mexico who are still dedicated to the fine art of weaving. Their *tapetes* are considered to be among the finest hand-woven carpets in the world and are highly sought after—not only in the United States, but also around the world. In other states, such as Puebla, Guerrero, and Chiapas, *artesanos* produce a large variety of items made of ceramic, clay, paper maché, glass, tin, wood, wool, straw, stone, metal, and many other materials.

Lectura: Cómo Hacer una Piñata

You already know what a *piñata* is. The *piñata* is hung high from a pole or tree by a rope. As it swings from side to side, children put on blindfolds and swing sticks at it until the poor *piñata* is ruptured and its concealed treats fall to the ground. When that happens, children scramble in delightful pandemonium to pick up all the goodies.

While some *piñatas* are relatively simple, others may take weeks to complete and are truly works of art. The following text gives instructions on how to make one:

Hay piñatas de todos tamaños y figuras. Las más clásicas son flores, barcos, estrellas, loros, pavos reales, tecolotes, gallos, gallinas, patos, guajolotes, borregos, burros, toros, elefantes, pescados, frutas y vegetales, aeroplanos, payasos, y personajes de moda o políticos.

La piñata tradicional se hace con una olla. Existen pueblos de alfareros que se dedican a hacer "ollas piñateras," como ellos las llaman. Estas ollas llegan a los mercados a donde la gente puede adquirirlas. Posteriormente les aplican engrudo con el que pegan el papel periódico que servirá de base para darle la forma que se desea, usando papeles de colores más apropiados. Hoy día, también se fabrican muchas piñatas de papel y cartón solamente, pero son de una calidad inferior a la tradicional.

Para hacer una piñata tradicional, siga los siguientes pasos:

1. Compre una olla piñatera.

2. Elija un diseño para su piñata y dibújelo en una hoja de papel en blanco.

3. Pegue papel periódico alrededor de la olla para así construir el modelo deseado, ya sea con cartoncillo o papel grueso, usando engrudo.

4. Cubra el armazón con papel de china enroscado, papel lustre o crepé.

5. De los extremos de la figura, cuelgue tiras largas multicolores de listón para darle mayor lucimiento.

6. Llene la piñata de galletas, dulces, cacahuates o frutas de la estación: naranjas, limones, mandarinas, jícamas, y otras.

Cuando se va a romper la piñata, ésta se cuelga con un lazo sostenido desde sus dos extremos por personas que la mueven tratando de que no la rompan pronto. Por su parte, quienes intentan romperla, deben tener cubiertos los ojos, y les darán vueltas hasta hacerles perder la noción del espacio de manera que no sea fácil romperla.

Vocabulario Útil:

figura figure

clásico classic

pavo real peacock

tecolote owl (Mex.)

borrego lamb

guajalote turkey (Mex.)

alfarero potter

olla piñatera a pot used to form a piñata

posteriormente afterward

engrudo paste (flour and water)

papel periódico newspaper

apropiado fitting; appropriate

calidad quality

siguiente following

paso step

elegir to choose

diseño design

hoja page

en blanco blank

pegar to affix; to glue on

alrededor around

ya sea whether it be

cartoncillo construction paper

grueso thick

cubrir to cover

armazón frame

papel de china enroscado coiled Chinese (rice) paper; streamers

papel lustre silver paper

extremo end

listón ribbon

lucimiento sparkle; brilliance

galleta cookie; biscuit

lazo a rope in a loop

sostener to hang; to hold

romper to break

dar vueltas to spin around

noción del espacio depth perception

Cultura Latina

Words like *tecolote* (owl) and *guajalote* (turkey) are ancient Nahuatl words passed down from the Aztecs. They are used primarily in Mexico. In most other countries, an owl is *un buho* (sometimes *una lechuza*), and a turkey is *un pavo.*

Análisis del Texto

Now let's take a closer look:

La piñata tradicional se hace con una olla. The *se hace* is translated as "is made." It's a "se passive" construction: "The traditional piñata is made with a pot."

posteriormente les aplican engrudo *Posteriormente* looks like a fancy word, but all it means is "then" or "afterward." Don't try to translate this as "posteriorly."

servirá de base The preposition *de*, which normally might mean "of" or "from," should here be translated as "as a." Thus, *servirá de base* would mean "will serve as a base." *Servir* can also take *para*, as in *Esta cosa no sirve para nada*, which means "This thing is useless (doesn't serve for anything)."

Ten Cuidado

The word *extremo* is an unreliable *amigo* in many situations. Yes, it is a cognate of the word "extreme" in English, and when used as an adjective, it does mean that: *un caso de extrema gravedad* means "an extremely serious case." But as a noun, it usually means "end," as we see in our *lectura: los extremos de la figura* means "the ends of the figure."

Cuando se va a romper la piñata, ésta se cuelga. Here we have another example of a gender link: *ésta* refers back to *piñata*, and serves as a pronoun. So this would translate as "When the piñata is going to be broken, it is hung …." The sentence probably could be understood just fine without the *ésta*, but having the pronoun there makes the sentence sound a bit more formal.

Por su parte, quienes intentan romperla, deben tener cubiertos los ojos, y les darán vueltas hasta hacerles perder la noción del espacio de manera que no sea fácil romperla. This is quite a sentence, isn't it? Let's break it up. First, the *por su parte* is just there to set this sentence apart from the previous one. Before we were talking about the piñata, and now we're talking about the people who are going to swing at it. You could translate it as "for their part," or you could just leave it out.

Quienes means "those who." *Deben tener* means "should have." Notice that *cubiertos*, which here means "covered," is placed before the noun modified (*ojos*). It could have been after as well. The verb of the sentence, *ser*, is in the subjunctive (*sea*) because we do not know how many times they will have to turn the children around until they lose their depth perception. Translated, this sentence would mean:

Acuérdate _____

The verb *tener* is actually a cognate for the verbal suffix "–tain" in English. So "to detain" is *detener*, "to sustain" is *sostener*, "to maintain" is *mantener*, and "to retain" is *retener*.

> "For their part, the people who are going to try to break the *piñata* should have their eyes covered and be spun around until they lose their depth perception so that it won't be easy to break it (the *piñata*)."

Gramática: Suffixes, Part Two

Now let's get back to those darn suffixes. In addition to the many suffixes of Latin and Greek origin that Spanish shares with English, there are a number of suffixes that are used in Spanish alone.

For example, let's take the basic word *palo*, which means "stick" or "pole." Add the suffix *–illo*, and we get *palillo*, which in some countries means "a toothpick." *Palito* could be a small shovel or a twig. If we add the ending *–eta* to *palo*, we get *paleta*, which in Mexico is a "Popsicle," and to an artist is a "palette" for mixing paint. If we add *–azo*, a suffix meaning "a hit or blow with," we get *palazo*, which could imply hitting something or someone with a shovel. If you hit somebody with your Popsicle, you'd be giving them a *paletazo*.

Or how about the popular musical instrument *la guitarra?* If we add the augmentative suffix *–ón*, we get *guitarrón*, a very large guitar used in mariachi bands. We could add another suffix right onto this new word, such as *–ista*, and get *guitarronista*, a person who plays the *guitarrón*. Now, if our *guitarronista* has warm sentiments for his beloved *guitarrón*, he might refer to it lovingly as his *guitarroncito*. And if, after a long night playing in dusty cantinas, he decides to hit one of the *trompetistas* over the head with his dear *guitarróncito*, we could say that he gave the trumpet player a *guitarroncitazo*.

The following sections cover a lot of suffixes, and you don't need to memorize all of them. Except for the more common ones, it is quite possible to live without them entirely. But your knowledge of Spanish will always remain incomplete if you don't at least have a passing knowledge of suffixes.

Ten Cuidado _____

The use and meaning of Spanish suffixes can be filled with subtleties. To use them effectively, you may need considerable practice talking with native speakers. Even if you follow the rules, you may find yourself conveying an unintended idea with the addition of a suffix. But words such as *poquito* and *muchísimo* are pretty standard and can be used at any time.

Diminutive Suffixes

Diminutive suffixes are common and are used to make a word refer to something smaller. The most common diminutive suffix is *–ito* (and its feminine equivalent, *–ita*). Thus, *un pájaro* is a "bird," and *un pajarito* is a "little bird." In English, we can also make a similar diminutive by adding *–y* or *–ie*, as in "birdie."

 Acuérdate _____

Sometimes a diminutive can be added to a word that might seem to result in an oxymoron: *La casa está enormecita* means "The house is a little too enormous"; while *Los zapatos me quedan grandecitos* means "the shoes are just a little too big on me." Don't let this boggle your mind.

Sometimes several suffixes can be added for an increased effect: *poco → poquito → poquitito → poquititito*.

Diminutive suffixes also can be used to create terms of endearment. They can be added to a person's name (*Esteban → Estebanito*; *Lupe → Lupita*) or to any noun or adjective (*el niñito está pequeñito* means "The dear little boy is teeny weenie.").

Here are some of the more common diminutive suffixes with examples:

-ito, –cito, –ecito I'm sure that you've seen these already. Monosyllabic words that end in a consonant, and words containing diphthongs or that end in *–e* usually take *–cito* or *-ecito*. Thus, *flor* becomes *florecita*, which means "little flower"; *bebé* becomes *bebecito*, which means "a little baby"; and *puerta* becomes *puertecita*, which means "a little door." Notice that the ending must agree in gender with that of the original noun, except in words that end in "the wrong letter," such as *un problema → un problemita*.

–illo, –cillo These are similar to *–ito*, but not quite as common: *un poquillo* means "a little bit." The second version, *–cillo*, is used with multisyllabic words that are accented on the last syllable: *cartón* (cardboard) *→* becomes *cartoncillo* (construction paper).

–tico   Much the same as *–ito*, this is used mostly in the Caribbean and especially in Costa Rica: *Espere un momentico por favor* means "Please wait one little moment."

-zuelo, –achuelo   Not particularly common, these suffixes can be added to nouns and sometimes adjectives to create slightly smaller versions of larger things: *río* → *riachuelo* (brook or stream); *cazo* (saucepan) → *cazuela* (casserole dish).

> **Cultura Latina**
>
> The *–tico* suffix is so popular in Costa Rica that *los costaricenses* are nicknamed *ticos*.

> **Cultura Latina**
>
> In Mexico, the word *ahorita* (*ahora* + *ita*) is common and can be used in a variety of ways. Depending on the context, *ahorita* can mean anything from "right away" to "in a while" to even "never." If you ask, "When will (something) be ready?" and the response is *ahorita*, you may wish to clarify exactly what the speaker means.

Augmentative Suffixes

The augmentative suffixes are the opposite of diminutives. They have the effect of making something larger or more intense.

–ísimo   You probably already know this superlative suffix, which is added to adjectives and some adverbs as an intensifier: *Te quiero muchísimo* means "I love you very much." Similarly, *Fue una tarea dificilísima* means "It was an extremely difficult task." You may even hear it used more than once in the same word, as in *muchisísimo*. The King of Spain isn't just *rico*, he's *riquisísimo*. .

–ote, –ota   These suffixes are added to nouns and adjectives: *grande* → *grandote* (huge); *perro* → *perrote* (big dog); *abrazo* (hug) → *abrazote* (a huge "bear" hug); *bandera* (flag) → *banderota* (a big flag or banner).

–ón, –ona   These are similar to the previous suffixes: *libro* → *librón* (a large book). The *–ón* ending does not need to change to match the gender of the original word (*guitarra* → *guitarrón*), unless it is added to an animate noun (*mujer* → *mujerona*, which means "a big woman"). However, this suffix can also be used adjectivally, when the gender must match the noun described: *oreja* → *orejona* (describes a female person or animal with big ears), and *simpática* (friendly) → *simpaticona* (a very friendly girl/woman).

–azo   This suffix generally means "a hit or blow with …," as in *ladrillo* (brick) → *ladrillazo* (a blow with a brick). The suffix can also be used simply as an augmentative: *hombre* → *hombrazo* (a big and, presumably, good man). *Ella le dio un telefonazo* would

mean "She hit him with a telephone," but in a slangy sort of way, it could also mean "She called him on the telephone."

Pejorative Suffixes

The pejorative suffixes can be attached to words to indicate contempt or undesirability. They are not terribly common but are nonetheless good to know:

–uco, –uca, –ucho, –ucha *casa* → *casucha* (a house in disrepair); and *hermana* → *hermanuca* (a sister that you don't like).

–aco, –aca, –acho These suffixes usually are pejorative, as in *libraco*, which also means "a lousy book," or *poblacho* (from *pueblo*), which means "a one-horse town." The suffix *–aco* can also be seen as an adjectival ending with no negative connotation, as in *austríaco* (Austrian) and *polaco* (Polish).

–ejo/a Add these suffixes to make things smaller and bothersome: *animal* → *animalejo* (a little irritating animal); *calle* → *calleja* (a small, uninteresting street).

Miscellaneous Suffixes

Now let's look at the final suffixes in this chapter:

–ería This refers to a place where items are made or sold: *zapatería*; (shoe store or factory); *mueblería* (furniture store or factory). You already know *pizzería* from Italian.

–dad This one corresponds to *–ity* in English. With it, you can create abstract nouns from adjectives: *generoso* (generous) → *generosidad* (generosity); *sensible* (sensitive) → *sensibilidad* (sensitivity).

–aje This makes nouns from verbs and other nouns: *hospedar* (to provide with accommodations) → *hospedaje* (lodging); *aprendiz* (apprentice) → *aprendizaje* (apprenticeship).

–al, –tal These suffixes indicate a tree or grove: *manzana* → *manzanal* (apple orchard); and *café* → *cafetal* (coffee plantation). They can also be used figuratively to express abundance: *dinero* → *dineral* (a whole field of money).

–anza With this, you can make nouns from some verbs: *enseñar* → *enseñanza* (instruction). It sometimes corresponds to *–ance* in English: *ordenar* (to order) becomes *ordenanza* (ordinance).

–dura This suffix indicates the effect of an action: *picar* (to puncture; to bite) makes *picadura* (a puncture or insect bite).

–ense   This indicates place of origin: *nicaragüense* means "Nicaraguan."

–eo   This indicates collective nouns, such as *papeleo*, which means "paperwork."

–ero   This suffix has a variety of uses that expand on the meaning of the root word: *sombra* (shade) → *sombrero* (hat); *vaca* (cow) → *vaquero* (cowboy).

Acuérdate

The common verb ending *–ear* is often used with coined verbs, as in *bacupear*, which means "to back up a computer file."

–eza   With this, you can make abstract nouns from adjectives: *bello* (pretty); *belleza* (beauty); *rico* (rich) → *riqueza* (richness or wealth).

–edo/–eda   These suffixes make collective nouns, often with trees: *roble* (oak tree) → *robledo* (oak grove); *álamo* (poplar tree) → *alameda* (poplar grove).

–erio   This suffix appears in nouns derived from verbs or other nouns: *ministro* (government minister) → *ministerio* (government ministry); *imperar* (to rule; to prevail) → *imperio* (empire).

–ero, –era, –dero, –dera   In nouns and adjectives, these suffixes express the idea of a trade, instrument, or place: *pan* (bread) → *panadero* (baker); *coche* (car) → *cochera* (carport, or garage); *lavar* → *lavadero* (laundry room); *ropa* → *ropero* (wardrobe).

–ado, –ido   These suffixes can express a certificate or degree, a similarity to a root word, or a sound: *dolor* (pain) → *dolorido* (painful); *doctor* → *doctorado* (Ph.D.); *maullar* (to meow) → *maullido* (a cat's meow).

–oso/–osa   In adjectives derived from nouns or verbs, these suffixes indicate abundance of a condition: *furia* → *furioso* (furious); *contagiar* → *contagioso* (contagious).

–dor, –dora   These suffixes show up in adjectives derived from verbs: *hablar* → *hablador/a* (talkative). They also appear in some nouns: *inspeccionar* → *inspector/a* (inspector).

–és/esa   These indicate place of origin or the language from that place: *danés* (Danish/Danish language); *escocés* (Scottish); *holandés* (from Holland/Dutch language).

–ada   This one is similar to the English suffix *–ful*, as in *cuchara* (spoon) → *cucharada* (spoonful).

–udo, –uda   In adjectives, these express abundance: *lana* (wool) → *lanudo* (wooly); *barba* (beard) → *barbudo* (a man with a big beard).

–ez   This suffix shows up in abstract nouns, as in *escaso* (scarce) → *escasez* (scarcity).

–izo, –iza   These suffixes appear in adjectives derived from other adjectives: *rojo* → *rojizo* (reddish); *enfermo* (sick) → *enfermizo* (sickly).

El Web

If you are interested in *artesanías* but are unable to travel to Mexico anytime soon, you can see (and even purchase) them at www.mexcrafts.com.mx and www.mexonline.com/crafts.htm.

Risa del Día

I couldn't find any jokes about *artesanos*, probably because artisans are held in such high esteem. This joke is a bit off the wall:

> *El esposo se está bañando:*
>
> *María, ¿dónde está el champú?*
>
> *Ahí, delante de ti …*
>
> *Pero es que es para el cabello seco y yo lo tengo mojado.*

Vocabulario Útil:

> *bañarse*   to bathe
>
> *delante de ti*   in front of you
>
> *cabello*   hair
>
> *seco*   dry
>
> *mojado*   wet

The Least You Need to Know

◆ Mexico produces many beautiful handcrafted objects known as *artesanías*.

◆ If you can't travel to Mexico, you can see and purchase *artesanías* over the Internet.

◆ Some Spanish suffixes do not have an equivalent cognate with an English suffix.

◆ Suffixes can be diminutive, augmentative, pejorative, adjectival, or nominative (make more nouns). They can also be used to create terms of endearment.

22

Los Viajes

In This Chapter

- ◆ *Diálogo I:* En el Aeropuerto Internacional
- ◆ *Gramática:* Interrogatives
- ◆ *Diálogo II:* El Planetario de Madrid

I have some good news and some bad news. The good news is that there is no *lectura* in this chapter. You needed a break from all those readings, anyway. Even the grammar section is short. *¡Qué suerte!*

Of course, there is a price to pay for my generosity: this chapter contains challenging dialogues. Your mission, should you choose to accept it, is to read each dialogue aloud and see how much of it you understand. Underline or highlight any words that are new or unknown to you. Then read the English translation to see how you did. After a few days, try it again to see if you've improved.

Diálogo I: En el Aeropuerto Internacional de San José, Costa Rica

Mike has just arrived in San José, Costa Rica (not California!). Here is his conversation with the immigration officer:

Mike: *Buenas tardes, señor.*

El agente: *Buenas tardes. ¿De dónde es?*

Mike: *Soy de Australia.*

El agente: *Su pasaporte, por favor.*

Mike: *Sí, cómo no. Aquí lo tiene.*

El agente: *Muy bien. ¿Cuál es el motivo de su viaje a Costa Rica?*

Mike: *Será un viaje de placer. Tengo amigos aquí en San José, y he venido a vistarlos. También me gustaría hacer un viaje alrededor del país. Me encantaría ver los volcanes.*

El agente: *Claro, los volcanes son muy interesantes. ¿Por cuántos diás permanecerá usted en el país?*

Mike: *Hasta el 3 de marzo. O sea, son 30 días en total, más o menos.*

El agente: *Bien. Su visa vencerá en 60 días. Espero que su estadía sea agradable.*

Mike: *Gracias. Disculpe, ¿me puede decir una cosa?*

El agente: *A ver …*

Mike: *¿Qué hora es aquí? Quiero ajustar mi reloj.*

El agente: *Ya son las 11:45.*

Mike: *Gracias, señor. Usted es muy amable.*

El agente: *No hay de qué.*

Translation:

Mike: Good afternoon, sir.

The agent: Good afternoon. Where are you from?

Mike: I'm from Australia.

The agent: Your passport, please.

Mike: Yes, of course. Here you go ("here you have it").

The agent: Very good. What is the reason for your trip to Costa Rica?

Mike: It will be a pleasure trip. I have friends here in San José, and I've come to visit them. I'd also like to take a trip around the country. I'd love to see the volcanoes.

The agent: Sure, the volcanoes are very interesting. How many days will you remain in the country?

Mike: Until the third of March. In other words, it'll be 30 days in all, more or less.

The agent: All right. Your visa will expire in 60 days. I hope that you have a pleasant stay.

Acuérdate

If you are planning to travel, find out ahead of time what the visa requirements are for the countries you plan to visit. In most cases, you'll just need a valid passport. However, for some countries you may be required to have all your paperwork taken care of ahead of time.

Mike: Thank you. Pardon me. Can you tell me something?

The agent: All right … ("let's see what it is …")

Mike: What time is it here? I want to adjust my watch.

The agent: It's 11:45 now.

Mike: Thank you, sir. You are very kind.

The agent: Don't mention it ("there is no need to thank me").

If you found any words that were new or difficult in the previous dialogue, write them down. Look them up in your dictionary to see if these words have any secondary meanings.

Gramática: Interrogatives

You have already encountered most of these, so this may be a review. But just in case, let's take a quick look at those "question words" *una vez más*.

Notice that these interrogatives have *tildes* on them. I'll explain why they are required in a minute.

Interrogatives

Interrogative	Translation
¿quién?	who? or whom? (singular)
¿quiénes?	who? (plural)
¿qué?	what? or which? (singular and plural)
¿cuál?	which?
¿cuáles?	which? (plural)
¿cuándo?	when?
¿dónde?	where?
¿cómo?	how?
¿cuánto?	how much?
¿cuántos/as?	how many?
¿por qué?	why?

Cultura Latina

If you are looking for accommodations, it is quite acceptable (and a good idea) to ask the receptionist to show you the room before you agree to take it. In Guatemala, I once ended up in a room with a broken bed (no mattress), no bathroom facilities, and two rabid dogs just across the hall barking furiously at me through a half-torn wire gate, ready to tear me to shreds. Guess I should have asked to see the room first ....

Here are a few sentences using interrogatives:

¿Quiénes estaban ahí en ese momento?
Who (plural) was there at that moment?

¿Quién va a llamar mañana?
Who will be calling tomorrow?

¿Qué tengo que hacer?
What do I have to do?

¿Dónde está la estación de policía más cercana?
Where is the nearest police station?

¿Cómo era el hombre que le asaltó?
What was the man like ("look like") who mugged you?

Ten Cuidado

The *tildes* on the interrogatives don't change their pronunciation; they are important only when writing the language. There is no need to say these words any differently. But don't forget to write the *tildes* when these words are used as interrogatives.

Now, as I mentioned before, you have no doubt seen some of these very same words without the *tilde*. This is because these words also work as relative pronouns. And what is a relative pronoun? Just a little word that hooks two clauses together: "the man *who* came to dinner"; "the house *which* is yellow"; "the person *whom* I saw yesterday."

Read the following examples:

♦ *Where* do you live? (would have accent mark in Spanish)

  That's the house *where* I live. (no accent mark in Spanish)

♦ *Who* robbed you? (would have accent mark)

  That's the guy *who* robbed me. (no accent mark)

♦ *Which* guy is it? (would have accent mark)

  I already told you *which* guy it is. (no accent mark)

♦ *When* did this happen? (would have accent mark)

  It happened *when* I was going home. (no accent mark)

♦ *Why* did he do it? (would have accent mark in Spanish)

  I don't know *why* he did it. (no accent mark)

♦ *How* did it happen? (yes accent mark)

  I don't know *how* it happened. (no accent mark)

> **Acuérdate** _____
>
> Remember that the words for "why" and "because" are practically the same. Literally, *¿por qué?* means "for what?" When written as one word and without the *tilde*, *porque* means "because." So *¿Por qué lo hiciste?* means "Why did you do it?"; *Porque sí* means "Just because."

If the previous sentences had been in Spanish, we would have needed a *tilde* on the first *italicized* word in each pair.

Diálogo II: El Planetario de Madrid

Here we have a tourist asking for directions:

El turista: *Disculpe, señor.*

El madrileño: *Sí, dígame. ¿En qué le puedo ayudar?*

El turista: *Muchas gracias, señor. Es que soy turista y estoy en Madrid por primera vez.*

El madrileño: *Muy bien. ¿A dónde quiere ir?*

Ten Cuidado

Remember that when *que* is used in expressions of emotion or surprise, you must write the *tilde*: *¡Qué bonita!* means "How pretty!" *¡Qué lástima!* means "What a shame!" *Que* also requires a *tilde* when used as a question word. But don't write the *tilde* when it is used as a relative pronoun: *El hombre que vive aquí* means "the man who/that lives here."

El turista: *Voy al Planetario de Madrid. Quiero ver el nuevo programa. Se llama La Vida Más Allá de la Tierra.*

El madrileño: *¡Qué casualidad! Soy astrónomo. Sé perfectamente donde está el planetario.*

El turista: *No me diga. Entonces, ¿cómo se llega al lugar?*

El madrileño: *Mire, si quiere ir en el metro, súbase en la línea 6. Bájese en la estación de Méndez Álvaro. Si va a ir en autobús, puede tomar la línea 148, que es la que va de la Plaza de Callao al Puente de Vallecas.*

El turista: *Muy bien. Muchísimas gracias por su ayuda. Ahí veo una parada de autobuses.*

El madrileño: *Espero que disfrute del programa. Adiós.*

El turista: *Adiós.*

Translation:

The tourist: Excuse me, sir.

Person from Madrid: Yes, tell me, how can I help you?

The tourist: Thank you very much, sir. You see, I'm a tourist and I'm in Madrid for the first time.

Person from Madrid: All right. Where are you trying to go?

The tourist: I'm going to the Madrid Planetarium. I want to see the new program. It's called "Life Beyond the Earth."

Person from Madrid: What a coincidence! I'm an astronomer. I know perfectly well where the planetarium is.

The tourist: You don't say. So, how do you get to the place?

Person from Madrid: Look, if you want to go by metro, you're going to get on line 6. Get off at the Méndez Álvaro station. If you're going to go by bus, you can take line 148, which (is the one that) goes from the Plaza de Callao to Puente de Vallecas.

The tourist: Very good. Thank you very much for your help. I see a bus stop over there.

Person from Madrid: I hope you enjoy the program. Goodbye.

The tourist: Goodbye.

Algo Nuevo
The verb *controlar* borders on being a false *amigo*, as it usually means "to check or inspect." When tickets are checked on an airplane or bus, it is known as *control de boletos*. If someone says "*Necesito controlar su boleto,*" he doesn't mean "I need to control your ticket," but simply "I need to check it to see if you actually paid for this trip."

El Web

Visit www.spanishclassonline.com/vocabulary/interrogatives.htm for more information on the interrogatives covered in this chapter.

U.S. citizens can check visa requirements for foreign travel at http://travel.state.gov. If you are a citizen of another country, consult your local authorities, or contact the embassy or consulate of the country you wish to visit. They will be happy to tell you what you'll need.

Risa del Día

If you've ever lost your luggage during a trip, you'll appreciate the following *chiste*:

Un hombre en el mostrador de una aerolínea, despachando su equipaje:

Mire, quiero que me manden la valija grande a Londres. La más chiquita a Miami. Los dos bolsos de lona mándemelos a Río y el baúl a Beirut.

Disculpeme, pero eso no es posible, señor.

¿Cómo que no?, si ya lo hicieron la última vez que viajé … ¡y sin mi permiso!

Vocabulario Útil:

mostrador   counter

aerolínea   airline

despachar   to dispatch; to take care of; to send

equipaje   luggage

valija   suitcase

Londres   London

Acuérdate

Bajar means "to get down," but from a vehicle, it means "to get off." If you want the bus driver to let you out, yell *¡Baja!* or *¡Bajan!* (not *¡Bajo!*).

lona   canvas; cloth

baúl   chest

¿Cómo que no?   "What do you mean it isn't?"

The Least You Need to Know

♦ Interrogative pronouns and relative pronouns are the same, except that the interrogatives need *tildes*.

♦ The *tildes* do not change the pronunciation of the interrogative words.

♦ When looking for accommodations, it is quite acceptable to ask the receptionist to show you the room before you decide to take it.

Part 5

Money, Science, and Politics

¡Felicitaciones! You've almost made it to the end ….

This part contains some of the most challenging *lecturas* in the book. We'll look at computers, business correspondence, a political document, and other complex texts.

After you finish the book, I strongly suggest that you go back and read some of the earlier *lecturas* again. You'll be amazed at how much easier they are now. Once you feel comfortable with the *lecturas* in the book, you'll be more than ready to tackle Spanish at an advanced level. *¡Buena suerte!*

Chapter 23

El Comercio

In This Chapter

- ◆ *Lectura:* correspondencia mercantil
- ◆ *Gramática:* Polite Phrases and Expressions
- ◆ *Diálogo:* en el banco Bantico
- ◆ Idiot's guide to idioms

The United States is Latin America's most important trading partner. Each year the United States imports billions of dollars in goods and raw materials from Latin America and Spain, including textiles, footwear, fruits, vegetables, wine, precious metals, and minerals, just to name a few. The United States also exports many products to the Spanish-speaking world, in addition to the millions of dollars spent annually by American tourists traveling "south of the border."

In 1993, Canada, Mexico, and the United States signed a mutual trade agreement known as the North American Free Trade Agreement (NAFTA), thus creating what has been called the "largest free-trade zone in the world." Many U.S. companies have set up assembly plants across the Mexican border, known as *maquiladoras* (or simply as *maquilas*). In recent years, the *maquiladora* industry has taken a hit, as jobs that were once cheaper in Mexico are now even cheaper in China and Vietnam. Nonetheless, there is still a considerable amount of trade between all three countries.

Even if you never find yourself in a position to conduct official business in Spanish, a basic familiarity with the kind of language used for business purposes can come in handy.

Lectura: Correspondencia Mercantil

In Spanish, as in English, the kind of language used in official business can be a little difficult to understand. But the good news is that most business correspondence tends to be rather formulaic, using the same openings, closings, and cordialities throughout. Remember to have your dictionary on hand as you read the text, and note any words or phrases that you find difficult:

Industrias Agrícolas Echeverría S.A. de C.V._Fertilizantes—Maquinaria Pesada—Sistemas de Irrigación_Teléfono: 52 5 546 30 41; Fax 52 5 546 30 39_Parque Industrial del Norte_Apartado Postal 195_Torreón, Coah._C.P. 27170, México

> ### Algo Nuevo
>
> You will see the letters *S.A.* (sometimes with *de C.V.*) after the names of many businesses. These letters stand for *Sociedad Anónima (de Capital Variable)*, which means "Anonymous Society of Variable Capital." In plain English, it means "Incorporated." So *Industrias Agrícolas Echeverría S.A. de C.V.* would translate as "Echeverria Agricultural Industries, Inc."

Torreón, Coah., el 23 de junio de 2006

Estimados Señores:

Nos complace referirnos a su atenta carta del día 5 de este mes para proporionarles la infomación que se sirven solicitar:

Acuérdate

Another way to say, "it is my (our) pleasure to do X" in a business letter (in addition to *nos complace*) is *me (nos) es grato* plus infinitive: *Nos es grato contestar su atenta carta* ... means "It is our pleasure to respond to your kind letter ...." You wouldn't say this in conversation, but you may see it in a business letter.

Economía General: Ha mejorado sensiblemente, según los últimos informes proporcionados por instituciones tan serias como el Banco Nacional de México y el Crédito Comercial S.A.

Ventas a Plazo: Como una consecuencia de la recuperación económica, numerosas granjas están intensificando sus operaciones a plazo. Puede observarse al respecto en la "Estadística Comercial", que el volumen de las ventas aumentó en forma muy apreciable durante el mes pasado, y hay gran optimismo.

> **Acuérdate**
>
> The word *serio* has several meanings. It can mean "serious" or "grave," but it also can mean "reliable" and "respectable." If you say that a person is *serio/a*, this could also mean that he or she is "worried" or even "depressed." Context should make it clear.

Importaciones: Puede considerarse que, a medida que vaya desarrollándose la industria nacional, el capítulo de importaciones ha de reducirse en importancia, porque el país producirá cuanto necesite para su consumo. El gobierno está decidido a facilitar el establecimiento de nuevas industrias y a impartir amplia protección a las existentes.

Confiamos en que la información anterior sea de utilidad para las resoluciones que ustedes tomen en el caso de que nos hablan.

Quedando a su entera disposición para cualquier consulta, los saludamos muy atentamente.

Juan José Sarabía Martínez, Gerente del Depto. de Ventas

Vocabulario Útil:

mercantil mercantile; business (adjective)

maquinaria pesada heavy machinery

parque industrial industrial park

apartado postal P.O. box

Coah. Coahuila (a state in Mexico)

C.P. "*Código Postal*" (postal code)

Estimados Señores Esteemed Sirs

nos complace It is our pleasure ("It pleases us")

atenta carta kind letter

proporionar to provide

se sirven here, "are requested"

sensiblemente appreciably; considerably

informe report

serio serious; legitimate

venta a plazo installment plan

recuperación recuperation; upswing

volumen volume; amount

aumentar to increase; to expand

optimismo optimism

desarrollarse to develop

capítulo	chapter; period	*anterior*	previous
reducirse	to be reduced	*utilidad*	usefulness; of use
facilitar	to facilitate; to make easier	*resolución*	decision; resolutions
establecimiento	establishment	*quedando*	remaining
impartir	to impart	*a su disposición*	at your disposal
amplio	broad; wide-ranging	*saludar*	to greet; to give salutations
existente	current; existing	*atentamente*	sincerely
confiar en	to trust		

Análisis del Texto

¡Excelente! Now let's take a closer look:

el 23 de junio de 2006   Notice the form for writing the date: el + "day" + de + "month" (no capital letter) + de + "year."

> **Acuérdate**
>
> If you send a letter and you're not sure to whom it should be addressed, you can use *A quien corresponda*, which means "To whom it may concern." Notice the use of the subjunctive—because you don't know whom it concerns, you need to put the verb in the subjunctive to allow for this uncertainty.

Estimados Señores   Most business letters begin with *Estimados señores* …. This is much more formal than *Queridos*, which means "Dear" and implies affection. You can sometimes omit the *estimado* part if you want and just write *Señores*. This would include both men and women (I know it isn't fair …). If you are addressing a woman, it would, of course, be *Estimada*.

Nos complace referirnos a su atenta carta   Almost all business letters are *atenta*. This extends to the closing as well: *atentamente* means "sincerely" or "kindly."

se sirven solicitor   In formal writing, the verb *servir* has a secondary meaning of "to please" or "to be so kind as to": *Sírvase responder lo más pronto que sea factible* means "Please reply (take the liberty of replying) as soon as it becomes feasible." In this example, it is understood that the responses to various questions have been requested, and the *se sirven* makes the tone of the letter more polite.

según los últimos informes proporcionados por instituciones tan serias   Here, *últimos* would be translated as "latest" rather than "last."

en forma muy apreciable   Here again we see the avoidance of the *–mente* adverb. This could have been written as *apreciablemente*, but the *en forma* construction is more manageable in Spanish. Nonetheless, a good translation would read "appreciably," not "in an appreciable form."

a medida que vaya desarrollándose la industria nacional   I love this! Literally, it would mean "as the national industry may go developing itself." No, that doesn't make sense. Let's see what's going on. First, that subjunctive (*vaya*) is there because the writer is speculating as to how things may develop, and therefore must use the subjunctive to reflect this "unknown quantity." Second, the *ir* plus present participle suggests motion and progress, although the sentence could also have been written with *a medida que se desarolle la industria nacional.* But the use of *ir* suggests a period of time during which progress may be noted. A better translation is "to the extent that national industry (may) develop over time."

> **Ten Cuidado**
>
> The word for "colleague" is *colega*. It's a nice word to use in a business or educational setting. Just remember that the word doesn't change to *colego* when addressing a man; *estimados colegas* would be the way to address a mixed group. Say *una colega* if you are addressing a woman.

ha de reducirse en importancia   *Haber* + *de* + infinitive in this sentence means about the same thing as the verb *deber*: *Ha de ser posible* means "It should be possible."

el país producirá cuanto necesite para su consumo   Here's another subjunctive construction. We do not know how much the country will need, so the subjunctive allows for this uncertainty. You could translate this as "The country will produce whatever amount it may need (but we don't know how much)."

El gobierno está decidido   The verb *decidir* does mean "to decide," but in this context we might venture to translate this as "the government is resolute" rather than "decided."

Confiamos en que la información anterior sea de utilidad para las resoluciones que ustedes tomen en el caso de que nos hablan   Translated, this means "We trust that the preceding information may be useful vis-a-vis the decisions that you may make (more subjunctive) with respect to the issues under discussion." The word *sea* is the subjunctive of *ser* and is needed here because of the hope and uncertainty of the statement.

Quedando a su entera disposición para cualquier consulta, los saludamos muy atentamente   Here the letter reads "Remaining at your entire disposal for any consultation (questions, advice, and so on), we greet you (send salutations) most sincerely."

Gramática: Polite Phrases and Expressions

This section contains numerous courteous expressions that you should learn by heart. You're probably already familiar with some of them. That's okay. It's always a good idea to have these phrases at the tip of your tongue whenever you meet someone, especially in a business setting.

Things to Say When Being Introduced

When you first meet someone, don't just greet him or her with *Hola* or *Buenos días* (*tardes, noches*). It's hard to be too polite in Spanish, especially in the beginning. So try using one of the following polite expressions; it will be greatly appreciated:

Mucho gusto   Nice to meet you

Un placer   A pleasure

Encantado   Charmed (said by men, usually to women)

Encantada   Charmed (said by women to anyone)

Me da mucho gusto conocerlo/la   Nice to meet you

El gusto es mío   The pleasure is mine (if the other person says *mucho gusto* to you first)

(Your name), *a sus órdenes*   "at your service"

(Your name), *para servirle*   "at your service"

The last two are mostly used by men. *Encantado* (said if you're a man) and *encantada* (if a woman) are also quite popular. *El gusto es mío* is a good response if someone says *Mucho gusto* to you first. Be careful not to respond with *Sí* to *El gusto es mío* (I've heard this!), which would mean, "Yes, the pleasure *is* all yours, I'm sure."

Acuérdate

Remember that the gender-specific ending of *encantado/a* must match *your* gender, not the gender of the person whom you are addressing (*encantar* means "to enchant"). If a man were to say *encantada* to a woman, he would be saying: "You must be very enchanted to meet me, handsome devil that I am …." (That's probably not the best way to make a good first impression, guys.)

"Of Course"

Here are three ways to say "of course." They're good responses to a question when the answer is obviously going to be "yes":

> *Sí, cómo no*
>
> *Sí, por supuesto*
>
> *Sí, desde luego* (used mostly in Spain)

For "of course not," try these:

> *No, de ninguna manera* (No, in no way)
>
> *No, no puede ser* (No, that can't be)

Algo Nuevo

Business culture in the Spanish-speaking world is very different from that of the United States, Canada, and Britain. For one thing, the "get it done yesterday" perspective of many business people in the English-speaking world is not as common in Latin America or Spain. A business meeting may not start "on time" by American or European standards. Issues about money, sales, or contract negotiations may be postponed until the eating, drinking, and other social activities have all been concluded.

Polite Forms for Asking Questions

When doing business, you'll often find that at some point you will want to pose a question. Here's a list of courteous phrases you can use to ensure that you get the answers you need. The translations are all a bit on the literal side. In reality, all these expressions basically mean "please." Let's take a look:

Poder hacer el favor de + infinitive   This means "to be able to do the favor of X," as in: *¿Me podría hacer el favor de decir el precio por kilo?* ("Could you [do me a favor and] tell me what the price is per kilo?") You can also use it without poder, as in *Hágame el favor de decirme su dirección y teléfono durante el día.* ("Do me the favor of telling me your address and daytime phone number.")

Poder ayudar con ...   This is translated as "to be able to help with ...," as in: *¿Me puede ayudar con el idioma, por favor?* ("Can you please help me with the language?")

Poder decir una cosa ...   This means "to be able to tell someone something," as in: *Disculpe, ¿me podría decir una cosa? ¿Cuánto van a cobrarme por el manejo, envío, y los impuestos?* ("Pardon me. Could you tell me something? How much are they going to charge me for handling, shipping, and taxes?")

Ten Cuidado

The verb *molestar* is a false cognate. It doesn't mean "to molest" as we now use this word in English. *Molestar* simply means "to bother" or "to cause inconvenience." Thus, the expression *No se moleste* does not mean "Don't molest yourself," but rather "Don't trouble yourself or create any unnecessary inconvenience in your life on my behalf."

Permitir hacer una pregunta "To be permitted to ask a question," as in *Señorita, ¿me permite hacerle una pregunta? ¿Cuál es su número de seguro social?* ("Miss, may I ask you a question please? What is your Social Security number?")

Tener la bondad de + infinitive "To be so good as to …," as in *Señora, ¿no puede usted tener la bondad de decirme su nombre y apellido?* ("Madam, would you please be so kind as to tell me your first and last name?")

¿No le importa si + conjugated verb This means "Do you mind if I …?" as in: *¿No le importaría si enviamos la mercancía el viernes?* ("Would you mind if we sent the merchandise on Friday?")

"Thank You" and "You're Welcome"

I know that you already know how to say "Thank you" and "No, thank you" and "You're welcome." But it can't hurt to have a few more phrases to expand on what you already know. After you say *Gracias*, consider adding one of the following phrases:

After *Gracias*, add …

> *muy amable*   (you are) very kind
>
> *por su ayuda/paciencia*   for your help/patience
>
> *por su atención*   for helping me
>
> *por todo*   for everything
>
> *Estoy muy agradecido/a por su tiempo.*   I'm very grateful for your time.
>
> *Espero que no haya sido molestia.*   I hope that it hasn't been too much trouble.

When someone says *Gracias* to you, you should respond with one of the following:

> *De nada.*   You're welcome.
>
> *Por nada.*   You're welcome.

No hay de qué.   Don't mention it.

No faltaba más.   It goes without saying.

No se preocupe.   Don't worry about it.

A sus órdenes.   At your service.

A la orden.   At your command (mostly in the Caribbean).

Para servirle.   At your service.

¡A usted (por su cortesía/paciencia)!   Thank you! (for your courtesy/patience)

> **Cultura Latina**
>
> Yes, you can say *de nada* all day for "you're welcome." But I suggest that you try using the more formal expressions now and then. Your efforts to be courteous will not go unappreciated. Don't forget that you can always add *señor* or *señora* to the end of most courteous phrases: *A sus órdenes, señora.*

> **Cultura Latina**
>
> Spanish-speakers tend to have a slightly different perception of time and punctuality than Anglos. Arriving somewhere "on time" may mean being "late" by up to several hours. In many cases, a 2:00 business meeting in Latin America might not begin until 3:00 (although this is changing in some sectors). If you're in doubt, you can ask *¿A la hora en punto?* ("Should I arrive exactly at the specified hour?")

When someone wishes something good for you (such as *Buena suerte,* which means "Good luck"), respond with one of the following:

Gracias, igualmente.   Thanks, same to you.

Que le vaya bien.   Good luck (may it go well for you).

Gracias, muy amable.   Thanks, you are very kind.

> **Ten Cuidado**
>
> The expression *Que le vaya bien* is popular, especially in Mexico, but it is usually said to people leaving by those remaining behind. Don't say *Que le vaya bien* when you are the one leaving (I've done this—it's embarrassing). If you're leaving, say *Adios* or *Hasta luego.* If you're staying behind, you can say *Adios, que le (te, les) vaya bien.*

Diálogo: En El Banco Bantico S.A.

Here's a conversation in a Costa Rican bank between Bridget O'Kelly and various people there. This time the dialogue is followed by a "Vocabulario Útil" section only.

Cajero: *Buenas tardes, señorita. ¿En qué le puedo ayudar?*

O'Kelly: *Buenas tardes. Soy Bridget O'Kelly y quisiera abrir una cuenta corriente y otra de ahorros.*

Cajero: *Está muy bien. Con todo gusto. Nomás que aquí sirve sólo a los que ya tienen sus cuentas. Tiene que pasar a la ventanilla tres. Ahí la pueden atender.*

O'Kelly: *Muy bien. Gracias. (Va a la ventanilla tres)*

Cajero: *Buenas tardes, señora.*

O'Kelly: *Señorita.*

Cajero: *Ah, sí. Señorita. Perdón. ¿En qué puedo servirle?*

O'Kelly: *Quiero abrir dos cuentas, una corriente y la otra de ahorros.*

Cajero: *Bien, ¿de dónde es usted?*

O'Kelly: *Soy de Irlanda.*

Cajero: *Bienvenida a Costa Rica. Espero que le guste su estadía aquí. A ver, ¿tiene usted su pasaporte y permiso para trabajar en Costa Rica?*

O'Kelly: *Sí señor, aquí los tiene.*

Cajero: *Gracias. ¿Me espera un momentico por favor?*

O'Kelly: *Sí, cómo no.*

Mientras espera O'Kelly, llega una señora costarricense y se pone delante de ella. Le da sus papeles al cajero, y comienza a hablar con él de una forma muy cordial.

O'Kelly: *Perdone, señora, pero fíjese que hay fila ¿eh?*

La señora: *Ay, perdón, señorita. Lo que pasa es que pensé que usted ya había terminado.*

O'Kelly: *No se preocupe, pero es que no he terminado todavía.*

La señora: *Bueno, Gustavo (dirigiéndose al cajero), tengo prisa. Saludos a tu mamá de mi parte. Nos vemos mañana.*

Cajero: *Que te vaya bien, tía.*

O'Kelly: *Ahora, ¿qué pasa con mis cuentas?*

Cajero: *Todo está bien, señorita. He aquí los papeles para abrir las cuentas. Llene las dos solicitudes y pase por favor a la ventanilla cinco.*

O'Kelly: *¿A otra ventanilla? Bueno, está bien. Muchas gracias.*

Cajero: *A sus órdenes.*

Vocabulario Útil:

cajero/a   teller; cashier; clerk

quisiera   would like; might like

cuenta corriente   checking account

cuenta de ahorros   savings account

con todo gusto   "with pleasure"

ventanilla   window (not always with glass)

Irlanda   Ireland

bienvenido   welcome

estadía   stay; visit

saludos   greetings

de mi parte   on my behalf

he aquí   here; I have here

llenar   to fill out

Ten Cuidado _____

*Atender (*atiendo, atiendes*) doesn't mean "to attend" as in "to show up for." It means "to serve or help." If you enter a store and can't find anyone to help you, ask ¿Quién atiende aquí? for "Who's here to help the customers?" The noun atención sometimes means "attention" in the English sense, but it can also mean "assistance."*

Idiot's Guide to Idioms

As promised, the chapters in this final part of the book contain lists of idiomatic phrases for you to memorize. The translations are not literal; instead, you'll find the English equivalent expression. You may want to look up any new words. Most of these are highly idiomatic (a word that linguists use when a phrase doesn't make any sense):

A buen hambre no hay pan duro.   Beggars can't be choosers.

ahogarse en un vaso de agua   to make a mountain out of a molehill

al azar   at random

al cantar del gallo   at the crack of dawn

Al hierro caliente batir de repente.   Strike while the iron is hot.

Antes que te cases mira lo que haces.   Look before you leap.

al pie de la letra   to the letter

a pedir de boca   to your heart's content

A quien madruga, Dios le ayuda.   The early bird catches the worm.

a toda costa   at all costs

El Web

For more online information about doing business in Latin America check out www. latinbusinesschronicle.com.

For info about Spanish idioms, visit http://spanish.about.com/od/idiomsandphrases.

Risa del Día

Sometimes doing business in another language is not as easy as you might think. If you need something translated into Spanish for business purposes, make sure that you hire a qualified professional. Also, if you plan to market a product in a Spanish-speaking country, have your advertising reviewed by a native speaker of that country before you release the material. Cutting corners can be embarrassing. Even the big companies end up making huge mistakes sometimes. Take a look at these:

◆ The Dairy Association's huge success with the campaign "Got Milk?" prompted them to expand advertising to Mexico. It was soon brought to their attention the Spanish translation read "Are you lactating?" (*¿Tiene leche?*)

◆ An American T-shirt maker in Miami printed shirts that promoted the Pope's visit for the Spanish market. Instead of "I saw the Pope" (*el Papa*), the shirts read "I Saw the Potato" (*la papa*).

◆ Frank Perdue's chicken slogan, "It takes a strong man to make a tender chicken," was translated into Spanish as "It takes an aroused man to make a chicken affectionate." (*Tierno* means tender, but with living things, it means "sweet and affectionate.")

◆ When Parker Pen marketed its ball-point pen in Mexico, the ads were supposed to have read "It won't leak in your pocket and embarrass you." The company thought that the word *embarazar* (to impregnate) meant to "embarrass," so the ad read: "It won't leak in your pocket and make you pregnant!"

◆ When American Airlines wanted to advertise its new leather first-class seats in the Mexican market, it translated its "Fly In Leather" campaign literally, which meant "Fly Naked" in Spanish! (The word *cuero* does mean "leather," but in the phrase *vuela en cuero*, it hints at nakedness.)

The Least You Need to Know

♦ The United States is the number-one trading partner for Latin America.

♦ Business culture in Spain and Latin America is very different from that of the United States—negotiations and discussions about money are often put off until the end of your visit.

♦ Courteous expressions, in addition to the basic *Gracias* and *De nada*, can open doors for you and are a must when doing business.

♦ If you're writing for the Spanish-speaking market, have all translations done (or reviewed) by a professional translator, or suffer the consequences.

Chapter **24**

La Tecnología

In This Chapter

◆ *Lectura:* ¿Qué es un módem?

◆ *Gramática:* possessives revisited

◆ *Lecturita:* 404 No encontrado

◆ Palabras para ti

◆ More idioms

For many of us, computers have become an integral part of our daily lives. In fact, I am writing these words on my home computer right now—can't imagine using anything else.

La Tecnología y el Mundo Latino

While it is certainly true that much of the Spanish-speaking world remains underdeveloped, the number of Spanish-speakers who are online or who use computers on a daily basis is growing steadily every year. Even in some of the most remote areas, computer technology is rapidly integrating itself into everyday life. As international trade and communication continue to expand, a strong knowledge of computers and computer terminology will become increasingly important. So I thought that this would be a good time to introduce you to some Spanish technospeak.

Lectura: ¿Qué Hace el Módem?

There are three words for computer in Spanish. In Latin America, both *computadora* and *computador* are used, although the feminine *computadora* seems slightly more popular. In Spain, people say *ordenador*. If you read a text about computers and see the word *ordenador* used throughout, you can be sure that the material was intended for the Spanish market.

Be aware that the computer terminology in your bilingual dictionary may be unreliable. Part of the problem is that computer terms change so often that it's almost impossible for the lexicographers to keep up with it all. For more accurate terminology, search for *glosarios de términos de la informática* on the Internet.

Here is a short *lectura* that discusses how a modem works. The passage will expose you to the kind of language you'll be faced with if you ever need to read a computer-related text in Spanish:

La computadora (computador, ordenador) consiste en un aparato digital que funciona al encender y apagar interruptores electrónicos. Las líneas telefónicas, de lo contrario, son dispositivos análogos que envían señales en forma de un corriente continuo. Como consecuencia de ello, se necesita un módem para unir el espacio entre estos dos tipos de dispositivos. El módem envía los datos digitales de la computadora a través de líneas telefónicas análogas. Puede lograr esto modulando los datos digitales para convertirlos en una señal análoga; es decir, el módem varía la frecuencia de la señal digital para formar una señal análoga continua. Y cuando el módem recibe señales análogas a través de la línea telefónica, hace el opuesto: demodula, o quita las frecuencias variadas de la onda análoga para convertirlas en impulsos digitales. De estas dos funciones, modulación y demodulación, surgió el nombre del módem.

En la mayoría de los casos, su computadora viene con alguna clase de software de comunicaciones y un gran número de programas fabricados por terceros que están disponibles para uso con el módem. Debido a que el módem solamente funciona en versiones, debería asegurarse de comprar programas de software de comunicaciones que son compatibles con las versiones de sus aplicaciones y con el sistema operativo.

Vocabulario Útil:

consistir	to consist	*interruptor*	switch
aparato	machine; device	*de lo contrario*	"on the other hand"
encender	to turn on	*dispositivo*	device
apagar	to turn off	*análogo*	analog

señal signal

corriente current

continuo continuous

consecuencia result; consequence

ello that; all of that

unir to unite; to link

a través de across

lograr to achieve

modular to modulate

es decir "that is to say ..."

variar to vary; to fluctuate

frecuencia frequency

recibir to receive

el opuesto the opposite

onda wave

impulso impulse

mayoría majority

alguna clase some kind

software de comunicaciones communication software

terceros third parties

debido a due to

asegurarse to make sure

sistema operativo operating system

You will find that Spanish has adopted many English words directly into its computer vocabulary: *el software*, *el hardware*, *el mouse*, *el monitor*, and *el módem*. This has been partly due to the fact that until relatively recently, most technical manuals, as well as the computer applications themselves, were written only in English. So all the Spanish-speaking computer programmers had to learn the English words. Also, because there are so many Spanish-speaking countries, the adoption of the English terms has allowed for greater uniformity in the use of these terms from place to place.

Análisis del Texto

Now let's take a look at a few selected parts of the *lectura:*

al encender y apagar You've seen the *al* plus infinitive before. It means "upon" or "when you do X."

de lo contrario This translates as "on the other hand," even though one might argue that "on the contrary" would be closer to the Spanish. Often, "on the other hand" is *por otro lado* in Spanish. But sometimes you have to read between the lines. *De lo contrario* can also mean "if not," as in: *Creo que el técnico va a poder reparar el problema. De lo contrario, voy a tener que comprar un nuevo módem.* ("I think that the technician is going to be able to fix the problem. If not, I'm going to have to buy a new modem.")

como consecuencia Here, *como* means "as," not "how." That's why there's no *tilde.* You knew that already, right?

Algo Nuevo

You know that the verb *buscar* means "to look for," or "to search." *Buscar* also has a few secondary meanings. In some contexts, it means "to try to achieve," as in: *un programa que busca mayor inversión en el sector público* ("a program that aims to achieve a greater investment in the public sector"). *Buscar* can also mean "to get or pick up," as in *Te voy a buscar en el aeropuerto* ("I'm going to pick you up at the airport"). A *búsqueda* is "a search" of any kind, including on a computer.

---

líneas telefónicas análogas   This means "analog telephone lines." So why couldn't this have been *líneas análogas telefónicas*? Well, that also would have been a possibility. However, putting the word *telefónicas* at the end would have changed things a bit. In Spanish, the last word in a series of adjectives has the most impact. If I say *líneas análogas telefónicas*, I would be setting up a comparison between the analog phone lines and the analog "something else" lines. But with *análogas* coming last, the emphasis is on the fact that the telephone lines are analog, not that the analog lines are telephone lines.

puede lograr esto modulando   Just a reminder that the present participle form of *modular* (*modulando*) needs to be translated here as "by modulating."

en la mayoría de casos   Yes, this means "in the majority of cases," but you could probably be a bit more loose with the translation and just say "Most of the time ...."

Algo Nuevo

To make *tildes* on an IBM-compatible PC running a Windows operating system, hold down the Ctrl key, hit the apostrophe ' (part of the " key), and then release. Now type the letter (*a, e, i, o, u*) on which you want the *tilde* to appear. You can also insert any of these from the symbol list in MS Word, but it takes a long time. For Macintosh computers, hold down the Option key, hit the letter *e*, and release. Now type the letter (*a, e, i, o, u*) on which you want the *tilde* to appear.

Gramática: Possessives—I Got Mine, You Got Yours

You've probably already learned most of these. But as I always say, a little review won't kill you. The possessives are pretty easy. Just remember that when more than one thing is being "possessed," an *–s* must be added for the plural.

The pronoun *ello* is a little-used, but very handy, way to say "all of that." When you are discussing a variety of points and wish to group them together as a whole, you can use *ello*. So if I'm talking about my life story—my childhood, my adolescence, my first computer, and so on—I can wrap all that history together with *ello: A pesar de ello, he podido mantener una perspectiva muy optimista* means "In spite of all of that (my entire life's experience), I have still been able to maintain a positive perspective."

Note also that these do not have *tildes* on them. This is important because *tú* means "you," while *tu* means "your." In the *nosotros* and *vosotros* form, you must match the gender and number to those of the noun:

Possessives, Singular and Plural

Singular	Plural	Definition
mi	*mis*	my
tu	*tus*	your
su	*sus*	his/her/your/its
nuestro	*nuestros*	our (masculine nouns)
nuestra	*nuestras*	our (feminine nouns)
vuestro	*vuestros*	you all's (masculine nouns)
vuestra	*vuestras*	you all's (feminine nouns)
su	*sus*	their (you all's)

Ten Cuidado

Be careful not to overdo it with possessives when talking about the things that belong to you. It is quite common, and indeed preferable, to use the definite articles (*el, la, los, las*) rather than the possessives in many cases. Don't talk about everything as *"mi carro, mi perro, mi casa, mi comida, mi ropa"*—you'll give the impression that you're *egoísta* (selfish). When ownership is obvious or implied, the article works just fine.

Here are a few examples of possessives:

Él es mi papá, y ella es mi mamá.
He is my dad, and she is my mom.

Nuestra computadora es nueva, pero nuestro software es viejo.
Our computer is new, but our software is old.

Mi casa es su casa.
My house is your house.

Su red está sobrecargada.
Your (his/her) network is overloaded.

Vuestros monitores son muy antiguos.
Your monitors are very out-of-date.

In addition to these possessives, there is a second set of possessives called possessive adjectives. In English, we also make this distinction when we say "my car" and "the car is mine." These work the same as other adjectives:

Possessive Adjectives, Plural and Singular

Singular	Plural	Definition
mío/mía	*míos/mías*	mine
tuyo/tuya	*tuyos/tuyas*	your
suyo/suya	*suyos/suyas*	his, hers, your
nuestro/nuestra	*nustros/nuestras*	our
vuestro/vuestra	*vuestros/vuestras*	you all's (familiar)
suyo/suya	*suyos/suyas*	their; you all's

Acuérdate

Some English-speakers have trouble remembering that the possessive adjectives match the gender of the object owned, not the gender of the person speaking. So there's no need to feel uncomfortable saying *la casa es mía* if you're a man, or *el coche es mío* if you're a woman. Possessive adjectives have nothing to do with *your* gender, just the gender of your possessions.

Here are a few more examples:

Todos los archivos de la carpeta tuya se han borrado.
All the files in your folder have been erased.

Este disquete es mío, pero el otro es de Oscar.
This floppy disk is mine, but the other one is Oscar's.

Oye, ¿son tuyos estos documentos?
"Hey, are these documents yours?"

Su disco duro puede archivar más datos que el nuestro.
His (her) hard drive can store more data than ours.

Lecturita: 404 No Encontrado

If you're trying to log on to a Spanish website
and are having trouble, you may come across
the following message. I thought I'd give you
the translation just in case:

El servidor Web no puede encontrar el archivo
o la secuencia de comandos que ha solicitado.
Compruebe la dirección URL para asegurarse
de que la ruta de acceso es correcta. Póngase en
contacto con el administrador del servidor si el
problema persiste.

> **Cultura Latina**
>
> Internet use among Latin Ameri-
> cans as a whole has increased
> substantially over recent years and
> is expected to reach 80 million
> in 2008. In Spain, the number is
> expected to reach 16 million.

Translation:

"The web server cannot find the file or script you asked for. Please check the URL
to ensure that the path is correct. Contact the server's administrator if this problem
persists."

Palabras Para Ti

The following list introduces you to some basic computer terminology in Spanish. In
some cases, you may find that the English word is more common than the Spanish
word—even in Spain. Still, it never hurts to know the terms in both languages:

bandwidth   *ancho de banda*

bookmark   *marca*

button   *botón*

browser   *navegador*

CD (compact disc)   *disco compacto*

chat   *charla*

to click on (something with your
mouse)   *hacer clic en*

to delete   *borrar*

DNS (Domain Name System)   *Sistema
de nombres de dominio*

DOS (disk operating system)   *sistema
operativo de disco*

file   *archivo*

frame   *estructura*

gateway   *puerta de acceso*

GIF (Graphics Interchange Format)
Formato gráfico de intercambio

GUI (graphic user interface) *Interfaz gráfico de usuario*

hard drive *disco duro*

home page *página principal o inicial de un sitio Web*

host *host; anfitrión*

HTML (Hypertext Markup Language) *Lenguaje de marcas de hipertexto*

HTTP (Hypertext Transfer Protocol) *Protocolo de tranferencia hipertexto*

key *tecla*

keyboard *teclado*

LAN (local area network) *Red de area local*

link *enlace*

monitor *monitor*

mouse *el mouse; ratón*

motherboard *placa matriz; el motherboard*

printer *impresora*

to push (a button) *oprimir; presionar; aplastar*

RAM (random access memory) *Memoria de acceso aleatorio*

ROM (read only memory) *Memoria solo de lectura*

to run a program *ejecutar*

to save *guardar; archivar*

scanner *escáner*

SPAM *"Bombardeo" con correo electrónico*

URL (uniform resource locator) *Localizador uniforme de recursos*

WAN (wide area network) *Red de area amplia*

wireless network *red inalámbrica*

Idiot's Guide to Idioms

Now that you'll be able to say "There's more than one way to skin a cat" in Spanish, I'm sure your life will be complete. Notice that the word *gato* does not appear in the Spanish version (*pulga* means "a flea"):

boca abajo face down

boca arriba face up

borrón y cuenta nueva to turn over a new leaf/wipe the slate clean

buscar una aguja en un pajar to look for a needle in a haystack

Cada quien tiene su manera de matar pulgas. There's more than one way to skin a cat.

caminar con pies de plomo to go with caution

caer bien (*me cae bien*)   to like (a person)

caer mal   to dislike (a person)

Caras vemos, corazones no sabemos.   You can't judge a book by its cover.

cerrar los ojos a la realidad   to bury one's head in the sand

criar cuervos, que te sacarán los ojos   to bite the hand that feeds you

dar en el clavo   to hit the nail on the head

De eso ni hablar.   That's out of the question.

dejar mucho que desear   to leave much to be desired

El Web

For more info on Spanish computer terms, visit www.css.qmul.ac.uk/foreign/ eng-spanish.htm or http://spanish.about.com/od/technologoydictionaries.

Risa del Día

Throughout history, people have always needed somebody else to tease or make jokes about. In *el Cono Sur*, *argentinos* and *uruguayos* love to pick on Spaniards, whom they call collectively (and sometimes lovingly) *gallegos*, which means "Galicians" (even though all Spaniards obviously do not come from Galicia). Elsewhere, Peruvians and Ecuadorians trade insults, as do Mexicans and Guatemalans, Colombians and Venezuelans, Costa Ricans and Nicaraguans, and so on. Other countries pick on *argentinos*, *cubanos*, *gringos*, or just about any nationality they can think of.

This situation may be unfortunate, but at least between Latinos these jokes are usually made in good fun. Everyone seems to get their revenge sooner or later by hurling the same jokes back at the people who first told them. Still, it is true that the idea of "political correctness" has yet to take hold in most sectors of the Spanish-speaking world.

In an effort to be "PC" (that's politically correct, not "personal computer"), I'm going to insert my Spanish name, *Esteban*, where you would normally see *argentinos*, *gallegos*, *gringos*, and so on. You can insert whomever you want; the jokes remain the same.

Acuérdate

For ¡ and ¿, use the following combinations if you're working on an IBM-compatible PC: Ctrl + Alt + Shift + ! = ¡; Ctrl + Alt + Shift + ? = ¿. Mac users: Option + 1 = ¡; Option + Shift + ? = ¿.

1. *¿Cómo se sabe si Esteban acaba de usar una computadora?*
   Si el monitor está lleno de liquid paper.

2. *Esteban pide una pizza a domicilio y le preguntan:*
   —¿En cuantos pedazos quiere que la cortemos?
   ¿6 ó 12?
   Hombre, pues 6 nada más, yo no como tantos.

3. *¿Por qué hay hielo sobre un televisor? … porque Esteban intentó congelar la imagen.*

The following joke had to stay in the original. No offense meant to any Spaniards out there ….

4. *Un avión de Iberia llegando a Ezeiza:*
   Aquí torre de control torre de control … ¿cuál es su posición?
   Pues, aquí estamos con José sentados delante de los relojitos.

So, to be fair …

5. *¿Para qué los argentinos le ponen azúcar a la almohada?*
   … para tener dulces sueños.

Vocabulario Útil:

a domicilio for home delivery	*Iberia* Spanish national airline
pedazo piece	*Ezeiza* main airport in Buenos Aires
congelar la imagen to freeze the image	*dulces sueños* sweet dreams

The Least You Need to Know

- It is useful to be familiar with computer terminology in Spanish.

- Many English words have been adopted into Spanish, but it's always best to know both the Spanish and English terms.

- Possessives such as *mi, tu,* and *su* are invariable with respect to gender, but *nuestro, vuestro, mío, tuyo,* and *suyo* must match the gender of the noun possessed. All possessives must match for singular or plural.

- Don't overuse the possessives *mi* and *mis;* it sounds odd in Spanish. Use the definite articles when ownership is obvious.

Chapter 25

La Política

In This Chapter

- ◆ *Lectura:* La Constitución de la República de Cuba
- ◆ *Gramática:* homonyms
- ◆ More idioms

It's no wonder that the Spanish-speaking world has long been a hotbed of political activity. Both Spain and Latin America have been plagued by civil wars, revolutions, counterinsurgencies, military dictatorships, foreign invasions, corruption, debt, hyper-inflation—the list goes on. The last 50 years have been especially tumultuous politically for nearly every Spanish-speaking country.

Pero Las Cosas Han Mejorado

In spite of its political troubles, things have begun to look up in recent years for *el mundo hispanohablante*. Francisco Franco's nearly 40 years as Spain's *generalísimo* ended with his death in 1975. Since then, Spain's constitutional monarchy has made great strides toward democratic reform. In 1996, control of the Spanish Parliament changed hands peacefully in a free and open election when Felipe González and his *Partido Socialista Obrero Español*, or PSOE (Spanish Socialist Workers' Party), lost to José María

Aznar and the *Partido Popular*. Since then, the political situation in Spain has continued to remain relatively stable.

Many of the political instabilities that Latin America faced during the 1980s and 1990s have also turned around, to some degree. In the wake of peace accords and free elections, Central America has finally put an end to most guerilla activity and right-wing counterinsurgencies. The countries of *el Cono Sur* have returned to democracy after decades of military dictatorships. Mexico's ruling party, the PRI, finally lost its nearly 80-year hold on power in the 2000 elections, and opposition parties such as the PAN (National Action Party) and PDR (Democratic Revolutionary Party) are becoming stronger at all levels. Even Cuba, which has long been politically and economically isolated from much of the West, has opened its doors to limited foreign investments and free enterprise.

Nevertheless, the Spanish-speaking world still has numerous obstacles to overcome in the political arena, and politics undoubtedly will continue to be an element in the lives of Spaniards and Latin Americans for many years to come.

Lectura: La Constitución de la República de Cuba

The following *lectura* is from the preamble to Cuba's constitution. Of course, you are free to agree or disagree with what it says. The text was not chosen for political reasons, but rather because it seemed perfect for this topic—it is filled with political rhetoric and challenging vocabulary.

Preámbulo:

Nosotros, Ciudadanos Cubanos;

Acuérdate

The word for "patriot" is *patriota*. There is no change to *patrioto*. You must say *un patriota*, or *una patriota*. The word also can be used as an adjective, where again there is no change. Of course, you will have to add *–s* whenever you're talking about more than one.

herederos y continuadores del trabajo creador y de las tradiciones de combatividad, firmeza, heroísmo y sacrificio forjadas por nuestros antecesores; por los aborígenes que prefirieron muchas veces el exterminio a la sumisión; por los esclavos que se rebelaron contra sus amos; por los que despertaron la conciencia nacional y el ansia cubana de patria y libertad; por los patriotas que en 1868 iniciaron las guerras de independencia contra el colonialismo español y los que en el último impulso de 1895 las llevaron a la victoria de 1898, que les fue arrebatada por la intervención y ocupación militar del imperialismo yanqui;

por los obreros, campesinos, estudiantes e intelectuales que lucharon durante más de cincuenta años contra el dominio imperialista, la corrupción política, la falta de derechos y libertades populares, el desempleo y la explotación impuesta por capitalistas y terratenientes;

por lo que promovieron e integraron y desarrollaron las primeras organizaciones de obreros y de campesinos, difundieron las ideas socialistas y fundaron los primeros movimientos marxista y marxista-leninista; por los integrantes de la vanguardia de la generación del centenario del natalicio de Martí, que nutridos por su magisterio nos condujeron a la victoria revolucionaria popular de Enero; por los que, con el sacrificio de sus vidas, defendieron la Revolución contribuyendo a su definitiva consolidación; por los que masivamente cumplieron heroicas misiones internacionalistas;

Guiados

por el ideario de José Martí y las ideas politico-sociales de Marx, Éngels y Lenin;

Apoyados

en el internacionalismo proletario, en la amistad fraternal, la ayuda, la cooperación y la solidaridad de los pueblos del mundo, especialmente los de América Latina y del Caribe;

> ### Cultura Latina
>
> José Julián Martí (1853–1895) was a Cuban writer and patriot whose poetry, political prose, and eventual death in battle made him the martyred symbol of Cuban aspirations of independence.

Decididos

a llevar adelante la Revolución triunfadora del Moncada y del Granma, de la Sierra y de Girón encabezada por Fidel Castro que, sustentada en la más estrecha unidad de todas las fuerzas revolucionarias y del pueblo, conquistó la plena independencia nacional, estableció el poder revolucionario, realizé las transformaciones democráticas, inició la construcción del socialismo y, con el Partido Comunista al frente, la continúa con el objetivo final de edificar la sociedad comunista;

Conscientes

de que todos los regímenes sustentados en la explotación del hombre por el hombre determinan la humillación de los explotados y la degradación de la condición humana de los explotadores; de que sólo en el socialismo y el comunismo, cuando el hombre ha sido liberado de todas las formas de explotación: de la esclavitud, de la servidumbre y del capitalismo, se alcanza la entera dignidad del ser humano;

y de que nuestra Revolución elevó la dignidad de la patria y del cubano a superior altura;

Ten Cuidado

The word *regímen* is an unreliable cognate in English. *Regímen* is a cognate of "regime," which in English usually means "an oppressive government." In Spanish, it just means "government or administration" and isn't necessarily a negative word. Interestingly, when talking about food, *un regímen* can mean "a diet," as in "to go on a diet to lose weight."

Declaramos

Nuestra voluntad de que la ley de leyes de la República esté presidida por este profundo anhelo, al fin logrado, de José Martí:

"Yo quiero que la ley primera de nuestra República sea el culto de los cubanos a la dignidad plena del hombre."

Vocabulario Útil:

Here are some vocabulary words to help you with this *lectura:*

preámbulo preamble

ciudadano citizen

heredero heir

continuador person who continues

creador creative

combatividad fighting spirit

firmeza firmness

heroísmo heroism

sacrificio sacrifice

forjar to forge; to shape

antecesor forefather; ancestor (formal)

aborígenes native peoples

exterminio extermination

sumisión submission

esclavo slave

rebelarse to rebel

ansia longing; wish (formal)

arrebatar to steal; to rob

imperialismo imperialism

yanqui Yankee; of the United States

obrero worker

luchar to fight

dominio dominion

definitivo final; definitive

popular popular; of the people

explotación exploitation

terrateniente landholder

promover to promote

difundir to broadcast; to publish

fundar to found

integrante   someone who belongs to a group; member

centenario   hundred-year anniversary

natalicio   birth (formal)

nutrir   to nurture

magisterio   teaching

masivamente   en masse

ideario   ideas; ideology

guiar   to guide

apoyar   to support

internacionalismo   internationalism

llevar adelante   to promote; to bring forward

triunfador   triumphant

encabezado por   led by

sustentar   to sustain; to hold

estrecho   close; narrow

pueblo   here, "the people"

al frente   to the foreground; in the lead

objetivo   goal; objective

edificar   to edify; to construct

regímenes   governments; regimes

liberar   to free; to liberate

servidumbre   servitude

alcanzar   to reach

entero   entire; whole

ser humano   human being

voluntad   will

presidido por   to be presided over by

anhelo   wish; desire; hope

culto   reverence; worship

plena   open; full

Análisis del Texto

Now let's take a closer look at a few excerpts from the *lectura*:

Nosotros, Ciudadanos Cubanos   There really isn't any better translation for this than "We, the Citizens of Cuba."

Acuérdate

Remember that words such as *creador*, *hablador*, and *trabajador* can usually be used as both nouns and adjectives: *Los trabajadores son muy creadores y habladores* means "The workers are very creative and talkative"; *Los habladores son muy trabajadores* means "The talkative people are very hard workers."

tradiciones de combatividad, firmeza, heroísmo y sacrificio forjadas por nuestros antecesores
Notice that the *forjadas* refers to *tradiciones*. With all these extra words in the sentence,

it's easy to get confused. Remember, the gender and number of *forjadas* links it back to the feminine plural of *tradiciones*.

prefirieron muchas veces el exterminio a la sumisión   If you prefer one thing over another in Spanish, it's *preferir + a*, as in: *Prefiero la democracia al totalitarismo* ("I prefer democracy over (to) totalitarianism").

por los que despertaron la conciencia nacional   The *los que* translates as "those who."

que lucharon durante más de cincuenta años contra   If you are fighting against something, it's *luchar contra*, as in: *Luchó contra la pobreza de su país* ("She fought against the poverty in her country"). Remember that while the word *durante* does mean "during," with time expressions, as in the previous phrase, it usually means "for."

por lo que promovieron e integraron y desarrollaron las primeras organizaciones de obreros y de campesinos   Notice here how the subject comes after the conjugated verb. The subject here is actually *las primeras organizaciones* Because Spanish verbs are linked to their subject by conjugation, placement of the subject may be at the end of the sentence, unlike in English, where the subject nearly always comes before the verb. Don't let this throw you off.

You can also see that in Spanish, you can say "promoted and integrated and developed," where in English, we would prefer to avoid too many "ands" and just say "promoted, integrated, and developed." Also, in a similar way, the second half "… of workers and of peasants" is worth mentioning. We English-speakers would prefer not to repeat the second "of," but in Spanish, it is acceptable to say *de esto y de eso y del otro*.

por los integrantes de la vanguardia de la generación del centenario del natalicio de Martí, que nutridos por su magisterio nos condujeron a la victoria revolucionaria popular de Enero   Here again we have a situation where the gender and number of the adjective links it back to something far away. The word *nutridos*, which means "nurtured," modifies *integrantes*, which means "members." How do I know this? Because *nutridos* is in the masculine plural form, and the only other masculine plural noun it could possibly modify is *integrantes*. Yes, gender and number continue to be our friends.

Castro marched into Havana in January 1959, and this event is often called "the January Revolution." Translated, the sentence would read: "… by the members of the vanguard of the one hundredth anniversary of the birth of Martí, who, nurtured by his teachings, brought us to the popular January Revolution."

Decididos a llevar adelante la Revolución triunfadora del Moncada y del Granma, de la Sierra y de Girón encabezada por Fidel Castro   Time for a quick history lesson ….

On July 26, 1953, the Moncada army barracks in Santiago de Cuba were attacked by a revolutionary force led by Castro. The engagement, though unsuccessful, marked the beginning of the Cuban Revolution. Castro's forces became known as the 26th of July Movement. Castro was captured and sentenced to prison; he ultimately fled to Mexico.

Ten Cuidado

Both *más que* and *más de* are possible in Spanish, but there is a difference between the two, so be careful. *Más de* means "more than something countable," as in *No puedo comprar más de tres* ("I can't buy more than three"). *Más que* means "more than" with uncountable nouns or between two dependent clauses, as in *Yo no peso más que Juan* ("I don't weigh more than Juan does").

Granma, believe it or not, actually comes from the English word "Grandma" (yes, "grandmother") and refers to an old boat that brought Castro back to Cuba in 1956. Today, it is the name of the country's official Communist Party newspaper. The *Sierra* refers to *la Sierra Maestra*, the mountains from which Castro organized and launched many of his revolutionary activities. *Girón* refers to *Playa Girón*, the beach that was the scene of the failed CIA-backed Bay of Pigs invasion of 1961.

Translated, this section would read: "Determined to bring forth the triumphant Revolution of the Moncada, the Granma, of the Sierra (Maestra), and of Girón (Bay of Pigs), led by Fidel Castro …."

la continúa con el objetivo final de edificar Make sure you don't read the *la* as definite article "the." That would really throw you off. The *la* is acting as a pronoun and refers back to *la construcción del socialismo* (see the sixth paragraph in the *lectura*).

sustentados en la explotación del hombre The *en* here should be translated as "by," rather than "on" or "in." So this would read "sus-

Acuérdate

The definite article is required with most abstract nouns or when you are speaking in general about a specific subject. So *la libertad* means "liberty" even though we would never say "the liberty" in English.

tained by the exploitation of men." Remember that *el hombre* here means "men and women in general," not "the man." It may not be politically correct, but Spanish rarely is when it comes to gender.

Yo quiero que la ley primera de nuestra República sea Just a reminder: the *sea* must be in the subjunctive because it is preceded by the *Yo quiero*.

Gramática: Sorting Out Those Homonyms

You were already introduced to a few homonyms (words that are pronounced the same but are written differently) when we discussed *tildes* and the monosyllabic pronouns versus possessives way back in the beginning of this book. Now we'll take a look at a few more homonyms in Spanish and see how the slight variation in spelling can make a big difference in what words mean. Some of the words in the following list are "true homonyms" in that they would be pronounced exactly the same by everyone and in all cases. Others are only homonyms in Latin America. You'll also see that the *tilde* (or lack thereof) can make a big difference.

The following list is not complete (that would require an entire book all to itself) but will nonetheless give you an idea of the kinds of spelling variations that you may come across, and highlight the types of spelling errors you should do your best to avoid:

Monosyllabic homonyms (or near homonyms):

a   (preposition)/*ha*   (from *haber*)

as   ace (in cards)/*has*   (from *haber*)

¡Ay!   (an exclamation)/*hay*   there is/are

¡Eh!   (an exclamation)/*he*   (from *haber*)

oí   I heard/*hoy*   today

ahí   there/*hay*   there is/are

Two-syllable homonyms (or near homonyms):

aré   (from *arar*) I plowed/*haré*   I will do

arte   art/*harté*   I got fed up with

asar   to cook; to broil/*azar*   chance

baso   (from *basar*) I base/*vaso*   a drinking glass

bello   beautiful/*vello*   body hair

bienes   goods/*vienes*   (from *venir*) you come

botar   to throw away/*votar*   to vote

basar   to base/*bazar*   market

barón   baron or nobleman/*varón*   male

basto   ordinary/*vasto*   vast; extensive

casar   to marry/*cazar*   to hunt

echo   (from *echar*) to toss/*hecho*   (from *hacer*) done

calló   he/she/it fell silent/*cayó*   he/she/it fell down/*callo*   a callus on the skin

errar   to miss (not hit)/*herrar*   to shoe a horse

Three-syllable homonyms (or near homonyms):

avía   (from *aviar*) to prepare/*había*   (from *haber*)

ávido   eager/*habido*   (from *haber*)

ablando, ablandar   to soften/*hablando*   talking

abría   (from *abrir*)/*habría*   (from *haber*)

alado   winged/*halado*   (from *halar*) to haul

aprender   to learn/*aprehender*   to apprehend

arroyo   small river/*arrollo*   (from *arrollar*) to roll up

bacilo   a microorganism/*vacilo*   (from *vacilar*) I vacillate

bestia   beast/*vestía*   (from *vestir*) to dress

Idiot's Guide to Idioms

Here are some more idioms and expressions to add to your collection:

El que no se tira al agua no pasa el río.   Nothing ventured, nothing gained.

en bandeja   on a silver platter

en menos de lo que canta un gallo   faster than a speeding bullet

en resumidas palabras   in short

entre la espada y la pared   between a rock and a hard place

en un abrir y cerrar de ojos   in the blink of an eye

Eso es harina de otro costal.   That's a horse of a different color.

estar al margen   to be out of the loop

estar echando chispas   to be hopping mad

estar hasta la coronilla   to be fed up

Hay gato encerrado.   I smell a rat.

Genio y figura hasta la sepultura.   Old habits die hard.

Hablando de la caída de Roma.   Speak of the devil.

Hombre prevenido vale por dos.   Forewarned is forearmed.

Ir al grano   to come to the point

largarle a otro el mochuelo   to pass the buck

llover a cántaros   to rain cats and dogs

llovido del cielo   a godsend

más pobre que una rata   poor as a church mouse

Más vale un pájaro en la mano que cien volando.   A bird in the hand is worth two in the bush.

Más vale prevenir que lamentar.   Better safe than sorry.

matar la gallina de los huevos de oro   to kill the goose that lays the golden egg

meter planca   to pull strings (to have influence)

Algo Nuevo

In Spanish, both *conservador* ("conservative") and *liberal* exist in a political context. But believe it or not, these words are actually unreliable cognates. With respect to the economy, *conservador* in Spanish implies that the government would "conserve" its control over the economy, which is different from the "small government, free market, and local control." Conversely, a *liberal* government in Spanish implies that the government would maintain a hands-off approach to the economy, allowing for less government control, lower taxes, and more free enterprise.

El Web

For an up-to-date look at the political situations of Spain and several Latin American countries, visit the official website of the United Nations at www.un.org. Both English and Spanish languages are available.

Risa del Día

It's no wonder that with all the political instability the Spanish-speaking world has had to endure, politicians are not always held in the highest regard. As you might imagine, much of the humor surrounding politics and politicians is far too *verde* to tell here. These two jokes are a bit watered down.

By the way, in the second joke, *Pepito* is the same personage as the *Jaimito* you met in previous jokes.

1. *Escuela para políticos:*

   Desde afuera de la escuela para políticos se escuchaba:

   ¡Corrupto! … ¡Incapaz! … ¡Coimero! … ¡Ladrón!

   Y un hombre le dijo a otro:

   Caramba, ¿a quien insultan tanto?

   No son insultos, sólo están pasando lista.

2. *Gatos revolucionarios:*

   Una maestra cubana dice a los niños que hagan una composición con un tema de la revolución y al terminar manda a Pepito a que lea la suya:

   Yo tengo una gata que ayer tuvo cinco gaticos y todos los gaticos son revolucionarios.

   La maestra, al ver que Pepito sabía que hasta los gaticos deben ser revolucionarios, propone al director de la escuela que llame al inspector para que oiga la composición. Pasados tres días llega el inspector a la escuela y la maestra muy diligente le pide a Pepito que lea su composición y Pepito lee:

   Yo tengo una gata que hace cinco días tuvo cinco gaticos y tres son revolucionarios.

   Al oír esto, la maestra reacciona rápidamente y le dice:

   Pepito, la primera vez que leíste tu composición dijiste que todos los gaticos eran revolucionarios, ¿qué pasó?

   Bueno maestra, es que dos ya abrieron los ojos.

Vocabulario Útil:

corrupto	corrupt	*coimero*	someone who accepts bribes
incapaz	incapable	*ladrón*	thief

caramba "my goodness"

insultar to insult

insulto insult

pasar lista to take roll call

tema topic; issue; theme

mandar to order; to have someone do something

la suya his

gatico kitten (*gatito* also possible)

proponer to propose; to suggest

pasados here, "after"

diligente diligent

hace cinco días five days ago

reaccionar to react

abrir los ojos to open one's eyes; "to realize the truth"

Acuérdate

The word *tema* is a cognate of "theme" but can be heard in everyday conversation as meaning "issue, quaestion, subject, or topic." It can also be used as a filler to begin a statement, as in: *El tema es que el gobierno no respeta la voluntad del pueblo* ("The issue (thing, deal) is that the government doesn't respect the will of the people").

The Least You Need to Know

◆ Politics have been a hot topic in the Spanish-speaking world for a long time.

◆ There has been considerable progress in recent years toward increasing political stability in Latin America.

◆ Numerous homonyms exist in Spanish; even the smallest changes in spelling or accentuation can mean a difference in the meaning of a word.

Chapter 26

La Medicina

In This Chapter

◆ *Lectura:* Complicaciones Neuro-vasculares Periféricas en el Diabético

◆ *Gramática:* reflexive verbs

◆ Esteban's advice on cognates

◆ More Idiot's Guide to Idioms

There is currently a great demand in the United States for bilingual health-care practitioners. If you are considering a career in some aspect of medicine, you'll have little difficulty finding a job if you can speak both English and Spanish. If you are already working in medicine and don't speak Spanish, I'm glad you bought this book.

Although many of us find the jargon used by doctors to be a big headache, the good news is that much of the "doctor-ese" used by English-speaking doctors is the same in Spanish because both languages use Latin and Greek roots to form such words. Of course, while it's great to recognize that *angiopatía* means "angiopathy" in English, if you don't know what "angiopathy" means, the cognate is of little help. Sometimes you'll need to look up the meaning of a word, even if you know what the equivalent is in English.

Lectura: Complicaciones Neuro-vasculares Periféricas en el Diabético

The following medical text is not too bad. If it causes you any discomfort, take two *aspirinas y llámame en la mañana:*

Actualmente es poco común que un enfermo fallezca de coma o cetoacidosis diabética. No obstante, en un 70 por ciento de los casos existen serias complicaciones vasculares. Las alteraciones vasculares que dan origen al pie diabético están presentes en mayor o menor grado en el 80 por ciento de los diabéticos que tienen más de 10 años de evolución. Es digno de recordarse que en 1934 se afirmó en forma contundente y clara: Las complicaciones más graves en el pie se pueden evitar siguiendo unas cuantas reglas básicas en la educación del paciente.

Una de cada cinco internaciones hospitalarias de diabéticos es por lesiones en el pie. El riesgo de amputación es 15 veces mayor que en pacientes no diabéticos y ocupa 50 a 70 por ciento de las amputaciones no traumáticas que se efectúan en hospitales generales. De aquí que, el explorar en forma rutinaria el pie del diabético cada vez que asiste a consulta para el control metabólico, constituye el método ideal de prevención al permitir la detección de las lesiones en forma temprana.

Las dos lesiones básicas que se presentan en alguna etapa de la evolución de la diabetes son la neuropatía y la angiopatía. Pueden encontrarse aisladas aunque lo más común es que se asocien, y que médica y clínicamente se vea que predomina alguna de las dos. La neuropatía produce una pérdida de sensibilidad y una pérdida del sentido de posición del pie. La neuropatía motora afecta a todos los músculos del pie y en ocasiones provoca deformaciones características; la neuropatía de los nervios vaso-motores da falsamente un pie caliente a pesar de existir un riego sanguíneo defectuoso.

Las infecciones son muchas veces no detectables hasta que la extremidad, e incluso la vida estén amenazadas. El paciente diabético no suele percibir la progresión de la úlcera y los signos y síntomas de la infección no se manifiestan hasta más tarde.

Vocabulario Útil:

periférico	peripheral	*un coma*	a coma
actualmente	currently; these days	*diabético*	diabetic (adjective and noun)
enfermo	here, "a person who is ill"	*no obstante*	nonetheless
fallecer	to pass away; die (kinder than *morir*)	*alteración*	change; alteration
		dar origen	to originate

mayor o menor   more or less; about

digno   worthy

afirmarse   to affirm; to maintain

contundente   conclusively; convincingly

regla   rule

educación   instruction

internación   admission (to a medical facility)

hospitalario   hospital (adjective)

lesión   injury; wound

riesgo   risk

ocupar   to occupy

no traumático   nontraumatic

efectuarse   to be performed

de aquí que   thus

el explorar   exploring

rutinario   routine

asistir   to attend; to go to

consulta   consultation

metabólico   metabolic

detección   detection

etapa   stage

neuropatía   neuropathy

angiopatía   angiopathy

aislado   isolated

asociarse   here, "to be found together"

predominar   to predominate

pérdida   loss

sensibilidad   sensitivity

sentido   feeling

motor   motor (adjective)

en ocasiones   sometimes; occasionally

riego   here, "supply"

sanguíneo   blood (adjective)

defectuoso   defective

manifiestar   to show; to manifest

Acuérdate

The verb *soler* (*suelo, sueles,* and so on) plus an infinitive means "to usually …": *Suele tener muchos problemas médicos* means "He usually has a lot of medical problems." In certain countries, *soler* is not used a lot in daily speech. The verb *acostumbrar* and verbal phrases such as *tener la costumbre de* tend to be more common, especially in Mexico.

Análisis del Texto

Time to perform a physical exam on our little *lectura:*

es poco común que un enfermo fallezca   *Fallezca* is the subjunctive of *fallecer.* Even though it is not common for people to die from this condition, it is still possible and could happen from time to time. The uncertainty and possibility of the statement will require *fallezca* instead of *fallece*.

10 años de evolución   I might have understood this as "evolution" the first time I read it, too. Obviously, though, these patients aren't "evolving." You need to see beyond the obvious cognate here and think of alternate meanings for this word, such as "progression" or "development."

siguiendo unas cuantas reglas básicas   Here, *siguiendo* needs to be translated as "by following." Remember that *cuánto*, as an interrogative (question word), is left in the singular gender-neutral form, but must match gender and number when used adjectivally. Translation: "by following a few basic rules."

una de cada cinco internaciones hospitalarias de diabéticos   Here we have the "four out of five doctors" construction. Note that *una* is feminine because it is linked to *internaciones*. Translation: "one out of every five hospital admissions of diabetics."

Algo Nuevo

In this *lectura*, we have a fine example of "*el* + infinitive" in *el explorar en forma rutinaria*. In Spanish, it is possible to create nouns from verbs by using the masculine singular article *el* plus an infinitive verb. This is not generally the preferred construction where a more common noun exists; I wouldn't say *el trabajar* for "work" when I can simply say *trabajo*. But if I wanted to express the idea of "working with Spanish-speaking patients" as a singular idea, I could say *el trabajar con pacientes de habla hispana*.

---

a pesar de existir   The phrase *a pesar de* means "in spite of." It can be followed by *que* when there is another clause after it: *A pesar de que Juan está enfermo* translates as "In spite of the fact that Juan is ill." In cases of doubt or uncertainty, the verb will be in the subjunctive mood: *A pesar de que el médico pueda tratarlo* means "In spite of the fact that the doctor may be able to treat him." It can also be followed by an infinitive (without the *que*): *A pesar de haber intentado curarlo, el pobre falleció* would mean "In spite of having tried to cure him, the poor guy passed away."

Acuérdate

When a *–mente* adverb is followed by a second (or third) *–mente* adverb, only the last in the series actually takes the *–mente* suffix. In the *lectura*, you saw *médica y clínicamente*. This should be understood as "medically and clinically." Another example: *Te quiero profunda y eterna y cariñosamente* means "I love you deeply, eternally, and affectionately." As a noun, the word *mente* means "mind," which you'll go out of if you use this suffix too much.

e incluso   Don't forget that the word *y* becomes *e* before *i*, *y*, and *hi*. And *o* becomes *u* before *u* and *hu*.

Gramática: Reflexive Verbs

Reflexive verbs are usually covered in basic Spanish textbooks. But this chapter offers a good opportunity to review those reflexives with a new perspective.

Esteban's Guide to Reflexive Verbs

When you wash yourself, talk to yourself, or ask yourself a question, your actions are considered reflexive: "I talk to myself." In other words, when the object of a verb (in this case, "myself") is the same as the person doing the action (in this case, "I"), we have a reflexive construction. So while "The dog bit Bob" is not reflexive, "The dog bit his tail (his own tail)" is.

Many introductory textbooks make a big deal out of reflexive verbs, as if they were creatures all to their own. However, most reflexive verbs aren't "reflexive verbs" at all, but simply reflexive constructions using regular old verbs. What makes them reflexive is that the indirect object pronoun (INDOP)—or sometimes just the direct object pronoun (DOP)—and the person doing the action of the verb are one and the same. That's all there is to it.

As you know, a "reflexive verb" is written as an infinitive with *se* attached to it:

> *lavarse*   to wash oneself
>
> *preguntarse*   to ask oneself
>
> *tocarse*   to touch oneself (such as your nose)
>
> *cuidarse*   to take care of oneself
>
> *bañarse*   to bathe oneself

As a quick review, here are those reflexive pronouns again:

The Reflexive Pronouns

Pronoun	Example
me	*me lavo*
te	*te lavas*
se	*se lava*

continues

The Reflexive Pronouns (continued)

Pronoun	Example
nos	*nos lavamos*
os	*os laváis*
se	*se lavan*

Notice how the conjugations of the verb follow the changes in the pronoun. This is our big clue to reflexiveness, unlike many other DOPs and INDOPs, where the verbs don't conjugate according to the object pronoun, but according to who or what was doing the action.

Take a quick look at the following example to see what I'm talking about:

Te amo   I love you. (not reflexive)

Te aman   They love you. (not reflexive)

Te amamos   We love you. (still not reflexive)

Te amas   You love yourself. (Finally, we have a reflexive—the *te* and the *tú* are linked because they are both in the second-person singular.)

There is a construction in Spanish that looks like a reflexive but is actually an expression of mutuality ("each other"). When you see *se* followed by a plural, you may be dealing with such a construction: *Los novios se besan* means "The boyfriend and girlfriend kiss each other" (not "they kiss themselves"). When you come across one of these, pay attention to the context of the sentence. For example, *Los niños se lavan* could mean "The children are washing themselves" or "The children are washing each other."

So why is *te amas* reflexive? There is no reflexive verb jumping into the picture out of nowhere. It's the same old *amar*. But the construction is reflexive because the person doing the action (*tú*) and the object of that action (*te*) are one and the same. Yes, we could say that the reflexive verb here is *amarse*, but that doesn't matter—the construction is the important thing.

Many verbs that are reflexive in Spanish are not reflexive in English (and vice versa). However, the idea of yourself being the object is still understandable if you stretch your imagination a little:

preocuparse   to worry (oneself)

sentarse   to sit down (to sit yourself down)

preguntarse   to wonder (to ask yourself)

lastimarse   to hurt (yourself)

emborracharse   to get (yourself) drunk

encontrarse   to be (to find yourself)

There are exceptions:

enamorarse   to fall in love (not with yourself)

sentirse   to feel (not "to feel yourself," but to feel in terms of your health and/or emotional state)

irse   to leave (not "to leave yourself")

> **Acuérdate**
>
> The verb *dormir* means "to sleep," but when it's reflexive (*dormirse*) it means "to fall asleep." It's a subtle difference, as in *Siempre duermo bien, pero anoche no pude dormirme,* which means "I always sleep well, but last night I couldn't fall asleep."

You'll find that your dictionary will give you definitions for reflexive verbs, but in reality very few verbs exist *only* as reflexives. So my advice is that you not think of these verbs as "reflexive verbs" but rather as reflexive constructions using regular old verbs when the subject and object are the same.

Here are some additional examples to show you what I mean:

Me lastimé la espalda.
I hurt my back.

¿Cómo se siente?
How do you feel?

Tengo que irme.
I have to leave.

Me pregunto si eso va a ser possible.
I wonder (ask myself) if that is going to be possible.

Me duele el codo y no quiero tocármelo.
My elbow hurts and I don't want to touch it.

Mis amigos quieren que yo me emborrache, pero yo no lo voy a hacer.
My friends want me to get drunk, but I'm not going to do it.

El hombre no quiso sentarse.
The man refused to sit down.

Acuérdate _____

If you are injured or need to cry for help, yell *¡Socorro!* Yes, *ayuda* also means "help," but it isn't quite as shout-able as *socorro*: *¡Socorro! Me he caído y no puedo levantarme!* means "Help, I've fallen and I can't get up!" It is cognate with "succor." *Socorro* is also a small city in central New Mexico.

Diálogo: No Me Siento Bien

No matter how fascinating your surroundings may be, being sick is never fun. In this *diálogo*, Kathy has gotten ill during a trip to Colombia and has gone to the doctor in search of relief. She's a bit of a hypochondriac, so you'll get to hear about a lot of different illnesses, both real and imagined:

El médico: *Buenas tardes, señora.*

Kathy: *Señorita.*

El médico: *Ay perdón, señorita. ¿Cómo se siente el día de hoy?*

Kathy: *Ay, doctor, no me siento nada bien.*

El médico: *¿Qué le pasa?*

Kathy: *Bueno, cada vez que salgo para hacer algo me enfermo.*

El médico: *No me diga. A ver. ¿Cuáles son sus síntomas?*

Kathy: *Tengo hinchazón en la mano izquierda, ampollas en el pie derecho, y un sarpullido en la espalda. Y ando muy mal del estómago, doctor. Tengo dolores de cabeza y de la garganta. Me siento mareada e inquieta. Tengo mucha tos, y estornudo todo el tiempo. Creo que tengo también la ictiricia, la hepatitis, la alta presión, la diabetes, e inclusive el cáncer pulmonar. Ya va para dos días que tengo … usted sabe … la diarrea. ¿Usted cree que voy a morirme?*

El médico: *Pues, no sé. Déjeme examinarla primero. (La examina el médico. Parece que no tiene nada.) Bueno, no creo que se vaya a morir. De hecho, me parece que usted es una persona físicamente muy sana. Vamos a ver si no le podemos quitar lo de la diarrea. ¿De acuerdo?*

Kathy: *Sí, está bien.*

Ten Cuidado _____

Be aware that the *se* passive (*Se habla español* means "Spanish is spoken") can look like a reflexive construction. Usually the context of the statement will tell you what's going on. Spanish can't speak to itself, obviously, but *Juan se habla* would mean "Juan is talking to himself."

El médico: *¿Quisiera que le prepare un té de manzanilla?*

Kathy: *¿Té de manzanilla? No puede ser. ¿En serio?*

El médico: *No, señorita. Se lo dije en broma. Estudié la medicina en la Clínica Mayo en Minnesota y en el Hopsital de la Universidad de Stanford en California. Le voy a dar una reseta para unas pastillas. Puede ir a la farmacia para comprar la medicína. Tome dos, tres veces al día, hasta que se sienta mejor.*

Kathy: *Bueno, y si todavía estoy mal, ¿qué debo hacer?*

El médico: *Llame al consultorio para hacer una cita.*

Kathy: *Pues, espero que estas pastillas me hagan efecto. ¿Pero qué voy a hacer para las otras enfermedads que tengo?*

El médico: *Conozco a un buen psicólogo.*

Translation:

The doctor: Good afternoon, Madam.

Kathy: Miss.

The doctor: Oh, sorry, Miss. How do you feel today?

Kathy: Oh, doctor, I don't feel well at all (nada here means "at all").

The doctor: What's wrong (with you)?

Kathy: Well, every time I go out to do something I get sick.

The doctor: You don't say. Let's see. What are your symptoms?

Kathy: I've got swelling in my left hand, blisters on my right foot, and a rash on my back. And I've got stomach problems, doctor. I have headaches and (pain in my) throat. I feel dizzy and uneasy. I cough a lot, and I sneeze all the time. I think I also have jaundice, hepatitis, high blood pressure, diabetes, and even lung cancer. It's been nearly two days that I've had—you know—diarrhea. Do you think I'm going to die?

The doctor: Well, I don't know. Let me examine you first. (The doctor examines her; she looks fine.) Well, I don't think that you're going to die. In fact, you seem to be a very healthy person, physically. Let's see if we can't take care of (remove) the diarrhea. Agreed?

Kathy: Yes, all right.

The doctor: Would you like me to make you some chamomile tea?

Cultura Latina

Folk remedies, homeopathy, and herbal medicines are all quite popular in Latin America. Depending on where you are, you may be offered a traditional remedy for your ailments, such as chamomile tea *(té de manzanilla)* or *las ventosas* (suction cups applied to the skin to draw out disease). You may or may not believe in such practices, but for some people they are part of everyday life.

Kathy: Chamomile tea? That can't be right. Are you serious?

The doctor: No, Miss. I was just kidding (I said it to you in jest). I studied medicine at the Mayo Clinic in Minnesota and at Stanford University Hospital in California. I'm going to give you a prescription for some pills. You can go to the pharmacy to buy the pills. Take two, three times a day, until you feel better.

Kathy: All right, and if I still feel bad, what should I do?

The doctor: Call the office to make an appointment.

Kathy: Well, I hope these pills are effective (on me). But what am I going to do about the other illnesses I have?

The doctor: I know a good psychologist.

Idiot's Guide to Idioms

Here's your last list of idiomatic expressions. There are hundreds more where these came from. If you are so inclined, you may purchase books that contain hundreds of these sayings and idioms at many bookstores and online:

No es nada del otro mundo.   It's nothing to write home about.

Ojos que no ven, corazón que no siente.   Out of sight, out of mind.

por un pelo   by the skin of one's teeth

quitarse un peso de encima   to take a load off one's mind/chest

saber nadar y guardar la ropa   to sleep with one eye open

salir de Guatemala para entrar en Guatepeor   out of the frying pan into the fire

ser plato de segunda mesa   to play second fiddle

sin ton ni son   without rhyme or reason

tener en cuenta   to bear in mind

toparse con la horma de sus zapatos   to meet one's match

venir como anillo al dedo   to fit like a glove

Esteban's Advice About Cognates

Yes, Spanish and English really do share a lot of words. Most of these words come from our "dead amigos" of Latin and Greek. The prefixes and suffixes that you learned in this book will help you tremendously in recognizing and producing words that are cognates in both languages. Cognates can help you to understand many Spanish words with minimal effort. They can also help you produce new Spanish words practically out of thin air. But as with most things in *la vida*, there's a catch. Read on to learn more ....

Recognizing Cognates

While there are some words in Spanish and English that are identical, far more words are *nearly* the same in both languages except for a slight change in spelling. In many cases, the only difference between the Spanish word and the English word is the addition or change of a vowel at the end of the word, or the use of only one consonant where the consonants are doubled in the English word ("committee" = *comité* in Spanish). A *th* in English may be written as a *t* in Spanish; *t*'s may be *d*'s, and *ph*'s are written as *f*'s. There may also be additional changes here and there to compensate for the bizarre way we spell in English:

- *carro*
- *rata* (yes, "a rat")
- *senador*
- *demócrata*
- *republicano*
- *crema*
- *vitamina*
- *aspirina*
- *calendario*
- *fotografía*
- *excelente*
- *guitarra*
- *teléfono*
- *presidente*
- *autor*
- *grupo*
- *americano*
- *medicina*
- *lámpara*
- *automóvil*
- *banco*
- *catedral*
- *diferente*
- *elegante*
- *famoso*

Many Spanish words that begin with *es–* have an English *amigo*. If you remove the *e* (and possibly the final vowel), the cognate becomes even clearer:

espacio space

especia spice

especial special

espía spy

esquí ski

estudiar study

estimado esteemed (careful, sometimes the *e* stays)

estupendo stupendous

estúpido not so stupendous

Algo Nuevo

Some Spanish words are cognates of uncommon English terms. For example, the Spanish verb for "to end" is *terminar*. It is a cognate of "to terminate," a word that you know but might not use every day. The Spanish word for someone who walks in his sleep is *sonámbulo*. The verb "to somnambulate" exists in English and means "to walk in your sleep." It's not a common word, but if you already knew it, you're in luck. When you hear a Spanish word, you may have to go through several synonyms for the same English word before you actually locate the cognate.

Some cognates don't always jump out and bite you on the nose. You may need to study such words a bit before you can recognize them:

champú shampoo

humedad humidity

ejecutar to execute

Words that end in *–um* in English tend to end in *–o* in Spanish:

gymnasio gymnasium

acuario aquarium

auditorio auditorium; audience

Ten Cuidado

In many English words, an internal consonant is doubled: a*pp*endix, comme*m*orate, asse*ss*ment, and so on. In Spanish, doubled consonants are very rare. The only exception is the doubled *cc* in words such as *acción*. Otherwise, if the consonant is doubled in the English word, don't double it in the Spanish cognate. You'll be right 99 percent of the time.

The ending *–a* is common in Spanish and may correspond to *–e* (or nothing) in English:

persona person

agricultura agriculture

causa cause

disciplina discipline

gasolina gasoline/petrol

forma form

planeta planet

idiota idiot

mapa map

There are many other ways to recognize a cognate. The more Spanish you read and hear, the better you will become at recognizing these *amigos*. But read on to see why things aren't as simple as all that ….

False Cognates

Yes, it is true that many words in Spanish and English look similar and mean the same thing, but cognates can also lead you astray. Some *amigos* may have a long list of secondary meanings that do not exist in the other language. These can be considered as unreliable cognates because they may serve you well in some situations, but not in others.

Algo Nuevo

For an example of an unreliable cognate, let's look at the verb *cancelar*. In many cases, you will be able to get by with *cancelar* when you want to say "to cancel." However, in Spanish, *cancelar* has a secondary meaning of "to pay off in full." You can say *Quiero cancelar esta factura* for "I want to pay off this bill." If you're not careful, you could misunderstand this as "I want to cancel this bill," which wouldn't mean the same thing and could lead to problems. Cognates are indeed very useful, but you must be careful when using them; don't assume that the words are always full cognates just because they look or sound similar.

Other false friends can have entirely different (or even opposite) meanings than the one you are thinking of. You must always verify either by the context or your dictionary that a cognate really does mean what you think it does. Here are a few examples:

asistir to attend (not "to assist")

caro expensive (not "car")

fábrica factory (not "fabric")

flor flower (not "floor")

librería bookstore (not "library")

colegio   elementary and/or secondary school (not "college")

horno   oven (not "horn")

constipado   a stuffy nose or head cold (not "constipated")

curioso   strange (not "curious" like a cat)

sensible   sensitive (not "sensible")

sensato   sensible (not "sensitive")

apuntar   to write down (not "to appoint")

restar   to subtract (not "to rest")

pan   bread (not "pan")

sopa   soup (not "soap")

familiar   having to do with family (not "something you already know a lot about")

Ten Cuidado

Remember: you can use cognates as an aid to communication and for building up your vocabulary, but *not* as a way to fumble through the language.

So, Now What?

At this point, you're probably feeling both elated and frustrated. First I tell you about all these cool free words, then I say that you can't always trust them and should always make sure they aren't *false amigos*. Well, I know it's frustrating. Tell you what—here's my advice:

When you speak Spanish, you can figure that about 70 percent of the time, your instincts about cognates will lead you in the right direction (at least close enough for you to get your idea across). So go ahead and use a cognate when it occurs to you. If you need to say "communication" and haven't learned the Spanish word yet, try *comunicación* and see what happens. If someone doesn't understand you, they'll let you know. Even if the cognate you choose isn't 100 percent correct, it may be a lot better than saying nothing at all.

Nevertheless, when it's *your* turn to understand Spanish rather than produce it, you might want to be even more cautious. Don't assume that you know exactly what is meant by a word just because you think you recognize it. You may indeed be right, but too many people have gotten into a lot of trouble by blithely using cognates as a way to muddle through Spanish. If the subject at hand is important, make sure that you really understand what the words mean. Follow your instincts, but let your dictionary be your guide.

La Última Palabra ...

You may have heard or seen people (Hollywood movies are notorious for this) who take this *amigo* concept a bit too far, believing that they can somehow conjure up Spanish by making their English sound Spanish: "I want-o to buy-o a Mexican-o blanket-o. How much-o cost-o?" Nice try, but that isn't Spanish, and talking like that is a bad idea and an embarrassment to those English-speakers who are really trying to learn the language correctly. I may be a complete idiot, but I will personally slap with a wet tortilla anyone who goes around talking like that after reading this book!

El Web

For more info on medical Spanish, visit the following sites:

http://users.ugent.be/~rvdstich/eugloss/ES/lijst.html

www.southtexascollege.edu/library/guides/medicalspanish.htm

Risa del Día

The doctor/patient joke is classic in Spanish:

Paciente olvidón:

>*Doctor, doctor ... ¿cómo sé si estoy perdiendo la memoria?*
>
>*Eso ya se lo dije ayer.*

Más allá del oficio:

>*Un hombre va a la consulta del médico y le dice:*
>
>*¡Doctor, me he caído y me duelen mucho las piernas!*
>
>*El doctor después de examinarlo le dice:*
>
>*No se preocupe, no es nada. Dentro de unos días ya estará usted trabajando.*
>
>*Caramba Doctor, qué maravilla, además de curarme ¿me dará trabajo?*

Consejos dentales, y de moda:

>*Un hombre va al dentista y le dice:*
>
>*Doctor, tengo los dientes muy amarillos, ¿que me recomienda?*
>
>*Corbata marrón.*

Acuérdate _____

The prefix *in–* often corresponds to *"un–"* in English. So *inesperado* is "unexpected," and *intocable* would be "untouchable."

Respuesta inesperada:

Una paciente le dice a su médico:

Doctor, ¡la pierna que me operó me quedó más corta!

Y el médico le responde:

No se preocupe señora, le puedo hacer la misma operación en la otra pierna.

Vocabulario Útil:

olvidón	forgetful	*oficio*	trade; duty
perder	to lose	*maravilla*	a wonder; a marvelous thing
corbata	a tie	*curar*	to cure
marrón	brown	*consejo*	advice
más allá	beyond	*inesperado*	unexpected

The Least You Need to Know

◆ Medical jargon tends to be the same in both English and Spanish.

◆ Reflexive infinitives have a *se* on the end.

◆ You can recognize a reflexive construction when the subject and the object are the same.

◆ Reflexive verbs are often just regular old verbs placed in a reflexive construction.

Workbook

Here is the place where you can practice what you've learned. This section follows the sequence of the material in the book, starting with Chapter 5. Most of the answers are available in the book if you go back to the corresponding chapters and dig around for them. Keep your dictionary on hand, as there may be more than one good answer.

Of course, this is not the only place that you should practice. After you complete these sections, go online or sit down with someone who speaks Spanish and explore additional ways of practicing your skills.

Chapter 5

Please give the English equivalents for the following words. Cheating is perfectly acceptable:

1. frontera
   _____

2. limitar
   _____

3. situar
   _____

4. meseta
   _____

5. compartir
   _____

6. frente a
   _____

7. extensión
   _____

8. atravesar
   _____

9. asentarse
   _____

10. los Pirineos
    _____

11. Marruecos
    _____

12. contar con
    _____

13. suroeste

_____

A. Explain to someone how nouns work in Spanish. If there is no one around, write a few paragraphs on a sheet of paper

detailing everything you know about Spanish nouns.

B. Now that you've gone through the chapter, reread the _lectura_ to see if it's any easier the second time.

Chapter 6

Give the English translation for the following words. Cheating is still fine:

1. enseñanza

_____

2. ejército

_____

3. enriquecer

_____

4. proponer

_____

5. terreno

_____

6. provocar

_____

7. promesa

_____

8. campesino

_____

9. multiplicar

_____

10. prestar dinero

_____

11. repartir

_____

12. régimen

_____

13. latifundios

_____

14. carreteras

_____

15. red

_____

A. Explain to someone how verbs work in Spanish. If there is no one around, write a few paragraphs on a sheet of paper detailing everything you know about Spanish verbs.

B. Learn more about Mexico on the Internet or by researching the topic at your local library.

Chapter 7

Give the English equivalent of the following words. Cheating is okay, I guess, but don't get too used to it:

1. espectador

2. realizarse

3. género

4. consagrado

5. acontecimiento

6. resultar

7. Mercosur

8. perderse

9. convocar

10. jornada

11. inferior

12. asistencia

13. ubicar

A. Explain to someone how adjectives work in Spanish. If there is no one around, write a few paragraphs on a sheet of paper detailing everything you know about Spanish adjectives.

B. Explain to someone how demonstrative pronouns and adjectives work in Spanish. If there is no one around, write a few paragraphs on a sheet of paper detailing everything you know about Spanish demonstratives.

Chapter 8

Give the English equivalents for the following words. Cheat only if you absolutely have to:

1. imperio

2. convertir

3. esqueleto

4. belleza

5. debido

_____

6. atractivo

_____

7. cima

_____

8. edificios

_____

9. entero

_____

10. duda

_____

11. entorno

_____

12. durar

_____

13. adornados

_____

14. ciudadela

_____

15. recorrido

_____

16. por su cuenta

_____

17. ubicación

_____

18. arqueológico

_____

A. Create sentences using *ser* and *estar*. Use the examples in this chapter as your guide. Substitute new nouns and adjectives for the words given in the examples: *Mi amigo es ecuatoriano; El gato está en la casa;* and so on.

B. Make a list of 10 Spanish verbs. Change the verbs into past participles. Now, create sentences using *estar* + past participle to describe the state of things: *La puerta esté abierta.* Then add any appropriate adverbs to modify the verbs: *La puerta esté muy abierta.*

C. Create sentences using *hay* to tell people what's there and what isn't there. Use *hay que* + infinitive to say what you "gotta do."

Chapter 9

Provide the Spanish equivalents for the following words. Cheating isn't cool, but it's up to you:

1. warm

_____

2. procedures; paperwork

_____

3. surface

_____

4. speed

_____

5. highways

    _____

6. to prevail

    _____

7. average

    _____

8. to fluctuate; to vary

    _____

9. principally

    _____

10. season; time of year

    _____

11. to occupy

    _____

12. coastal

    _____

13. to be subject to

    _____

14. cool

    _____

15. valid; in force

    _____

16. hot and humid

    _____

17. units

    _____

18. specific

    _____

A. Create 15 statements or questions using a transitive verb + a direct object: *Tengo un gato; ¿Quiere pagar la cuenta?*; and so on. Then, using the examples in this chapter as your guide, substitute the DOP for the noun: *Lo tengo; ¿Quiere pagarla?* or *¿La quiere pagar?*

B. Choose a subject, a transitive verb, an object, and an indirect object to receive the object: somebody + verb + indirect object + direct object, or somebody + verb + direct object + "to" + indirect object: "I give Eduardo the money" or "I give the money to Walter." Translate these into Spanish. Use the chapter's examples as your guide.

C. Create sentences that will help you to practice the third-person INDOP + the third-person DOP: *Se lo dije* = "I told it to him/her/usted/ustedes/them"; *Vamos a contárselo* = "Let's tell it to him/her/usted/ustedes/them." Remember to use *se*, not *le* or *les*. Use the previous examples as your guide. Add *a él, a ellas*, and so on, as needed for clarity.

Chapter 10

Give the Spanish translations of the following words. Cheat? Not you, right? Well, we'll see:

1. to deepen; to go into depth

   _____

2. minister

   _____

3. defense

   _____

4. threat

   _____

5. common

   _____

6. related to

   _____

7. to meet; to get together

   _____

8. army

   _____

9. commander

   _____

10. integration

    _____

11. leader; "boss"

    _____

12. to review; to look over

    _____

13. security

    _____

14. to constitute; to make up

    _____

15. drug-trafficking

    _____

16. period; time

    _____

17. armed forces

    _____

A. Write the future tense endings on a separate sheet of paper. Then write the conditional tense endings on a separate sheet of paper. Now write the preterit tense endings on a separate sheet of paper. Finally, write the imperfect tense endings on a separate sheet of paper (boy, you sure use a lot of paper).

B. Create sentences in the past tense, and practice forming and using the Spanish preterit. Refer to the previous examples and explanations if you need guidance.

C. Create as many sentences as you can where you need the future and/or conditional tense. Use your dictionary for vocabulary. Think of things that you "will do," "would do," or "could do" (_poder_ = _podr_–). Learn and practice the verbs that change their stem in the future and conditional tenses.

Chapter 11

Give the Spanish translations of the following words. Cheat only if you really need to:

1. field; area

   _____

2. efforts

   _____

3. state (adj.)

   _____

4. treatment

   _____

5. racism

   _____

6. entertainment

   _____

7. to remain

   _____

8. minority

   _____

9. today; the present

   _____

10. stereotype

   _____

11. law

   _____

12. studies; investigations

   _____

13. to show evidence that

   _____

14. invisible

   _____

15. commonly

   _____

16. "reality-based"

   _____

A. Explain to someone the use of the Spanish subjunctive. If there is no one around, write down your explanation.

B. Write the present subjunctive endings on a piece of paper.

C. Create sentences using the present subjunctive tense. Follow the rules as outlined here, and use the examples as your guide. Consult your dictionary for any additional vocabulary you might need.

Chapter 12

Provide the Spanish equivalents for the following words. Cheat only if it's a *lunes*, *miércoles*, or *viernes*:

1. season

   _____

2. institution

   _____

3. proceed; to come from

_____

4. identity

_____

5. stability

_____

6. support

_____

7. sense; feeling

_____

8. security

_____

9. to demonstrate; to show

_____

10. dignity

_____

11. to reaffirm

_____

12. well-being

_____

13. position

_____

14. society

_____

15. to unite; to tie

_____

16. to remain

_____

17. member

_____

18. custom

_____

19. common

_____

A. Think of all the members of your family, including your extended family. Now determine what their relationship to you would be in Spanish.

B. Explain to someone the differences between *para* and *por.* Give examples. If there isn't anyone around, write it down in a notebook.

Chapter 13

Give the Spanish for the following words. Cheat if you must, but don't tell your friends:

1. birth

_____

2. to be born

_____

3. shift

_____

4. hill

_____

5. adolescence

_____

6. to attend

_____

7. old-fashioned way; the old way

_____

8. midwife

_____

9. to suppose

_____

10. to get ahead

_____

11. to be located

_____

12. the stock market

_____

13. to keep one company

_____

14. to get over; to come through

_____

15. e-mail

_____

16. to make a decision

_____

17. entire; whole

_____

18. to get; to acquire

_____

A. Explain to someone the differences between _tú_ and _usted_. If there's no one around, write your thoughts in your notebook.

B. Go to a public place (the mall, shopping area, library, or other location) where you can sit down and watch people for a while. Look at everyone who walks by and ask yourself whether you would address this person as _tú_ or _usted_.

Chapter 14

Provide the Spanish for the following words. Rather than cheat, study the Vocabulario Útil again before taking the quiz if necessary:

1. lid

_____

2. butter

_____

3. dough; filling

_____

4. corn cob

_____

5. gram

_____

6. to roast

_____

7. strip

_____

8. salt "to taste"

_____

9. food processor

_____

10. tablespoonful

_____

11. to peel

_____

12. to slice

_____

13. to soak

_____

14. to drip

_____

15. a tamale holder

_____

16. to beat; to mix

_____

17. to grind

_____

18. to spread

_____

A. Host an authentic Latin American or Spanish dinner. Surf online or visit your library for recipes and any cookbooks that feature recipes from the Spanish-speaking world. Invite friends and family. Enjoy *sobremesa* after eating. During your dinner, discuss what you have learned about meals and food. If you need more information, do more research on the Internet or at the library.

B. Create sentences for practicing your prepositions. Use the list here as your guide, and utilize new vocabulary or words from your dictionary as you build your sentences.

Chapter 15

You know what to do. If you cheat this time, you risk punishment by a higher being:

1. to appear

_____

2. sign

_____

3. bishop

_____

4. again; another time

_____

5. message

_____

6. following

_____

7. meeting; encounter

_____

8. request

_____

9. to get sick

_____

10. top; summit

_____

11. Jewish

_____

12. Muslim

_____

13. ashamed

_____

14. because of; due to

_____

15. to transpire; to happen

_____

16. and so; for this reason

_____

17. to go around

_____

18. to pray

_____

19. chapel

_____

20. cleric; priest

_____

21. mosque

_____

22. communion

_____

23. to bless

_____

24. condition; state

_____

A. Create sentences using the present progressive tense. If you want, start with a few "somebody-is-doing-something" sentences in English, then try to translate them into Spanish. Use the examples and the explanations as your guide. Vary the tense of the helping verb to express more complex ideas of time.

B. Write a brief essay about yourself and your religious background. You don't need to share it with anyone. If you have no religious preference or affiliation, write about that.

Chapter 16

Please provide the Spanish. If you cheat, you won't be invited to the party ....

1. still; yet

_____

2. village; town

_____

3. soul

_____

4. to experience; "to taste"

_____

5. sense; feeling

_____

6. enchantment; charm

_____

7. neighborhood

_____

8. sounding of a bell; ringing

_____

9. visitor

10. enchanting; charming

11. to occur

12. to be watchful; to be waiting for

13. crowd

14. to take place

15. to unfold; to spread out

16. to parade

17. traditional; pure

18. city government

19. stand; stall; kiosk

20. beginning

A. Create sentences using various tenses of *haber*. Use the examples in the chapter as your guide. Try incorporating some of the new vocabulary you have learned here.

B. Make more sentences (they can be really short) using *tan* or *tanto*. Make even more sentences using words from the "Here, There, Everywhere" section.

C. Invite some friends over for a little *fiesta* of your own. Talk about how exciting this book is and suggest that all your guests run out and buy a copy ASAP.

Chapter 17

I pray thee that thou shalt provide the Castilian for the following locutions, if it pleaseth thee muchly …. Cheat not, lest thou be eaten by giant windmills:

1. face; countenance

2. idle; leisurely

3. chivalry

4. said; aforementioned

5. to acquire

6. reason

7. injustice; wrong

8. estate

9. battle

_____

10. knight

_____

11. himself; oneself

_____

12. after; at then end of

_____

13. wounds

_____

14. to be happy with; to be content

_____

15. homeland

_____

16. corner

_____

17. to equal; to be as good as

_____

18. master

_____

19. windmill

_____

20. fearsome

_____

A. Surf the Internet or visit your local library and search for more information about _Don Quixote_. Even if you read the book in English, it will still help you to understand a very important part of Spanish culture.

B. Create sentences using the past subjunctive tense. Use the examples as your guide. Make sentences using a "contrary to fact" construction: "If I were a knight from La Mancha (but I'm not), …."

Chapter 18

You know what to do. Spanish words, por favor. If you cheat, they won't let you in the museum:

1. address

_____

2. due to; "with the reason of"

_____

3. seat; office; headquarters

_____

4. younger than

_____

5. holiday

_____

6. as of

_____

7. having obtained previously

_____

8. older than

_____

9. fee; price

_____

10. holder of; named owner of

_____

11. ID card

12. educational

13. schedule; timetable

14. retired person

15. unemployed; out of a job

16. available

17. following

18. ticket window

19. season ticket; payment

20. to carry; to be equipped with

21. school (adjective)

22. at least

23. disabled; handicapped

24. in advance

25. to apply

26. to be obligated to

27. painting

A. Create sentences that use ordinal numbers. If needed, try using the word *vez* (time, occurrence) if you get stuck: *la primera vez*, *la quinta vez* ("the first time," "the fifth time"), and so on. Also, create sentences that help you practice your fractions, percentages, and the reading of longer numbers such as phone numbers. Use your telephone directory if needed.

B. Visit the Prado's website and learn more about the museum's collection. Or check out what's available at your local library about Spanish and Latin American artists.

Chapter 19

No vocabulary list today …. Go listen to some Latin music instead!

A. Go to your local music store and see what's available in the Latin section. Ask about flamenco music as well. But before you spend a lot of *dinero*, see if your local library has any tapes or CDs that you can check out for free.

B. Go online and search for more websites about Spanish or Latin American music. It won't take you long to find many good sites in both English and Spanish.

C. Memorize (or at least become familiar with) as many prefixes as you can. Create sentences using words from this chapter (or your dictionary) that begin with a prefix you learned here.

Chapter 20

Give the Spanish equivalents of the following words. Any cheating will result in a penalty kick against your team:

1. to surround

2. supposedly

3. overtime

4. to culminate; to end

5. surprising

6. champion

7. competition; contest

8. to pack one's bags

9. stadium

10. to react

11. astonishment; stupefaction

12. ground

13. signal

14. celebration

15. premature

16. tournament

17. net; goal

18. to get close to

19. shot

20. corner

21. to come together; to meet

22. in a matter of

23. to climb up

_____

24. ghost

_____

25. environment; atmosphere

_____

26. finished off; completed

_____

27. ball

_____

28. to dare

_____

29. field (for sport)

_____

30. at the end

_____

31. goalie

_____

32. hurriedly

_____

A. Write the Spanish suffixes in this chapter on note cards. On the other side, write the English equivalent. Go through the cards and learn the suffixes well enough to recognize them when you see them.

B. Memorize the following lyric: _Dale dale dale, no pierdas el tino, porque si lo pierdes, pierdes el camino._ This is the song that is sung at parties (in Mexico) when they do the _piñata_ part.

Chapter 21

Please provide the Spanish for these words. If you cheat, I'll steal your _piñata_ and eat all its delicious contents by myself:

1. following

_____

2. peacock

_____

3. owl

_____

4. potter

_____

5. pots for piñatas

_____

6. fitting; appropriate

_____

7. quality figure

_____

8. step

_____

9. to choose

_____

10. design

_____

11. page

_____

12. blank

_____

13. afterward

_____

14. newspaper

_____

15. construction paper

_____

16. thick

_____

17. to cover

_____

18. frame

_____

19. end to affix; to glue on

_____

20. around

_____

21. whether it be

_____

22. ribbon

_____

23. sparkle; brilliance

_____

24. to say goodbye

_____

A. Research Mexican handicrafts, either on the Internet or in your local library, and see what appeals to you. If you've got some extra cash, you can purchase *artesanías* from catalogs or over the web.

B. Choose 20 vocabulary words (nouns and adjectives) and practice adding some of the suffixes that you learned here to these words. Then try to guess what they might mean, using the explanations here as your guide. If you know a native Spanish-speaker, ask that person how your newly "suffixed" words sound.

Chapter 22

A. Review both the Spanish and the English translations of the four dialogues in this chapter and write down any words or phrases that are new or interesting to you. Use your dictionary for additional definitions.

B. Create questions asking "who, what, where, when, why," and so on. Use the examples in this chapter as a guide, and consult your dictionary for additional words. Don't forget to write those *tildes*.

Chapter 23

Give the Spanish equivalents. Cheating will result in the immediate bankruptcy (*bancarrota*) of your company and no more special discounts (*descuentos*):

1. are requested

   _____

2. appreciably; considerably

   _____

3. reports

   _____

4. Esteemed Sirs

   _____

5. "It is our pleasure"

   _____

6. kind letter

   _____

7. installment plan

   _____

8. recuperation; upswing

   _____

9. industrial park

   _____

10. P.O. box

    _____

11. chapter; period

    _____

12. to be reduced

    _____

13. to increase; to expand

    _____

14. appreciable

    _____

15. to impart

    _____

16. broad; wide-ranging

    _____

17. current; existing

    _____

18. to trust

    _____

19. usefulness; of use

    _____

20. decision; resolutions

    _____

21. to facilitate; to make easier

    _____

22. establishment

    _____

23. stay; visit

    _____

24. greetings

    _____

25. here; I have here

    _____

26. sincerely

    _____

27. teller; cashier; clerk

    _____

A. Using the letter as a guide, write a short letter to a business, asking for the price of some product. You can borrow (steal) the openings and closings of the letter from the example here. It's all very formulaic ….

B. Spend some extra time learning the courteous expressions discussed in this chapter. Do whatever it takes. I guarantee that it will be time well spent and that these polite phrases will open up many doors to you—even if your Spanish is less than perfect.

Chapter 24

Give the equivalent Spanish words. Cheating will result in a crashed hard drive and the loss of all your data:

1. switch

2. continuous

3. result; consequence

4. to turn off

5. device

6. analog

7. to consist

8. across

9. to vary; to fluctuate

10. machine; device

11. to turn on

12. signal

13. to achieve

14. frequency

15. some kind

16. communication software

17. to modulate

18. current

19. that; all of that

20. to unite; to link

21. wave

22. the opposite

23. third parties

24. piece

25. impulse

_____

A. Sit at a computer and try to name the basic parts in Spanish. If you don't know something, go online and see if you can find it. Then try to make the special Spanish characters á, é, í, ó, ú, ü, ñ, ¿, and ¡.

B. Talk about all the things that you own. Then talk about other people's stuff. Practice using the possessives with these sentences. Refer to the examples and explanations for guidance.

Chapter 25

Please provide the Spanish. If you cheat, your local government will be overthrown by rebel forces:

1. heroism

_____

2. citizen

_____

3. sacrifice

_____

4. creative

_____

5. to rebel

_____

6. imperialism

_____

7. fighting spirit

_____

8. dominion

_____

9. final; definitive

_____

10. slave

_____

11. worker

_____

12. to found

_____

13. someone who belongs to a group

_____

14. to fight for

_____

15. popular; of the people

_____

16. landholder

_____

17. to promote

_____

18. to broadcast; to publish

_____

19. to support

    _____

20. triumphant

    _____

21. sacrifice

    _____

22. ideas; ideology

    _____

23. to guide

    _____

24. goal; objective

    _____

25. government

    _____

26. to sustain; to hold

    _____

27. to reach

    _____

28. entire; whole

    _____

29. close; narrow

    _____

30. party (political)

    _____

31. wish; desire; hope

    _____

32. incapable

    _____

A. Go online or visit your favorite library and research the political situation of the Spanish-speaking country that most interests you.

B. Obtain a text in Spanish about a political event or issue (go online or check in a Spanish language publication), and underline any words that are unfamiliar to you. Or, if you want to start with English, take a political text from your local newspaper and underline some words that you wouldn't know how to say in Spanish. Either way, when you have a list of at least 15 words, try to translate them into the other language using your dictionary.

Chapter 26

Provide the Spanish equivalents. If you cheat, your insurance company will refuse to pay all your medical bills (unless you're Canadian, where it's free but takes forever to be seen):

1. to originate

    _____

2. progression

    _____

3. worthy

    _____

4. currently; these days

    _____

5. a person who is ill

   _____

6. to pass away; die (kinder than *morir*)

   _____

7. admission (to a medical facility)

   _____

8. hospital (adj.)

   _____

9. nonetheless

   _____

10. to affirm; to maintain

    _____

11. exploring

    _____

12. routine

    _____

13. conclusively; convincingly

    _____

14. rule

    _____

15. injury; wound

    _____

16. risk

    _____

17. traumatic

    _____

18. to be performed

    _____

19. thus

    _____

20. consultation

    _____

21. sensitivity

    _____

22. stage

    _____

23. isolated

    _____

24. blood (adj.)

    _____

25. defective

    _____

A. Using the examples in this chapter, create sentences with reflexive constructions. You don't have to look up reflexive verbs for this exercise. Remember that almost any old verb can be used reflexively.

B. Research a topic that relates to medicine, anatomy, or health care and create a vocabulary list from words that interest you.

C. Write down all the English words that you can think of in 10 minutes that end with *–tion* or *–um*. Change the *t* in *–tion* to *c*, and write a *tilde* on the *–ó*, making *–ción*. You have just created a list of words that are likely candidates for Spanish. Now, with your dictionary, verify some of the words that you have created.

Appendix A

Basic Grammar Resource

For your convenience, I have included some basic grammar in this appendix. If you don't find what you're looking for here, consult your beginning instructional text.

Phonetic Names of Letters

Sooner or later, you will need to spell something for someone, such as your name or hometown. So, it's a good idea to know the names of the letters in Spanish. In the following list, *ay* sounds like "day," "way," and "say." The combinations *ch* and *ll* are no longer considered as one letter.

a	ah	*j*	hotah
b	bay (*bay larga; bay grande; bay de "burro"*)	*k*	kah
		l	ehlay
c	say; thay	*m*	ehmay
d	day	*n*	ehnay
e	ay	*ñ*	ehnyay
f	ehfay	*o*	oh
g	hay	*p*	pay
h	ahchay	*q*	coo
i	ee (*ee lahteenah*)		

r	ehray		*v*	vay (*vay corta; vay chica; "vay de vaca"*)
rr	ehrrrray, or "dohblay ehray"		*w*	oovay (dohblay oo; vay dohblay)
s	ehsay		*x*	ehkees
t	tay		*y*	ee greeaygah
u	oo		*z*	setah; thayta

Present Indicative

These are your basic conjugations:

-ar Verbs

Pronoun	Ending	Conjugation
yo	*–o*	First person singular
tú	*–as*	Second person singular familiar
él, ella, usted	*–a*	Third person singular/second person formal
nosotros/as	*–amos*	First person plural
vosotros/as	*–áis*	Second person plural familiar
ellos, ellas, ustedes	*–an*	Second and third person plural

-er and *-ir* Verbs

Pronoun	Ending	Conjugation
yo	*–o*	First person singular
tú	*–es*	Second person singular familiar
él/ella/usted	*–e*	Third person singular/second person formal
nosotros/as	*–emos (–imos* for *–ir* verbs)	First person plural
vosotros/as	*–éis*	Second person familiar
ellos, ellas, ustedes	*–en*	Second and third person plural

Preterit Endings

These are the endings for the preterit, or "simple past." (Wonder why they call it simple when it can be so difficult?)

Regular –*ar* Verbs

Ending	Infinitive	Example
–é	*hablar*	*hablé*
–aste	*pagar*	*pagaste*
–ó	*cantar*	*cantó*
–amos	*contar*	*contamos*
–asteis	*mandar*	*mandasteis*
–aron	*comprar*	*compraron*

–*er* and –*ir* Verbs

Ending	Infinitive	Example
–í	*comer*	*comí*
–iste	*salir*	*saliste*
–ió	*vivir*	*vivió*
–imos	*entender*	*entendimos*
–isteis	*meter*	*metisteis*
–ieron	*decidir*	*decidieron*

When forming the preterit, don't forget the Spanish spelling rules. As with the subjunctive, the addition of some endings may require that an orthographic convenience be used to match the spelling to the pronunciation. For example, *pagar* becomes *pagué* in the *yo* form of the preterit because the *g* would be soft next to that *e*. We prevent that by inserting a *u*. You should still consider these verbs as regular.

If the verb stem ends in a vowel, the *i* in –*ieron* becomes *y*. So, *leer* becomes *leyeron* in the third person plural preterit tense because its stem is *le*–.

Imperfect Past Endings

They call this the "imperfect," but really, there's nothing wrong with it:

-ar Verbs

Ending	Example	Ending	Example
–aba	hablaba	–abas	cantabas
–aba	pagaba	–ábamos	contábamos
–abais	cantabais	–aban	compraban

-er and -ir Verbs

Ending	Example	Ending	Example
–ía	vivía	–ías	comías
–ía	sentía	–íamos	pedíamos
–íais	metíais	–ían	sabían

The first person and third person singular forms look the same, but the context usually makes it clear what's going on. Pronouns and names can also be added for clarity.

Irregular Imperfects

Imagine being both imperfect and irregular at the same time. What a life ....

Luckily, only three common verbs take an irregular imperfect form: *ser, ir,* and *ver.*

◆ **ser**   *era, eras, era, éramos, erais, eran*

◆ **ir**   *iba, ibas, iba, íbamos, ibais, iban*

◆ **ver**   *veía, veías, veía, veíamos, veíais, veían*

Tú Command Forms (Imperative Mood)

To tell someone to "speak," simply say *habla* (don't forget to be nice and add *por favor* now and then). Any DOPs and INDOPs are glued right onto the imperative verb, which will necessitate the addition of a *tilde* to maintain the correct stress (*habla, háblame,* and so on):

Forming Commands

Verb	Command	Definition
comer	*Come.*	Eat.
vivir	*Vive.*	Live.
cantar	*Cántala.*	Sing it.
escribir	*Escríbeme.*	Write me.
dar	*Dámelo.*	Give it to me.
contar	*Cuéntaselos.*	Tell them to him.

For the irregular *tú* commands, see the reference card in the beginning of the book. Also, remember that when you tell someone *not* to do something, you must use the subjunctive.

Stem-Changing Verbs

Here are a few examples of those stem-changers. Remember that these changes are not seen in the *nosotros* and *vosotros* forms of the verbs.

Some Stem-Changing Verbs

Verb	*Yo* Form	Change
contar	*cuento*	$o \rightarrow ue$
mostrar	*muestro*	$o \rightarrow ue$
poder	*puedo*	$o \rightarrow ue$
volver	*vuelvo*	$o \rightarrow ue$
jugar	*juego*	$u \rightarrow ue$
querer	*quiero*	$e \rightarrow ie$
perder	*pierdo*	$e \rightarrow ie$
pensar	*pienso*	$e \rightarrow ie$
pedir	*pido*	$e \rightarrow i$
repetir	*repito*	$e \rightarrow i$

Future and Conditional Tense Endings

For most verbs, just add the future ending right onto the infinitive. Notice how these endings, with the exception of the *nosotros* form, are all accented on the last syllable:

Future Tense

Ending	Conjugation	Ending	Conjugation
–é	hablaré	–ás	cantarás
–á	sentirá	–emos	viviremos
–éis	comeréis	–án	pensarán

Conditional Tense

Ending	Conjugation	Ending	Conjugation
–ía	pensaría	–ías	comprarías
–ía	tocaría	–íamos	creeríamos
–íais	jugaríais	–ían	beberían

For the irregular future and conditional stems, consult the reference card at the beginning of the book.

"Go" Verbs

Remember that these take the "go" part only in the first person indicative. However, in the present subjunctive, these verbs maintain the "go" part throughout:

"Go" Verbs

Verb	*Yo* Form	Verb	*Yo* Form
hacer	hago	poner	pongo
oír	oigo	salir	salgo
tener	tengo	traer	traigo
venir	vengo		

Some have stem changes:

"Go" Verbs with Stem Changes

Verb	*Yo* Form
decir	*digo*
seguir	*sigo*

Subjunctive Endings

It's almost like putting the wrong ending on the verb. Build it around the *yo* form. If there's a stem change, it will also show up here (except in *nosotros* and *vosotros* forms).

-ar Verbs

Ending	Verb	Subjunctive	Definition
-e	*hablar*	*hable*	I may speak
-es	*cantar*	*cantes*	you may sing
-e	*dudar*	*dude*	he/she/you may doubt
-emos	*pensar*	*pensemos*	we may think
-éis	*sentar*	*sentéis*	you all may sit
-en	*tomar*	*tomen*	they/you all may take

-er and *-ir* Verbs

Ending	Verb	Subjunctive	Definition
-a	*creer*	*crea*	I may believe
-as	*vivir*	*vivas*	you may live
-a	*correr*	*corra*	he/she/it/you may run
-amos	*vender*	*vendamos*	we may sell
-áis	*meter*	*metéis*	you all may insert
-an	*comer*	*coman*	they/you all may eat

Again, if a verb is a "go" verb or has some other change in the *yo* form, it maintains this throughout the subjunctive.

Verbs That Change Forms and the Subjunctive

Verb	*Yo* Form	Example
tener	*tengo*	*tenga*
traer	*traigo*	*traigas*
oír	*oigo*	*oiga*
salir	*salgo*	*salgamos*
hacer	*hago*	*hagan*
decir	*digo*	*digas*
conocer	*conozco*	*conozcáis*
poner	*pongo*	*pongamos*

For the irregular present subjunctives, refer to the reference card at the beginning of the book.

Demonstratives

Here are the pointing words. Remember, when used as an adjective there is no *tilde*. When used as a pronoun, the *tilde* is required (except for the neuters):

- ◆ Masculine singular nouns:

    este   este sombrero—"this hat"

    ese   ese reloj—"that watch"

    aquel   aquel edificio—"that building far away"

- ◆ Feminine singular nouns:

    esta   esta flor—"this flower"

    esa   esa alfombra—"that carpet"

    aquella   aquella mujer—"that woman far away"

- ◆ Masculine plural nouns:

    estos   estos platos—"these plates"

    esos   esos zapatos—"those shoes"

    aquellos   aquellos hombres—"those men far away"

- Feminine plural nouns:

  estas   estas muñecas—"these dolls"

  esas   esas camisas—"those shirts"

  aquellas   aquellas playas—"those far-away beaches"

The gender of the demonstrative pronoun links it to the nouns in question. You can often translate these as "this one," "that one," and even "these ones" in English:

- Masculine singular:

  éste   "this one"

  ése   "that one"

  aquél   "that one far away"

- Feminine singular:

  ésta   "this one"

  ésa   "that one"

  aquélla   "that one far away"

- Plurals:

  éstos   "these"

  éstas   "these"

  ésos   "those"

  ésas   "those"

  aquéllos   "those far away"

  aquéllas   "those far away"

- Neuter demonstrative pronouns:

  esto   "this (concept)"

  eso   "that (concept)"

  aquello   "that" (not used very often in conversation)

Reference Books

Butt, John, and Carmen Benjamin. *A New Reference Grammar of Modern Spanish*. New York: McGraw-Hill, 2004.

Editors of Larousse, Mexico. *El Pequeño Larousse Ilustrado*. Boston: Larousse Mexico and Houghton Mifflin, 2006.

Gerrard, A. Bryson. *Cassell's Colloquial Spanish: A Handbook of Idiomatic Usage, 3rd Revised Edition*. New York: Macmillan, 1981.

Jarman Galimberti, Beatriz, Roy Russell, Carol Styles Carvajal, and Jane Horwood, eds. *The Oxford Spanish Dictionary: Spanish-English/English-Spanish, 3rd Edition*. New York: Oxford University Press, 2003.

Appendix B

Occupational Spanish Phrases

As the Spanish-speaking population continues to grow in the United States, health-care professionals, as well as workplace managers and supervisors, are finding it increasingly important to be able to communicate in Spanish. With this in mind, I have included a section covering occupational Spanish in this second edition.

Spanish for Medical Professionals

Although an exhaustive Spanish/English medical glossary would be beyond the scope of this book, the phrases listed here will be helpful to health-care professionals who may need to obtain a Spanish-speaking patient's medical history. I have also included some basic requests that you might make during an exam, as well as a few standard discharge/aftercare instructions. Although you won't find every phrase here, with a little ingenuity you can modify most of these questions or phrases with other vocabulary as the situation requires. Remember to use your dictionary.

Many of these questions will be answered with a "Sí" or "No." You'll have to rely on the strength of your Spanish to understand more complex answers, but you should do fine if you've mastered the contents of this book.

Medical Spanish courses are offered at many teaching facilities around the country and online. If you are a health-care professional and need to use Spanish every day, you may wish to explore learning more medical Spanish in an academic setting.

Patient's Personal Information

What is your name?
¿Cómo se llama usted? ¿Cuál es su nombre?

What is your address?
¿Cuál es su dirección?

What is your phone number?
¿Cuál es su número de teléfono?

Why have you come to the hospital?
¿Por qué ha venido usted al hospital?

Where do you work?
¿Dónde trabaja usted?

Do you have medical insurance?
¿Tiene usted algún seguro médico?

Do you have a primary care physician?
¿Tiene usted un médico primario o de cabecera?

What is your doctor's name?
¿Cómo se llama su médico?

Do you know his/her telephone number?
¿Sabe su número de teléfono?

Do you have any medical or health problems?
¿Tiene usted problemas médicos o de la salud?

When was the last time you saw a doctor?
¿Cuándo fue la última vez que vio a un médico?

Have you ever been hospitalized before?
¿Ha estado hospitalizado alguna vez?

Why were you hospitalized?
¿Por qué estuvo hospitalizado/a?

Have you ever had surgery?
¿Ha sido operado/a alguna vez?

Do you work with hazardous chemicals?
¿Trabaja con químicas peligrosas?

Have you ever received a blood transfusion?
¿Ha recibido alguna vez una transfusión de sangre?

Do you have any relatives who have the same medical problem that you do?
¿Hay familiares que tienen el mismo problema médico que tiene usted?

Are your parents still living?
¿Todavía viven sus padres?

If not, what was the cause of your father's death?
Si no, ¿De qué murió su papá?

What was the cause of your mother's death?
¿De qué murió su madre?

At what age did your father/mother die?
¿A qué edad murió su padre/madre?

Please sign here, and here.
Por favor, firme aquí, y aquí.

General Health Questions

Have you had any recent changes in your weight?
¿Ha cambiado de peso últimamente?

How many kilos have you gained?
¿Por cuántos kilos ha aumentado de peso?

How many kilos have you lost?
¿Cuántos kilos ha perdido?

Do you have a fever?
¿Tiene fiebre?

Night sweats?
¿Sudores nocturas?

Do you smoke?
¿Fuma usted?

Did you used to smoke in the past?
¿Fumaba?

How many packs a day?
¿Cuántas cajetillas fumaba al dia?

When did you quit smoking?
¿Cuándo dejó de fumar?

Do you drink?
¿Toma usted bebidas alcohólicas?

Did you used to drink?
¿Tomaba?

How long have you gone without a drink?
¿Hace cuánto que no toma?

How is your appetite?
¿Come bien? ¿Tiene buen apetito?

Are you very thirsty?
¿Tiene mucha sed?

Do you sleep well?
¿Duerme bien?

Do you have a cough?
¿Tiene tos?

Do you have pain in your joints?
¿Tiene dolores de las articulaciones?

Have you had any swelling in your joints?
¿Se le hinchan las articulaciones?

Do you have back pain?
¿Le duele la espalda?

What symptoms do you currently have?
¿Qué síntomas tiene usted ahora?

Are you up-to-date on your vaccinations, including tetanus?
¿Está al día con sus vacunas, incluyendo el tétano?

Medicines

Are you currently taking any medications?
¿Está tomando medicamentos actualmente?

Which medications?
¿Cuales medicamentos?

Do you have your medications with you?
¿Trae sus medicamentos?

Do you have the prescription?
¿Trae su receta?

Allergies

Are you allergic to any medications?
¿Es alérgico/a a algunas medicinas?

Which medication(s)?
¿A qué medicina(s)?

Are you allergic to pollen?
¿Es usted alérgico/a al polen?

Do you have any food allergies?
¿Es alérgico/a a algún comestible o comida?

High-Risk Activities

Have you ever used IV drugs?
¿Se ha inyectado drogas alguna vez?

Which drug?
¿Cuál droga?

Are you sexually active?
¿Está teniendo usted relaciones sexuales?

Have you had unprotected sex?
¿Ha tenido usted el sexo sin protección?

Do you use condoms?
¿Usa condones?

Have you ever been tested for HIV?
¿Le han hecho la prueba para el virus que causa el SIDA?

What was the result of the test?
¿Cuál fue le resultado?

Sexually Transmitted Diseases

Have you ever had gonorrhea?
¿Alguna vez ha tenido la gonorrea?

Syphilis?
¿La sífilis?

Herpes?
¿El herpes?

Do you have sores on your penis/vaginal area?
¿Tiene úlceras en su pene/área vaginal?

Do you have any itching?
¿Tiene picazón?

Do you experience pain upon intercourse?
¿Le duele cuando tiene relaciones?

Pain

Are you in pain now?
¿Tiene dolor ahora mismo?

Where is the pain located?
¿En dónde tiene el dolor exactamente?

Is the pain strong, moderate, or light?
¿Es un dolor fuerte, moderado, o ligero (suave)?

When did the pain begin?
¿Cuándo le empezó el dolor?

How would you describe the pain?
¿Cómo es el dolor?

Sharp
Agudo

Dull
Sordo

Burning
Ardiente

Stabbing
Punzante

Like pressure
Cómo presión

It comes and goes.
Va y viene.

When the pain arrives, how long does it last?
¿Cuando le viene, por cuánto tiempo le dura?

Is it very frequent?
¿Con mucha frecuencia?

How many times have you had this pain in the last week?
¿Durante la última semana, cuántas veces ha tenido el dolor?

Does it come on with eating?
¿Ocurre al comer?

When exercizing?
¿Al hacer ejercicios?

Is there something that makes the pain better or worse?
¿Hay algo que le agrava o le mejora el dolor?

Skin

Do you have any skin problems?
¿Tiene problemas de la piel?

Rashes
Erupciones/sarpullidos

Hives
Ronchas

Itching
Picazón/comezón

Insect bites or stings
Picaduras de insectos

Any lumps?
¿Alguna bolita?

Open sores
Úlceras

Have you noticed any area of your skin changed color?
¿Ha notado cambios de color de su piel en alguna parte?

Head and Neck

Do you have headaches?
¿Tiene dolores de cabeza?

Migraines?
¿Migrañas?

Have you injured your head recently?
¿Se ha lastimado su cabeza últimamente?

How is your vision?
¿Puede ver bien?

Do you wear glasses or contacts?
¿Usa lentes o lentes de contacto?

Do you ever have blurry vision?
¿Ve borroso a veces?

Do you ever see double?
¿Ve doble a veces?

Do you have cataracts?
¿Tiene cataratas?

Glaucoma?
¿Glaucoma?

Do you see halos around lights?
¿Ve halos alrededor de las luces?

How is your hearing?
¿Oye bien?

Is your hearing the same in both ears?
¿Oye igual en los dos oídos?

Do you have pain in your ears?
¿Tiene dolor de oído?

Have you had a lot of ear infections?
¿Ha tenido muchas infecciones del oído?

Do you have frequent nosebleeds?
¿Le sale sangre de la nariz con mucha frecuencia?

Do you get sinus infections?
¿A veces le da la sinusitis?

Do you get colds frequently?
¿Le dan resfriados con mucha fecuencia?

Do you have any tooth pain?
¿Le duele un diente?

Do you wear false teeth/dentures?
¿Tiene dientes postizos?

Do you have a sore throat?
¿Le duele la garganta?

Do you have pain in your neck?
¿Le duele el cuello?

Do you have lumps in your neck?
¿Tiene bolitas en el cuello?

Lungs and Heart

Do you have difficulty breathing?
¿Le dificulta respirar?

Are you out of breath?
¿Le falta aire?

Can you go up stairs?
¿Puede subir escaleras?

Do you use oxygen at home?
¿Usa el oxígeno en casa?

Are you coughing up blood?
¿Ha notado sangre cuando tose?

Do you have wheezing in your chest?
¿Tiene chillidos en el pecho?

Do you have asthma?
¿Tiene el asma?

What brings on an asthma attack?
¿Hay algo que le provoca ataques de asma?

Have you ever had pneumonia?
¿Ha tenido pulmonía alguna vez?

Tuberculosis?
¿Tuberculosis?

Have you ever had a TB test?
¿Le han puesto alguna vez laprueba para la tuberculosis?

What was the result?
¿Qué fue el resultado?

Have you ever had a chest X-ray?
¿Le han tomado un radiografía del pecho alguna vez?

Do you have, or have you ever had, any heart problems?

¿Tiene ahora, o ha tenido en el pasado, problemas del corazón?

High blood pressure?
¿Alta presión?

Do you ever have chest pains?
¿Tiene dolor de pecho a veces?

How many pillows do you need when you sleep?
¿Cuantas almohadas usa para dormir?

Women's Health

Have you noticed any lumps in your breasts?
¿Ha notado algunas bolitas en los senos?

Have you ever had a mammogram?
¿Le han hecho un mamograma alguna vez?

Do you ever notice secretions or blood from your nipples?
¿Le sale secreciones o sangre de los pezones a veces?

When was your last menstrual period?
¿Cuando fue su última regla?

Was it normal?
¿Fue normal?

Do you have painful periods?
¿Tiene dolores con la regla?

Do you bleed excessively when you have your period?
¿Sangra mucho durante la regla?

How many pads do you use?
¿Cuántas toallas usa?

Do you use tampons?
¿Usa tampones?

Do you bleed between periods?
¿Ha sangrado entre las reglas?

When did you go through menopause?
¿Cuándo le vino la menopausia?

Have you had any bleeding since then?
¿Ha sangrado desde entonces?

How many times have you been pregnant?
¿Cuántas veces ha estado embarazada?

Did you have any problems with your pregnancies?
¿Tuvo problemas con los embarazos?

Have you had any miscarriages?
¿Ha tenido abortos espontaneos?

Do you use any form of birth control?
¿Usa algún método anticonceptivo?

Birth control pills
La píldora anticonceptiva

Diaphragm
El diafragma

An IUD
Un dispositivo intrauterino

Condoms
Condones

Could you possibly be pregnant now?
¿Podría estar usted embarazada ahora?

Gastrointestinal and Urinary Tract

Do you have any difficulties swallowing?
¿Tiene dificultades para tragar o pasar saliva?

Does food get caught in your throat?
¿Se le atora la comida?

Do you have heartburn?
¿Tiene agruras?

Nausea?
¿Náusea?

Vomiting?
¿Vómitos?

How many times have you vomited today?
¿Cuántas veces ha vomitado hoy?

Have you vomited blood?
¿Vomitó sangre?

Do you have stomach pains?
¿Tiene dolor de estómago?

Do certain foods cause you pain?
¿Hay ciertas comidas que le provocan los dolores?

Do you have difficulty going to the bathroom?
¿Tiene problemas para ir al baño?

Are you constipated?
¿Está estreñido/a?

Have you seen blood in your stool?
¿Ha notado sangre en el excremento?

Have you had any black or tarry stools?
¿Ha tenido excremento negro como el asfalto?

Have you ever had hepatitis?
¿Ha tenido la hepatitis alguna vez?

Have your eyes ever turned yellow?
¿Se le han puesto amarillos los ojos alguna vez?

Have you ever had gallbladder surgery?
¿Le han operado de la vesícula alguna vez?

Do you have any problems urinating?
¿Tiene problemas para orinar?

Do you wake up at night to go to the bathroom?
¿Tiene que levantarse durante la noche para orinar?

Do you feel any burning upon urination?
¿Le arde cuando orina?

Have you ever had a urinary tract infection?
¿Ha tenido alguna vez una infección de la vía urinaria?

Have you noticed blood in your urine?
¿Ha notado sangre en la orina alguna vez?

Have you ever passed a stone?
¿Ha eliminado un piedrita en la orina alguna vez?

Do you have any penile discharge (male)?
¿Le sale una secreción del pene?

Neurological and Mental Health

Have you ever had a stroke?
¿Ha tenido un derrame cerebral alguna vez?

Has any part of your body ever become weak?
¿Se le ha puesto débil alguna parte de su cuerpo alguna vez?

Does part of your body feel numb?
¿Siente dormida alguna parte del cuerpo?

Do you feel any tingling sensations?
¿Tiene hormigueo?

Do you have difficulty remembering things?
¿Tiene dificultades para recordar cosas?

Do you feel dizzy?
¿Tiene mareos?

Are you nervous?
¿Está nervioso/a?

Would you say that you are sometimes depressed?
¿Diría que padece a veces de la depresión?

Have you ever thought of committing suicide?
¿Ha pensado alguna vez en suicidarse?

Have you thought of how you would do it?
¿Ha pensado en cómo lo haría?

Have you ever thought of doing harm to another person?
¿Ha pensado en hacerle daño a otra persona?

Can you take care of yourself?
¿Puede valerse por si mismo?

Do you have thyroid problems?
¿Tiene problemas con la tiroides?

Do you often feel hot or cold when others do not?
¿Siente frío o calor muchas veces cuando los demás no lo sienten?

Basic Medical Instructions

The following are some basic instructions and phrases that you may need before, during, or after a medical exam.

When making these kinds of requests, remember to always say *por favor* either before or after you ask someone to do something. If you want to tell someone *not* to do something, just negate the sentence. All of these are in the *usted* form. When speaking to a child, remember to use the *tú* forms:

Please, sit down.
Siéntese, por favor.

Wait here (in the waiting room).
Espere aquí (en la sala de espera).

Please follow me.
Sígame, por favor.

Don't worry, the nurse/doctor is coming in a moment.
No se desespere, la enfermera/el médico viene en un momento (*change gender to match gender of person coming*).

Lie down.
Acuéstese.

Open your mouth.
Abra la boca.

Stick out your tongue.
Saque la lengua.

Stand up/Get up.
Párese/Levántese.

Move your ...
Mueva su/sus ...

Remove your ...
Quite su/sus ...

Like this (*showing them what you want them to do*).
Así.

Hold this.
Agarre/Detenga esto.

I'm going to examine your ...
Le voy a examinar su/sus/el, la, los, las ...

Don't worry, everything is fine.
No se preocupe, todo está bien.

We need a blood/urine sample.
Necesitamos una muestra de sangre/orina.

I am going to touch you here (*indicating the place on your own body*).
Le voy a tocar aquí.

Here are your discharge instructions.
He aquí sus instrucciones de alta.

You have been diagnosed with ...
A usted le hemos diagnosticado ...

Go to your preferred pharmacy and fill this prescription.
Vaya a la farmacia de su preferencia para surtir esta receta.

Please do not (drive, eat a heavy meal, consume alcoholic beverages, lift heavy objects).
Por favor, no (maneje, coma comida pesada, consuma bebidas alcohólicas, levante cosas pesadas).

Make an appointment with your doctor (as soon as possible/this week/in two weeks).
Haga una cita con su médico (lo mas pronto possible, esta semana, en dos semanas).

Take two aspirin and call me in the morning.
Tómese dos aspirinas y llámeme en la mañana. (I just had to add this one).

Do you have any questions?
¿Tiene usted algunas preguntas?

Spanish for Managers

This section provides you with some basic phrases and typical interview questions that should help you to improve communication when hiring or managing a Spanish-speaking employee. As with the previous section on medical Spanish, I can only cover the fundamentals here.

A number of academic institutions offer industry-specific courses for managers, such as "Spanish for Restaurant & Food Service Managers" and "Spanish for Landscapers, Lawn Maintenance & Golf Course Superintendents." If you feel that time in a classroom would be helpful, search the Internet to see what's currently available.

The Job Interview

Personal Data

What is your full name?
¿Cuál es su nombre completo?

Do you have your ID documents?
¿Trae usted sus documentos de identificación?

The documents that you will need to apply for this job are …
Los documentos que usted necesitará para solicitar este trabajo son …

Do you have a Social Security number? (In countries other than the United States, there may be another national identification number to ask for.)
¿Tiene usted un número de seguro social?

May I see your driver's license, please?
¿Me permite su licencia de conducir, por favor?

What is your address?
¿Cuál es su dirección?

Your phone number?
¿Su número de teléfono?

Are there any other phone numbers we can call in case of an emergency?
¿Existen otros números de teléfono a que podemos llamar en casos de emergencia?

What is your marital status? (May be asked for certain documents, but not as a screening question.)
¿Cuál es su estado civil?

Common Interview Questions

So, tell me about yourself ...
Entonces, explíqueme algo sobre usted ...

Can you give me a summary of your experience?
¿Podría hacerme un resumen de su experiencia?

Why do you want to work here?
¿Por qué le gustaría trabajar aquí?

Why are you interested in this position?
¿Por qué le interesa este puesto?

What professional experience do you have?
¿Qué experiencias profesionales tiene?

Why do you think that you are capable of doing this job?
¿Qué le hace pensar que está usted capacitado/a para este trabajo?

Why did you leave your last job?
¿Por qué dejó su último empleo?

What studies or education have you had?
¿Qué estudios o formación ha realizado?

Considering everything that you have done so far, what do you like to do the most and why?
Considerando todo lo que usted ha hecho hasta ahora, ¿qué es lo que más le gusta y por qué?

What are your best qualities?
¿Cuáles son sus mejores cualidades?

What are your weaknesses?
¿Cuáles son sus defectos?

How do you like to work: Alone? In a group? And why?
¿Cómo le gustaría trabajar: ¿sólo? ¿en equipo? ¿y por qué?

Do you fit in easily with your colleagues at work?
¿Se integra usted fácilmente entre los colegas de trabajo?

What do you hope to accomplish in the next five years?
¿Qué pretende usted realizar dentro de los próximos cinco años?

With respect to your professional life, what have been some of your accomplishments at previous jobs?
Y respecto a su vida profesional ¿cuáles han sido los logros que ha conseguido en sus anteriores puestos de trabajo?

How much did you make at your previous job?
¿Cuánto ganaba en su último trabajo?

What are your financial expectations from this job?
¿Cuáles son sus expectativias económicas de este trabajo?

Can you provide professional references for us to contact?
¿Nos puede proporcionar algunas referencias profecionales con los que podemos comunicarnos acerca de usted?

Work Hours and Protocols

Your workday will be from 8:00 A.M. to 5:00 P.M., Monday through Friday. *(change days/times as needed)*
Usted trabajará de las 8:00 de la mañana a las 5:00 de la tarde, lunes a viernes.

At 10:00 and 2:00 you can take a ten-minute break.
A las 10:00 y a las 2:00 se puede tomar un descanso de diez minutos.

There is a lunch break from 12:00 to 1:00.
Hay una pausa para comer de las doce hasta la una.

If you are sick and unable to work, please call us as soon as possible.
Si está enfermo/a y no puede trabajar, llámenos lo más pronto posible.

If you get hurt while working, tell your supervisor immediately.
Si se lastima mientras está trabajando, dígaselo inmediatamente a su supervisor.

You will be responsible for ...
Usted será responsible para ...

Your supervisor will be Mr./Mrs./Miss ...
Su supervisor/a será el señor/la señora/la señorita ...

Work-Related Commands

The following examples should be viewed as both linguistic models to emulate as well as statements that you might actually say on the job. I do not wish to imply with these examples that all Spanish-speakers are only employed at unskilled jobs, although a large number of monolingual Spanish-speakers in the United States are indeed working as unskilled or semi-skilled laborers in a variety of industries.

Using your dictionary, you should be able to change the wording of these commands to fit your particular situation. If you don't like the direct command form, you can use the softer "*Hágame el favor de* + infinitive." At the very least, remember to say *por favor* when giving direct commands, just like your parents always taught you.

Do/Make/Prepare/Arrange

Do the chores.
Haga los quehaceres. (hacer)

Make the beds.
Haga las camas. (hacer)

Make the food.
Prepare la comida. (preparar)

Arrange (fix up) the rooms.
Arregle las habitaciones. (arreglar)

Move/Remove/Take Out

Move the furniture.
Mueva los muebles. (mover)

Remove the flower pots.
Remueva las macetas. (remover)

Take out the garbage.
Saque la basura. (sacar)

Lift/Carry/Bring

Lift the boxes.
Levante las cajas. (levantar)

Carry them to the room.
Tráigalas al cuarto. (traer)

Bring the shovel.
Traiga la pala. (traer)

Put/Replace

Put the plates on the table.
Ponga los platos sobre la mesa. (poner)

Replace the batteries.
Cambie las pilas. (cambiar)

Cut

Cut the grass.
Corte el césped/zacate (Mexico).
(cortar)

Fix

Repair the tire.
Repare la llanta. (reparar)

Fix the motor.
Ajuste el motor. (ajustar)

Fix the problem.
Arregle el problema. (arreglar)

Fill

Fill the tank.
Llene el tanque.

Clean/Dust/Vacuum/Disinfect

Clean the floor.
Limpie el piso. (limpiar)

Dust off the chairs.
Quítele el polvo a las sillas. (quitar)

Disinfect the bathroom.
Desinfecte el baño. (desinfectar)

Vacuum the carpet.
Aspire/Pase la aspiradora por—la alfombra. (aspirar/pasar)

Water

Water the plants.
Riegue las plantas. (regar)

Fold

Fold the towels.
Doble las toallas. (doblar)

Organize

Organize the books.
Ordene los libros. (ordenar)

Organize the party.
Organice la fiesta. (organizar)

Pick Up

Pick up the leaves.
Recoja las hojas. (recoger)

Empty

Empty the bucket.
Vacíe el balde. (vaciar)

Drive

Drive the tractor.
Conduzca el tractor. (conducir)

Store/Pack Up

Pack up/Put away the clothes (for a long time).
Guarde la ropa. (guardar)

Turn On/Turn Off

Turn on the light.
Encienda la luz. (encender)

Turn off the drill.
Apague el taladro. (apagar)

Hang

Hang the rope.
Cuelgue la soga. (colgar)

Index

versus English, 3-6
  capitalization, 21
  punctuation, 20-21
Spanish-language programs,
  learning tools, 38
Spanish/English dictionaries,
  36
sports, soccer
  joke, 240-241
  lecture, 234-238
  website reference, 239-240
  World Cup, 233-234
Strauss, Richard, 205
subjunctive
  defined, 135-136
  forming present
    subjunctive, 136-137
  spelling rules, 137
  uses
    future time, 140-141
    impersonal expressions,
      139-140
    impersonal wishes,
      140-141
    indirect commands,
      138-139
    negative tú commands,
      140
    potential existence, 142
    standard phrases,
      141-142
    usted commands,
      137-139
subtraction (math), 220
suffixes, 238-239, 247-248
  augmentative, 249-250
  diminutive, 248-249
  non-standard, 250-252
  pejorative, 250
superlatives, adjectives, 81
sustantivos. *See* nouns
swallowed d, pronunciation, 20
swallowed s, pronunciation,
  18-19
syllables, accent marks, 25-27

T

Tamalitos Mexicanos, recipe
  lecture, 168-169
    text analysis, 170-172
    vocabulary list, 169-170
tampoco, 101
tan, haber verb, 194-195
tantito, 194
tanto, 194-195
technology, 277-278
  modem lecture, 278
    text analysis, 279-281
    vocabulary list, 278-279
  websites, 285
tecolote, 246
Telemundo, 19, 38
television, Spanish-language
  programs, 38
tener, 247
text analysis
  Cárdenas, Lázaro, lecture,
    59-60
  Spain geographic
    description, 47-48
thank you phrase, 270-271
ticos, 121, 249
tildes, 24. *See also* accent
  marks
    defining accentuation,
      24-25
    diphthongs, 27-28, 32-33
    direct and indirect object
      pronouns, 115
    distinguishing words, 33
    interrogatives, 256
    numbers, 217
    proper use, 28
      endings other than n or
        s, 30-31
      exceptions, 30-32
      penultimate syllable,
        28-30
    syllables, 25-27

time, subjunctive, 140-141
tips, 170
tongue-twisters, 211
transitive verbs, pronouns,
  108-109
translations, word-for-word,
  60
traveling
  dialogue, 254-255
  joke, 259-260
  website, 259
trilled r sounds, 13
el trio, 228
triphthongs, 12
tú
  negative commands, 140
  versus usted, 159-161
tutear, 160

U

u, vowel sounds, 13
ue, diphthong pronunciation,
  19-20
un, indefinite articles, 49
una, indefinite articles, 49
United States of America
  Hispanic
    history, 131-133
    website references, 142
  lecture, 133
    text analysis, 134-135
    vocabulary list, 133-134
  statistics, 135
Univisión, 19, 38
Uruguay, South America
  Southern Cone, 75
usted
  subjunctive use, 137-139
  versus tú, 159-161

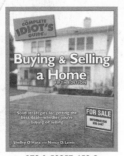

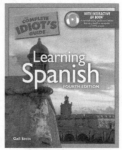

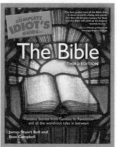
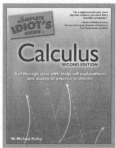